# The Emotional Needs of Young Children and Their Families

This book describes the value of psychodynamic ideas for understanding and treating a wide range of problems affecting the lives of young children and their families. It offers practical solutions for professionals involved in repairing the emotional damage caused by separation and loss and the more alarming problems of sexual and physical abuse.

The book assumes no previous knowledge of the subject, giving a clear account of basic psychodynamic concepts and showing how they have developed in theory and in practice. The introductory part sets out the social and legal contexts for working with children and families. Separate parts are devoted to working with individuals, families, groups and organisations. Each chapter suggests projects and practical work which may be carried out and developed by a wide range of professionals in a variety of community settings – including social services, schools and hospitals.

**The Emotional Needs of Young Children and Their Families: Using Psychoanalytic Ideas in the Community** is relevant both to those qualified and those still in training for a variety of disciplines. It stresses the importance of support and supervision for professionals in this area and provides valuable information about where to find it.

**Judith Trowell** is Consultant Child Psychiatrist and Psychoanalyst at the Tavistock Clinic, London. **Marion Bower** is Senior Psychiatric Social Worker at White City Child Guidance Unit, London.

# The Emotional Needs of Young Children and Their Families

## Using psychoanalytic ideas in the community

Edited by Judith Trowell and Marion Bower

London and New York

First published 1995
by Routledge
11 New Fetter Lane
London, EC4P 4EE

Simultaneously published in the USA and Canada
by Routledge
29 West 35th Street
New York
NY 10001

Routledge is an imprint of the Taylor & Francis Group

Reprinted 2000

Typeset in Times
by Keystroke, Jacaranda Lodge, Wolverhampton

Printed and bound in Great Britain by
Clays Ltd, St Ives plc

British Library Cataloguing in Publication Data
A catalogue record for this book is available from the British Library

Library of Congress Cataloging in Publication Data
A catalogue record for this book has been requested


ISBN 0–415–11612–0 (hbk)
ISBN 0–415–11613–9 (pbk)

# Contents

# List of illustrations

# Notes on contributors

**Zelinda Adam** trained as an analytic psychotherapist at the Lincoln Centre. She has a private practice and also works at Harlow House Psychiatric Day Hospital. She has been working with groups of depressed women for more than five years.

**Bobbie Cooper** currently works as a psychiatric social worker at a local authority Child Guidance Unit in Hammersmith and Fulham. She is also a qualified child psychotherapist working in private practice.

**Lynn Barnett** is a member of the Association of Child Psychotherapists, the British Psychological Society, and a past Fellow of the Royal Anthropological Institute. She chairs the Psychosocial Group of Medical Action for Global Security and contributes to child mental health programmes in the CIS, Central Europe and Balkans.

**Marion Bower** is Senior Psychiatric Social Worker at White City Child Guidance Unit, London.

**Christine Bradley** is Consultant in Social Work, Training Development at the Caldicott Community and in Local Authority with responsibility for Residential Care.

**Dilys Daws** is Consultant Child Psychotherapist, Tavistock Clinic. She also works at the baby clinic of the Wigg Practice, Kentish Town Health Centre. She is Chair of the Child Psychotherapy Trust, whose aim is to develop training for more child psychotherapists in the NHS, especially outside London.

**Maureen Fox** is Consultant Child Psychologist and teacher at the Tavistock Clinic and a psychoanalytic psychotherapist in private practice. She has a special interest in the needs of asylum-seeking children and families and is a founder member of the refugee charity 'Children of the Storm'.

**Eva Holmes** – is Principal Educational Psychologist of the London Borough of Enfield. She is Vice-Chair of 'Young Minds' and is the author of many professional papers.

**Rosalie Kerbekian** is Principal Child Psychotherapist, Parkside Clinic, Parkside Health Authority and is in part-time private practice.

**Anna Kerr** trained in psychiatric social work, worked in child abuse research, social work training and established a Family Centre. She is now a psychotherapist in training and a guardian ad litem, and co-author of *At Risk* (1975) and *On Behalf of the Child* (1990).

**Savi Mackenzie Smith** trained as a child psychotherapist at the Tavistock Clinic, where she works and teaches in the Child and Family Department. She currently has a placement at the Brixton Child Guidance Unit. At present she is training as an Adult Psychoanalytic Psychotherapist.

**Sheila Melzak** trained as a child psychotherapist. She works part-time at the Medical Centre for the Treatment of Victims of Torture.

**Isabel Menzies Lyth** is a social scientist, psychoanalyst and organisational consultant. She has a vast number of publications on institutions and their dynamics.

**Gillian Miles** is Senior Clinical Lecturer in Social Work at the Tavistock Clinic and a psychoanalytic psychotherapist. She has developed Observation Training in Social Work for basic training and PQ Child Care courses.

**Maggie Mills** is a university lecturer and clinical psychologist and currently is a psychotherapist at Shanti, the Women's Intercultural Psychotherapy Centre in Brixton. She was also associated with Newpin for many years. Mellow Mothering, the parenting intervention project, was started from joint research by Christine Puckering and herself.

**Michael Morice** trained as a child psychotherapist at the Tavistock Clinic. He teaches in London and abroad, and has worked in hospitals, Portman Clinic and Child Guidance. He is currently Head Psychotherapist at Richmond Child and Family Consultation Centre, and is in private practice in Richmond.

**Christine Puckering** is Senior Lecturer in Clinical Psychology at the University of Glasgow.

**Judith Trowell** is Consultant Child Psychiatrist and Psychoanalyst at the Tavistock Clinic, London.

**Felicity de Zulueta** is Consultant Psychotherapist and Honorary Senior Lecturer of the University of London, a biologist, psychiatrist and psychoanalytic psychotherapist, and Associate Member of the Institute of Group Analysis and Systemic Family Therapist. She is the author of a book on the traumatic origins of violence, *From Pain to Violence*.

# Preface

We hope that this book will be of interest to a wide variety of professionals, including social workers, doctors, teachers, health visitors, community nurses, psychologists, counsellors and psychotherapists, even if they have never encountered psychoanalytic ideas before.

At a time when many services are fragmenting we are increasingly exhorted to work together. Such collaboration ultimately requires better organisations, but at a personal professional level we believe that psychoanalytic ideas provide a valuable, shared framework which enhances the possibilities for working together. Our society is distressed by an increase in violence, juvenile crime and physical and sexual abuse of people who are vulnerable. Psychoanalysis provides a framework for both understanding and addressing these issues, as well as the 'ordinary' problems which beset many families.

We have concentrated mainly on work with young families as we believe this provides the best opportunity for true preventive work. However, we have also included chapters on work with slightly older children where a useful psychoanalytic concept is illustrated or in an area where psychoanalytic understanding is just beginning to be used, for example with refugee families.

For those who are new to psychoanalytic ideas we would recommend reading Chapters 2 and 3, which describe basic concepts and some of the advantages and difficulties of putting them into practice. The link pieces between sections highlight where particular concepts occur in the text, as well as putting the work described into a wider context. There is no glossary as we think that psychoanalytic ideas are best understood in practice. However, in addition to the bibliography there is a topic reading list which suggests reading to explore the work of individual psycho-analysts or particular therapeutic techniques in more depth.

We have emphasised that we feel that real changes also need to come at a social and political level as well as at professional levels. However, it is important to continue to build innovative and collaborative approaches in our own workplace, and we hope that at least some readers will be inspired to try out some of these ideas themselves as well as developing new initiatives of their own.

# Acknowledgements

We are very grateful to both our families for their tolerance and support while we were working on this book.

Special thanks are due to Jacob Bower who used his computer skills to help us with the practical aspects of putting the book on disk.

We are also very grateful to Gillian Miles for her support and encouragement, and for giving us valuable advice at moments of indecision.

## PERMISSIONS

Chapter 4 was previously published as 'The contribution of observation training to professional development in social work', *Journal of Social Work Practice* 5(1) 1991.

Chapter 8 was originally published in an earlier version as 'With the past in mind: a guardian ad litem's view of future planning in child care', *Journal of Social Work Practice* 5(1) 1991.

Chapter 10 was published in an earlier version as 'White City Toy Library, a therapeutic group for mothers and children', *Journal of Social Work Practice* 5(1) 1991.

*The Journal of Social Work Practice* is published by Carfax Publishing Company, PO Box 25, Abingdon, Oxfordshire, OX14 3UE.

Chapter 17 was previously published in *The Dynamics of the Social* by Isabel Menzies Lyth, Free Association Books, London.

The lines from the Yevgeny Yevtushenko poem 'The Unexpressed', published in *Almost at the End*, are reproduced by permission of Marion Boyars Publishers Limited.

Every effort has been made to obtain permission for the lines by

Ashley Montague originally published in *Direction of Human Development*. The publishers would be pleased to hear from anyone who could help trace the copyright holder of this work.

# Chapter 1

# Introduction

## The social context

*Judith Trowell and Marion Bower*

At a time when poverty and deprivation exist on a scale undreamed of ten years ago, it may seem ironic or even monstrous to produce a book which concentrates on the emotional needs and inner worlds of parents and children.

However, we hope to show that, like physical health, mental health and wellbeing (and their opposite) are intimately linked to social and economic factors. We believe that many professionals in health, education and social services are faced with the task of repairing the emotional damage created by years of poverty and deprivation. Perhaps it is not a coincidence that, in writing of the lack of support that parents receive in bringing up their children, John Bowlby uses the metaphor of malnutrition:

> For just as a society in which there is a chronic insufficiency of food may take a deplorably inadequate level of nutrition as its norm, so may a society in which parents of young children are left on their own with a chronic insufficiency of help take this state of affairs as its norm.
>
> (Bowlby 1988: 2)

Bowlby originally wrote this in 1980. In the fourteen years since then the number of children living in poverty has increased from 1 in 10 in 1979 to an estimated 1 in 3 in 1993. By May 1990 there were 2.5 million unemployed compared to around 600,000 in the previous decade (Yelloly 1993). Figures alone cannot adequately convey the miseries of poverty. Yelloly (1993) quotes an article from the *Guardian* which brings home the reality:

> I always called myself poor until I came to Meadow Well. Then I discovered what poverty really is. You see families counting out the pennies to see if they can buy a tin of beans. I thought

it went out with Dickens. You've got the Third World on Tyneside here. And nobody listens.

(*Guardian* 11 September 1991)

Here we see the roots of the psychological damage caused by poverty and unemployment. It is not only that parents cannot provide adequate clothes, food and shelter for their children. They also suffer depression, loss of dignity and self-respect.

Although psychoanalysts are often accused of ignoring the outer world in favour of the inner, the work of psychoanalysts such as Melanie Klein and D.W. Winnicott (whose ideas will be discussed in more detail in the following chapter) allows us to understand how external adversity can lead to emotional damage. Klein discovered that young children, even in good circumstances, suffer from intense anxieties and fears – including the fear that their parents are damaged or in a bad way. In good circumstances, external reality and the parents' love and support modify their anxieties. In bad circumstances, the external world reflects the child's anxieties, leading to an increase in insecurity and distress.

> Unpleasant experiences and the lack of enjoyable ones, in the young child, *especially lack of happy and close contact with loved people*, increase ambivalence, diminish trust and hope and confirm anxieties about inner annihilation and external persecution; moreover they slow down and perhaps permanently check the beneficial process through which in the long run inner security is achieved.
>
> (Klein 1940: 347, italics added)

This makes it clear how poverty *doubly* deprives children not only of material things, but of the emotional containment that preoccupied and depressed parents are unable to offer.

During the last fourteen years the pattern of family life has also changed dramatically and evidence suggests that this may make it more difficult for some parents to meet their children's needs. In 1979 there were 840,000 lone parents, by 1991 there were 1.3 million lone parents (*Independent on Sunday* 27 June 1993). Britain has one of the highest divorce rates in Europe – divorce rates doubled in the 1970s. Estimates indicate that, if divorce rates prevailing in the mid-1980s were to continue, a third of marriages would be likely to end in divorce (Kiernan 1991).

Although many couples remarry, the remarriage rates have

declined, which is thought to be related to an increased tendency for couples to cohabit without marriage. The reasons for these changes are complex and related to both social and economic changes. However, whatever the cause, these changes in family life have had an enormous impact on the happiness and emotional wellbeing of children.

In 1980 John Bowlby was able to state majestically 'looking after babies and children is no job for a single person' (Bowlby 1988: 2). While it is true that the incidence of poverty is greater among single-parent families, research has shown that the emotional situation is more complex.

A study by Cockett and Tripp (1994) broke new ground by examining *children's* feelings in a variety of different family situations. The researchers found that most children were desolated when their parents' relationships broke down – even when those relationships were riddled with conflicts. Children showed their distress in many different ways: lowered self-esteem, difficulties at school, problems making friends and health problems.

One interesting finding of the study was that it was the children in re-ordered families (i.e. where parents had remarried) who suffered most. Although the children of single parents did not fare as well as those in intact families, the study refuted attempts made by politicians in the 1990s to demonise single parents. The study also contradicted the common view that children are better off out of relationships where their parents are in conflict. It appeared that, for most children, having both their parents together was of enormous psychological importance, which makes the high incidence of marital breakdown a real cause for concern as far as children are concerned.

There is a darker side to childhood unhappiness. In February 1993 a 2-year-old boy was brutally murdered by two 10-year-old boys. The first newspaper reports described the two murderers as having 'no abnormality of mind'. Later the police described them as 'evil freaks'. The reality which gradually emerged was of two deeply disturbed boys, the victims of emotional and actual neglect and family breakdown. Between them their family backgrounds included child abuse, maternal depression, alcoholism and poverty. Both the boys had problems which are distressingly familiar to teachers and social workers in inner-city areas – poor academic achievement (despite average intelligence), tantrums, destructive behaviour and, later on, truancy.

Despite the sense of national outrage and shock, an important opportunity for raising public awareness has been lost. Although child murderers are very rare, emotional disturbance in children – with all its serious consequences – is very common. Conservative estimates put the incidence at 25.9 per cent of the population in inner-city children (Kurtz 1992: 6).

There is considerable evidence that the incidence of disturbance is rising. Research by Young Minds shows that the numbers of referrals to Child Guidance Units and Departments of Child and Family Psychiatry are rising and in some places have more than doubled. The Government's own research suggests that numbers of very young children showing signs of serious disturbances are increasing.

In the same year that James Bulger was murdered, a chronic schizophrenic patient, Christopher Clunis, committed a brutal murder. Newspaper reports and the subsequent Ritchie enquiry used this event to highlight the urgent need for more specialist services, a comprehensive list of what was needed was drawn up and £10 million have been allocated.

The murder of James Bulger produced no such response. Very few newspapers commented on the patchy, inadequate response to the long-standing disturbance of both the young murderers. Yet, at a time when the need for specialist child and family services has never been greater, many are being dismantled. (How this relates to changes in the legislation will be discussed below.)

We do not need only specialist services. We need a framework for understanding extreme emotions – love, hate, jealousy, envy, destructiveness. This is something that psychoanalysis can provide. It also helps us understand how these emotions come to be violently evoked and enacted and how they can be modified and channelled more constructively. We believe that psychoanalysis can function as a shared framework of understanding between professionals from a variety of disciplines, even if they are not using it as a therapeutic tool. This type of shared understanding can facilitate effective professional collaboration.

It could be argued that the children and families who most need this sort of help are least likely to attend Child Guidance or similar services. For this reason we have assembled a collection of papers which illustrate how psychoanalytic ideas can be used by a wide range of professionals in a wide range of settings to help disturbed children and their families.

Before going on to discuss the application of psychoanalytic ideas, we would like to examine briefly the way in which recent legislation has changed and the context in which many of us now work.

## CHANGES IN EDUCATION

How children should be taught has always been a subject for debate and controversy. In the last twenty years this debate has included such issues as the teaching of reading, styles of teaching and the integration of children with special needs into mainstream schools.

However, the most far reaching and radical changes in education in more than twenty years were introduced by the 1988 Education Reform Act. This Act introduced, among other things, the National Curriculum and assessment, the local management of schools and the publication of schools' examination results in 'league tables'. In effect, this is the introduction of a market system into education. Schools receive money for each pupil on roll. This means that schools must compete amongst themselves, not only for pupils, but for money. The theory was that parents would chose schools with high standards (i.e. good examination results) and these would be rewarded financially.

The National Curriculum was in itself an attempt to raise standards and attainments for all groups of children. The introduction of standard attainment tests (SATs) for all children at 7, 11 and 14 has created the possibility of identifying children who were underachieving, examining objectively subject areas or schools where children's needs were not being adequately met.

In addition to the SATs, schools are also now required to keep detailed records on children with special educational needs – what these needs are, the possible reasons for them and what has been done to meet them. Before examining whether these changes have benefited children with special educational needs, it is necessary to define the concept itself.

The term 'special educational needs' was introduced in the 1981 Education Act. Its meaning is very wide. It encompasses children who have learning difficulties because of organic physical or mental disabilities, and those of good potential who are handicapped because of emotional difficulties. The Act required pupils to be assessed multi-professionally to decide on the precise educational effects of the disability and the resources needed to meet them. This assessment is called a 'statement'.

A statement almost invariably means that additional financial resources are allocated to a child, and these days very substantial evidence is required that everything possible has been tried before there is even agreement to assess. However, in addition to the 2 per cent of children who are thought to need a statement of special educational needs, the Department of Education acknowledges that many other children (an estimated 20 per cent of the population) are affected by emotional and behavioural difficulties. There is now considerable evidence that it is these children who are suffering as a result of the 1988 Act.

There are two main reasons for this. Firstly, in a market system, children with emotional and behavioural difficulties are not good for business. Their educational attainments are often poor and their behaviour is seen as bad for the school's reputation. In fact in the last few years there has been a worrying rise in the number of 'difficult' children excluded from schools.

Secondly, with the delegation of financial resources away from Local Education Authorities to schools, the provision of support services is often patchy and uncoordinated. The possibility of the Local Education Authorities (LEAs) effectively planning or providing for children with special needs has been further reduced by the 1993 Education Act, which restricts their power and responsibilities to the 2 per cent of children with statements.

There is not only a loss of special units and schools, but there has been a decimation of multi-professional support services for children with emotional and behavioural problems, usually referred to as Child Guidance Units. This is not just a loss of provision, but a loss of the type of thinking which integrates emotional and educational problems and solutions.

In the 'old-style' child guidance services, Health, Education and Social Services professionals were able to work together to produce effective and varied solutions to emotionally related learning and behavioural problems. As schools cope with the increasing demands of the national curriculum and the erosion of child guidance and other centrally funded support services there is a danger that an appropriate balance of educational and therapeutic provisions will be lost or provided in only a fragmented and uncoordinated way.

This is particularly likely where provision for children with emotional and behavioural problems has been split off into 'Child

Mental Health Services' which are entirely funded by Health. In these cases links with schools and the complex special education needs procedures which now exist are harder to maintain. Yet schools are not only a valuable source of awareness of children's needs, but non-stigmatising arenas in which these needs can be met.

Later chapters in this book show how effectively children with emotional and behavioural problems can be helped in school, either by teachers, with support, or by other professionals working in collaboration with teachers.

Despite financial constraints, a few LEAs have retained partnerships with Health (and sometimes Social Services) to provide Child Guidance or similar services. Such collaborations reflect the reality of children's needs and lives. Unfortunately, it is not only within education that new organisation and legislation have created difficulties for professionals in working together. Alongside the Education Reform Act which has transformed the educational setting for children there have been other major pieces of legislation, particularly the Children Act and the NHS and Community Care Act.

## NHS AND COMMUNITY CARE ACT

The National Health Service has been transformed with the concept of the internal market. Resources have been split so that there are purchasers – Health Authorities, mainly concerned with hospital provisions, and Family Health Service Authorities (FHSA), mainly concerned with general practitioners and community services, and also independent fundholding general practices; and providers – these include hospitals, clinics, community services, ambulance services, all of which were previously NHS services. Provider units can also be voluntary organisations and private sector units.

Purchasers have to prioritise the services needed by their population and then, on the basis of competitive tendering, agree a time-limited contract with a provider unit for the services they require. Alongside this and within the same legislation, Social Service departments have also become divided into purchasers and providers. They have to focus their services, particularly on the elderly, the mentally ill out of hospitals, individuals with learning difficulties and children in need. Purchasers similarly have contracts with provider units – both from within Social Services and from Health, the voluntary sector and the private sector.

These changes in Education, Health and Social Services have had profound effects on services for children (Trowell 1991b; Berelowitz and Horne 1992).

Purchasers generally have little idea of the services required by children and families and so contracts and service specifications have very limited aims. Adrianne Jones and Keith Bilton in *The Future Shape of the Children's Services* (1994) argue that constant reorganisation, both of the organisations (Health, Social Services and Education) and of the geographical boundaries, have resulted in staff who can have as their task only the survival of change. Their work task and the populations they serve have changed so frequently that commitment and real awareness of need have been lost. They describe their most overwhelming impression as one of service fragmentation.

The UN Convention on the Rights of the Child (to which Britain came late as a signatory) places in international law for the first time a duty upon states to accord children rights on a par with adults (Kurtz 1992). It seems there is a long way to go before this is a reality. In *Services for the Mental Health of Children and Young People in England – A National Review* (Kurtz *et al.* 1994) there is a disturbing account of considerable disparity of service provisions across the country and of purchasers who frequently have little idea of the needs of or the appropriate services for their population.

Alongside service fragmentation there is the increasing social inequality mentioned earlier. The *BMJ* in April 1994 published a series of articles looking at the impact of social inequality on health. They highlighted: a) that the scale of excess mortality associated with lower social status dwarfs almost every other health problem, b) that mortality in those aged 0–64 years is four times higher in the poorest than in the most affluent electoral wards of the northern region of England and c) that three-quarters of the regional variation in the number of prescriptions provided per head of the population is associated with differences in regional levels of unemployment. There is a vicious circle of declining services and increasing needs.

## THE CHILDREN ACT

The Children Act 1989 came into operation in October 1991 and it is an enlightened and progressive piece of legislation. At the same time numerous documents of regulation and guidance were produced by the Department of Health to elaborate the Act. In addition, they produced *Working Together*, the document that sets the standards and conditions for implementing the Children Act in relation to child protection.

The Children Act brought together public and private law in relation to children and families and in addition set out proposals for a range of services that are needed to support families and meet children's needs. However, none of these is mandatory, but all are framed as suggestions so they have done very little to prevent the fragmentation and disintegration of services for children and families.

The Children Act enshrined in its opening section that the best interests of the child are paramount, but most of the Act then argues the need to work in partnership with parents. Most children grow up in and do best in families, but for the small number of abused children the outcome seems to have been that professionals feel obliged to go to enormous lengths to try to work with parents, some of whom may be beyond helping, to keep their child at home. The outcome has been that scarce resources have been consumed either on the investigative process, making sure this is done correctly (according to the Memorandum of Good Practice) or struggling heroically to go to any lengths to work with parents. What is left of any money seems to go in repeated 'directions' hearings. The Children Act gave the courts considerably greater powers in determining the details of case management, so that every proposed change needs a 'directions' hearing.

Social Service departments' budget for children and families is mostly consumed by this child protection work. The education service also has responsibilities for child protection, but these can frequently become lost as schools and LEAs struggle with organisational change. Health services have considerable child protection responsibilities, but unless purchasers recognise and include these in contracts they may be lost.

There is a contradiction and worry in all this. The Children's Act, written after the Cleveland inquiry, tries to provide a caring, humane basis for children's services – for children in need, children with disability, children caught in matrimonial breakdown. *Working Together* stresses the need and the obligation for inter-agency co-operation and joint working. At the same time, financial constraints and major reorganisation have resulted in service fragmentation and agencies turning in on themselves to ensure their own survival. To place the size of the child protection problem in perspective, in Camden at the end of the first quarter of 1994 there were 143 families with 253 children on the Child Protection Register and in Hammersmith and Fulham in the first quarter of 1994 there were four emergency protection orders and eleven care and supervision proceedings. A small number of children and families take a considerable proportion of the budget.

It is important this work is done well but the underlying question must be whether this is the best way forward. Social inequality is not being addressed, preventive work is almost non-existent and the proportion of the budget in Health, Education and Social Services being used by business managers, contracting officers and finance departments is escalating. Can this be understood? Our society is in transition. Social structures are changing alongside social deprivation, economic and financial realignment and, at the same time, an increase in religious fundamentalism. Our society has responded by espousing massive radical reforms across the whole arena of life. There is a belief that anxiety and uncertainty can be dealt with by encouraging individualism and rewarding individual initiative, the driving force being efficiency and the profit motive. This ignores, or at least undermines, the social needs of human beings to support and care for each other and unleashes competitiveness, rivalry and envy. The more assertive, the more aware, the more able people demand their rights and their needs are met. Health and Education now seem driven by consumer demands and Social Services is left to keep out of sight the disadvantaged and the needy.

Our society is functioning in a way which would be a cause for considerable concern if it were an individual. Societies, like individuals, have to find effective ways of managing conflict, sexuality, aggression, anxiety and vulnerability. In the following chapters we describe the early defences an infant erects against such feelings, which include splitting them off and projecting them onto others as denial. Individual development involves the capacity to integrate conflicts, to perceive people as whole persons and feel concern for them.

Society, like all large groups, tends to rely on the early types of defences. However, our own society seems particularly riddled with splits, divisions and fragmentation of the type described in this chapter. In this climate even those splits created for rational purposes, such as the purchaser–provider split are being used for defensive purposes, and for the denial of responsibility rather than the provision of more responsive services.

There is an urgent need for more genuinely integrated service provisions and this would have to begin at central government level with better links between departments such as Health and Education. In the absence of such structures professionals have to struggle to create integrated models of service. Most of the chapters in this book are models of intervention involving professionals from different disciplines and agencies. It will be seen how psychoanalysis provides an integrative structure which provides a means of understanding processes which go on at individual, family and larger group level. It also takes account of the forces which operate inside ourselves which resist collaborative work: envy, rivalry and jealousy. These emotions will always be with us, and the more we are aware of them the better able we will be to combat their effects.

# Chapter 2

# Key psychoanalytic concepts

*Judith Trowell*

Psychoanalysis began with Sigmund Freud and has been developed by analysts who have followed him. We have found many of these ideas very helpful as we try to understand children, their families and the community in which they live. The terms that are used to name or explain these ideas will be used throughout the book. Rather than have a glossary as an appendix, we felt it was important to have the ideas and brief descriptions of them at the start of the book because they are central to the themes of all the chapters.

## SIGMUND FREUD

Freud took as an essential starting point *the unconscious*, the idea that a large part of our mental life is not directly accessible to us. He did not discover the unconscious, it was already described, but he gave it very great importance. The unconscious reveals its existence in our dreams and in all the slips and mistakes we make, in which our real thoughts or wishes emerge. Experiences that are unacceptable to ourselves or in the social world are located in the unconscious and kept there by a censoring process. These experiences may be responses to external stimuli or they may arise inside ourselves: our own thoughts and feelings. These will have arisen in the unconscious and need to be kept there rather than allowed to emerge.

Freud viewed our mental life as a state of *innate conflict*, the conflict between Life and Death or love and destructiveness. There could be inappropriate (Life), loving feelings and thoughts often sexual, or inappropriate anger, destroying (Death-promoting) thoughts or feelings. The result of these conflicting and distressing feelings is *anxiety* and this leads to much of the mental distress that presents as symptoms.

All human beings have these conflicts, this anxiety, and Freud suggested various coping mechanisms or *defences* which enable us to deal with these. Sometimes these defences cannot keep the anxiety in the unconscious and so become over-elaborate, over-developed and produce problems themselves. For example, *repression* leading to forgetting can enable someone to get on, their conscious mind being clear, but if large areas of experience are 'forgotten' the person becomes rather cut off and out of touch. There are times when under external or internal stress a person starts to behave as though they were a younger age, they *regress*. A child may have acquired a skill, for example, toilet training or starting to feed themselves, then, with the birth of a new baby and the distress and uncertainty this produces, the child temporarily loses the newly acquired skill.

Sometimes an area of conflict can lead to *displacement*. A child in school may have a difficult time, be teased and mocked by the other children. The child becomes angry and distressed but does not respond at the time. However, once back home and provoked in a minor way by a younger brother or sister the full force of the rage and humiliation is unleashed on the sibling. These feelings have been displaced. Sometimes conflicts and difficulties can lead to a flurry of work or constructive activity: this is *sublimation*. Anxiety and uncertainty around the birth of a baby or a major change can lead to a child developing a keen interest in dinosaurs or drawing aviation models or a new hobby. The anxiety and the energy that go with it are released in this way.

Freud also described the *repetition compulsion*, when an individual deliberately, but unconsciously, places himself in distressing situations. These are repetitions of previous traumatic events and Freud thought this repetition was an unconscious attempt to master the situation.

Freud developed a schema of the mind: *the ego*, the part of the mind in touch with internal and external reality, *the id*, the unconscious feelings and thoughts, and the *superego*. The superego is a useful idea comprising both the ego ideal, the aims, wishes and aspirations to do things well and do them right, and the conscience which can be benign or malevolent. Our conscience can helpfully prevent us doing wrong or foolish things and can confirm wiser, more sensible courses of action, but it can also be a critical, harsh, punitive, destructive, judgemental voice convincing ourselves we are no good and useless, or by its constant recrimination leading to excessive *guilt*.

Freud understood how all this activity going on inside our minds inevitably affected our relationships with others in our lives. He described how our conflicts, feelings and expectations linked to past experiences of significant figures could be transferred on to other people in our lives – *the transference*. Initially he saw his patients' transference to him and their distorted perceptions and expectations, the transferred feelings, as a hindrance to the development of an understanding of their problems, but later he understood that observing the transference gave one a glimpse of the internal conflicts and difficulties just as dreams did. Transference was then seen as a useful tool for intervening effectively.

As well as the transference, Freud also experienced the *counter-transference*: that is, he became aware that his patients were stirring up inside him feelings, reactions and thoughts from his own background. He realised he needed to be very careful not to respond to his patients on the basis of these, his own emotional experiences; he saw patients needed to be protected from this.

In the world of children, Freud's major contribution was his recognition of *infantile* and *child sexuality*. He understood that children, however small, have very powerful sexual feelings for their parents and have an awareness of their own bodies and their pleasurable sexual feelings. Out of this emerged Freud's *Oedipus complex*. He recognised that little girls have strong longings for their father in a sexual way and that boys have powerful sexual longings for their mothers, which in part explains their vulnerability to abuse. He also saw that boys and girls also have strong sexual feelings for the same-sex parent. He recognised these were normal and part of each child's development and that they should remain as sexual fantasies, which goes some way towards explaining why if enacted in sexual abuse, for example, the outcome is so devastating for the child. He recognised the damage if these fantasies were enacted, although he was uncertain how often in reality this happened. *Castration anxiety* is part of this phase for boys and girls: that is, the fear of loss, or, for girls, a sense of having lost, the penis (or potency) as a punishment for sexual impulses.

Other ideas that Freud put forward are *acting out* and *projection*. The latter, along with internal objects and part objects, was taken up, in particular by the object relations school of psychoanalysis (the British School), which will be discussed later.

But perhaps the most important advance Freud made is that he listened to his patients and took what they had to say seriously. Most of his patients were women, often presenting with physical or hysterical symptoms. The prevailing culture did not consider that women had much that was useful or of interest to say. Freud gave women attention and respect, he listened and tried to understand. He also respected them as colleagues – women as psychoanalysts were encouraged by him.

## ANNA FREUD

She followed in her father's footsteps but developed and expanded the ideas. She worked extensively with children and, as her father had listened to women, she, in her direct work with children, listened to what they said and took it seriously. She was particularly aware in her work with latency-age children (5–11 years) of the importance of the external world and the role of the parents. In her work at the Hampstead Nurseries during the Second World War she became very conscious of the effects of deprivation and trauma on children. Her concept of *identification with the aggressor* has been immensely useful. Children who are beaten or abused take inside themselves the aggressor and then their vulnerability and smallness is reversed as they themselves become the aggressor in relation to smaller children, or when they have become adults and abuse their partner or their own children.

Anna Freud was very gifted in her thorough assessments and the rigour with which she insisted they were carried out. She believed it was vital to consider the whole child and this then led to a *profile* of the child. The child needed to be considered in its emotional development, its intellectual and educational development, its physical development and its psychological development within the family and with friends. Thus she was very committed to multidisciplinary teams who could work together to look at all the child's developmental lines and draw up its profile. This commitment has been confirmed and reasserted in the Children's Act 1989 which states in Part I (3) that the Court shall have regard to – (b) his physical, emotional and educational needs (page 2) and in Part IV (9) 'development' means physical, intellectual, emotional, social or behavioural development (page 28). Anna

Freud made a significant contribution in making psychoanalytical ideas available and useful to other professionals, particularly teachers.

## OBJECT RELATIONS: THE BRITISH SCHOOL

Psychoanalysts working in Britain, apart from the Classical Freudians (now Contemporary Freudians), began to move away from the instincts and drive theory as put forward by Freud to explain human behaviour. Freud understood human beings as driven by the need to discharge instinctive energy. As psychoanalysis developed, it became clear that the primary force that drives human beings is the seeking of human relationships. People like Klein, Winnicott, Fairbairn and Bion developed the concept of internal objects and part objects. These objects arise from external real relationships with people, plus the internal fantasies that become linked or attached to these internalised representations of the outside relationship.

From the beginning the baby is thought to see the mother not as a whole person but as a collection of her attributes. The internal objects we build up start from part objects; the baby is thought to be aware of the mother's eyes, hands, breast (bottle), smell and then the face. These in time come together to be a whole, a whole object. It is then the relationships with these internal objects and the external real people that become the centre of the child's or person's mental life. The conflicts are in relation to these relationships.

## MELANIE KLEIN

Klein, perhaps because she was a mother herself, became fascinated by and devoted a great deal of time and energy to understanding very young children and applying and developing psychoanalytic ideas around early development. She developed a play technique using the child's play and behaviour as a means of understanding the child, as the child's means of revealing their unconscious. The child's play and fantasy were seen as similar to dreams and could be understood as *free associations* (the speaking aloud of whatever thoughts come to mind by adult patients in analysis). She developed a set of toys that could maximise the communication through play: paper and coloured pens, small animals, both wild and domestic, small dolls, scissors, string, a soft ball, glue and plasticine.

She saw the young child as driven by conflicts and that this persists into adult life. She saw these conflicts as love versus hate and *envy*, that is destructive spoiling and denigration of 'a good object' (in origin the mother's breast). In both sexes it is an important factor in understanding the lack of value placed on mothering, or 'maternal' occupations in our society, by both sexes. The universal experience of envy is an important factor in understanding the problems in human relationships. The conflicts are revealed in the child's *fantasy life* and these fantasies provide a means of, a mechanism for, dealing with unbearable feelings. Klein did not, as Anna Freud did, concentrate on the elaboration of defence mechanisms.

Klein put forward the idea of *positions* rather than stages and phases of development, seeing that throughout life individuals move back and forth, oscillating in their mental state depending on internal and external stress or demands. The early position was described as *paranoid-schizoid*, i.e. the baby's experiences, early anxieties and ambivalence, psychotic anxiety (persecuting anxiety) and the resulting fantasy of a bad, hateful mother are expelled from the infant's mind by *projection*. But the infant remains linked to this aspect of itself which it has attempted to eliminate and is identified with it, hence *projective identification*. The fear is that the attack on mother will result in a retaliation by mother (punishment). But the infant who fears that mother is as envious as it is, in addition to possible retaliation, fears an envious attack by mother. Hence the baby is *paranoid* and, because part of itself is projected, is cut off from itself and is *schizoid*.

The mechanisms for dealing with the fantasies in this paranoid-schizoid position are *projection* and *projective identification and splitting*, which is when the good, loved is split from the bad, hated or envied, for example the witch and the good fairy, or, more insidious, 'them' and 'us'. Then one aspect of the split can be projected with projective identification or can be *denied*. *Denial* is the fate of thoughts, feelings, conflicts that arise deep in the unconscious. It is a particular psychoanalytic term used by Klein; it is not conscious lying or forgetting (repression). Another mechanism to deal with conflict is *manic flight*, which avoids the conflict with a highly excited, over-active state of mind; *omnipotence* is a means of surviving that involves believing one is all powerful and all knowing (omniscient). This usually involves splitting and projecting vulnerable needs and feelings. *Introjection* is what happens when split off and projected aspects of the self, plus aspects of the other, enter the internal world. It is the mechanism for building up internal objects.

Klein put forward the second position as the *depressive position*. This is depression not as a psychiatric term but as part of normal development and this has caused confusion and hostility because there is resistance to seeing young children described as 'in the depressive position'. It could usefully have been given another name (a new word), but it does describe a very important step recognised by most psychoanalysts and developmental psychologists. Around about six months the child changes, becomes aware of others as whole people, feels concern for them (as Winnicott puts it) and there is a recognition of the possible damage done, a wish to make better *reparation* and a sadness at what has happened in fantasy and perhaps in reality. The individual is seen as moving backwards and forwards between the depressive and paranoid-schizoid positions. Klein elaborated the concept of *repetition compulsion*. She saw that where conflicts had not been resolved an individual manages to engineer similar situations perhaps so that this time the unconscious conflict can be resolved.

Klein also made a significant contribution to the development of our understanding about sexuality and sexual development. Her view of the early centrality of the powerful mother, who is feared and envied, as well as longed for, by both boys and girls, is important. Her view on the resolution of the Oedipal conflict as resulting in a combined internal creative parental couple is also very important, particularly because the resolution she described comes from love and acceptance rather than fear. She places the Oedipal conflict and its resolution considerably earlier than Freud and Anna Freud, who continued to place it around the onset of latency.

## D.W. WINNICOTT

Winnicott was committed to object relations development but saw this occurring less as a result of unconscious fantasy as proposed by Klein and more as a reaction to environmental failure or impingement, hopefully moderated by a *good enough mother*. Klein too recognised the importance of the *environment* but

Winnicott stressed this. Winnicott saw that there was no such thing as a baby, there could only be a baby and a carer – usually mother, and that this couple at the outset were absorbed in each other. He called this, on mother's side, *primary maternal preoccupation*, a crucial state of mind which enables the mother and baby to be in communication in a deep way, unconsciously and consciously. This leaves the mother vulnerable to the external world and its demands and she needs to be protected by her partner or family. Gradually the mother comes out of this state and hopefully the baby by then is resilient enough to tolerate some frustration and failure.

He went on to describe the place of mirroring in the early mother/child relationship when the child sees herself as mother sees her, in mother's eyes and face. This *mirroring* develops as an idea to explain how individuals unconsciously are made aware of themselves by others' responses and how this can also occur in groups – families and professional networks where different individuals, through projective identification, mirror the conflicts inside an individual or in a family amongst its members.

Winnicott noticed how children have a special toy or blanket – this becomes the *transitional object*: that is, it is in part separate as an external object, but it is also part of the self, of me, and also part of the other, mother. So it can be seen as providing a bridge or a transition as the child separates out from mother, also something concrete to hold on to that represents mother and is, at the same time, separate. This is seen as complementing and consolidating the development of internal objects, out of which the individual develops *the capacity to be alone* when the internal world of internal objects feels secure and solid enough.

The transitional object gives way to a *transitional space*, and in this space Winnicott envisages play taking place; for adults it is the space in which to be creative. He did a great deal of writing and giving papers to make his ideas accessible to professionals, doctors, nurses and parents. Winnicott contributed to our understanding of the countertransference, particularly in, 'Hate in the countertransference', (1947) where he elaborates the negative feelings that therapists have for their patients and makes sense of so many of the difficulties professionals have in their interactions with patients and clients. Acknowledging one can hate one's patients and seeing why makes working with them so much more effective.

Just as transference was once seen as a hindrance by Freud and others, and then later was seen as a valuable tool, psychoanalysts began to examine countertransference. Winnicott remained of the view that the countertransference should be seen as a hindrance to the work and arose because of the analyst's own unresolved issues. *Paula Heimann's* contribution to the understanding of the *countertransference* is very important in taking psychoanalytic ideas forward. She suggested that, as with the transference, which was first seen as a hindrance and then recognised as a very useful therapeutic tool, so with countertransference. She recognised that there are two aspects to countertransference: that which comes from the therapist/analysts' own issues, but also that which the therapist/analyst feels because of the projections and projective identifications that are going on between the patient and analyst. This has proved enormously helpful and makes sense of the experience we all share when for no obvious reason in ourselves we find that we are thinking, feeling or doing something which is not how we ourselves were before the meeting. When we become angry or enraged or depressed or hopeless and yet a little while before we were all right, it is helpful to consider 'Am I in touch with something the other person is communicating unconsciously?'

## WILFRED BION

Wilfred Bion is a post-Kleinian who significantly developed psychoanalytic ideas through his work with seriously disturbed psychotic patients. He described how we can avoid knowing and prefer not knowing as a means of dealing with conflict and this involves attacking our own and others' capacities to think and make links. He sees this not just in psychotics, but in all of us. He also then describes how we must sometimes think the unthinkable if we are to take any leaps forward; which he did.

He developed his own ideas about early infant development, which both explain and predate the paranoid-schiziod position. He describes how infants in the grip of psychotic or persecuting anxiety transmit what he calls beta elements (the mechanism for projective identification) and that the mother receives these elements and if she is good enough (Winnicott) and able, and if her own internal world is secure enough, she can function as a container in her mind. There these elements can be thought about, detoxified, made bearable and the mother transmits back to the baby the feeling that, although it felt awful, the feelings can be managed and understood and she and the baby will survive. When this is repeated times beyond number, the baby develops a sense that it is *contained*, that the mother is a *container* that can be trusted; then slowly the baby internalises this containing function until it can contain itself and its own feelings. When the mother cannot contain the infant is left in terror which can result in a state of *nameless dread*, fear of annihilation or a feeling of being dropped, fragmented, not just split but in splinters so that its internal and external world becomes inhabited by these splinters – bizarre objects: for example, the incoherent and inconsistent thoughts and feelings encountered when with severely traumatised individuals.

Bion also made a major contribution to our understanding of groups, group process and group behaviour. He saw that large groups in some ways function with mechanisms similar to those used by his psychotic patients. The group can become dependent, or there can be fights or flights (running away) or there can be sexual arousal and pairings. He recognised that all these were ways of avoiding conflict and hence were anti-task, preventing work occurring. This understanding can be very helpful in making sense of what happens in families, in staff groups and in multi-professional meetings, where one person can carry/express something for everyone or where the group behaviour blocks progress.

There are many more psychoanalysts who have or are contributing important ideas. We have concentrated on key people as we see it but, in doing so, in no way want to minimise the work of the others. A full review of psychoanalytic ideas would be another book in itself.

# Chapter 3

# Early applications

## Children and institutions

*Marion Bower*

From the very beginning psychoanalytic ideas have been used to understand a wide variety of human activities, and Freud himself was the first to do this. His recent biographer Peter Gay (1988) notes that between 1905 and 1915 Freud published papers on literature, law, religion, education, art, ethics, linguistics, folklore, fairy tales, mythology, archaeology, the psychology of schoolboys and war.

However, these early applications were limited to attempts to deepen our understanding of certain activities whereas psychoanalysis itself aims not only for understanding, but also for change and development. In a sense Melanie Klein's development of the play technique was the earliest full application of psychoanalysis. It made it possible for the first time to psychoanalyse very young children and at the same time opened up new areas of understanding of very early mental development. At the time her ideas of the complexity of early mental life were greeted with derision; however, modern developmental psychology using sophisticated observation techniques and video has independently confirmed the immense richness of early mother–baby interaction and the complexity of infant mental life.

Prior to the Second World War there were few attempts to apply psychoanalytical ideas in a practical way. However, during the Second World War many psychoanalysts enlisted as army psychiatrists and were involved in the selection of officers and the rehabilitation of soldiers who had broken down under the stresses of war. An example of this was the work of Wilfred Bion who pioneered the use of groups both as a means of selecting officers and as a therapeutic technique. Although Bion's work was very successful he was not allowed to continue it. This resistance to psychoanalytic ideas and techniques, however practical, is something which will be encountered again and again.

As well as the work of the army psychiatrists, there were also psychoanalysts who became involved in the care of children who were separated from or who had lost their parents, and this work will be described in more detail below. After the war these initiatives developed along a number of different streams. One of these has been the attempt to develop institutions which can care for children in a way which is beneficial for their emotional and intellectual development. Related to this was a new field which was the understanding and 'therapy' of institutions themselves. This work was carried out not just by psychoanalysts but by sociologists and anthropologists with considerable knowledge of psychoanalytic ideas.

Another stream was the modification of 'classic' psychoanalytic practice where a patient is seen five times a week into other forms of psychoanalytically based therapy. This included the development of the child psychotherapy training initiated by Martha Harris and John Bowlby at the Tavistock Clinic in 1948. The work begun by Bion with groups has developed into a treatment used with both adults and children. Bion's hospital experiments, along with the work of other pioneers including Tom Main, has been extended into the concept of therapeutic communities for the treatment of very disturbed adults and children.

The third area of development was the recognition that psychoanalytic ideas could be of value to professionals working in a wide variety of settings in institutions and in the community, including doctors, social workers and teachers. An example of this application were the 'Balint' groups set up by the psychoanalyst Michael Balint to enable GPs to deepen their understanding of their patients. On a wider scale Martha Harris initiated 'work discussion' groups at the Tavistock Clinic where professionals from a variety of backgrounds have been able to discuss their work with children and families within a psychoanalytic framework of understanding.

A natural extension of this has been the growing practice of carrying out therapeutic work in a wide variety of institutions including hospitals and schools and health centres. Examples of all these types of application will be given in later chapters of this book. This chapter describes three early projects in institutions which have had a considerable influence on how children are cared for in institutions today. I also describe briefly the work of John

Bowlby who laid enormous stress on the value of family life for children and the need to support parents in caring for their children, which is an important theme of our book. These early applications provide a vivid picture of some of the psychoanalytic ideas presented in the previous chapter, particularly the influence of early experience on later development, the power of the *unconscious* and the operation of *defences* against emotional pain and anxiety.

The three institutional projects, which all took place within fifteen years of each other, show the rapid evolution of psychoanalytic thinking and the increasing sophistication with which it is being used in the community. They also illustrate the fruitful marriages that can be made between psychoanalytic thinking and other disciplines, such as developmental psychology and sociology.

This work also illustrates the struggle involved in working with psychoanalytic ideas. Helping people or institutions face emotional pain, anxiety and conflict is not necessarily a popular activity, and can take a long time to achieve. However, we believe the rewards make this struggle very worthwhile.

## THE HAMPSTEAD WARTIME NURSERIES

These were started in 1940 by Anna Freud and her friend Dorothy Burlingham. These residential nurseries cared for children who had either lost their parents or were separated from their parents because of the demands of the war. This included children whose mothers were engaged in war work or who were in hospital for various reasons. The psychoanalytic ideas which Anna Freud brought to this work included an awareness of the great significance to the first few years of life for later development, and the enormous importance of parents for children's emotional wellbeing. She observed and recorded the various defences and adaptations that children made to these painful separations.

These observations were the precursors of an enormous explosion of post-war research into early mother/child relationships, including the psychoanalytic technique of baby observation which Esther Bick developed in the 1950s (see Chapter 4). The techniques which Anna Freud developed to mitigate the effects of separation are standard practice in many institutions for children today. These included encouraging parents to visit freely and as often as possible rather than the 'clean break' advocated for children evacuated during the war. This allowed children to develop an understanding that although parents went away they would return. Children were organised in family-sized groups with one nurse and a regular back-up nurse for her days off. This ensured continuity of care and gave children the opportunity of forming a close relationship with a mother substitute. Anna Freud observed the beneficial effects of this regime on the children's development. They became more possessive of 'their' nurse, but were more willing to make sacrifices for her and they related better to each other.

Although Anna Freud underestimated the emotional significance of the mother in the first few months of life, her work stresses the serious consequences of separating children under 3 from their mothers for long periods. She shrewdly observed that, where children were separated from parents because their parents had died, there was the expectation that their behaviour would show signs of disturbance and this was treated with sympathy and understanding. Where children were separated from their parents for other reasons their signs of distress did not receive the same support.

This apparent insensitivity could be attributed to ignorance. However, subsequent work has shown that there is an emotional *resistance* to the awareness of children's emotional needs and distress. The strength of this resistance is vividly illustrated by the work of James Robertson who began as a social worker in the Hampstead Nurseries and was considerably influenced by his experiences of children and the effects of separation on them.

## THE WORK OF THE ROBERTSONS

In 1948 James Robertson joined John Bowlby at the Tavistock Clinic to study the reactions of young children to separations from their mothers. Initially the plan was to observe children whose mothers had gone into hospital, but it was found to be more practical to observe children who had gone into hospital themselves. In February 1948 James Robertson visited the children's ward of the Central Middlesex Hospital and stumbled across misery which was to be the subject of his work for many years to come. His own description of the ward conveys the science very powerfully.

In a ward that was busy with the movement of nurses, and with the activities of the older children, these younger ones sat in their cots desolate and tearful or deeply silent. They did not understand why the parents who had cared for them were not there; their needs were immediate and they had no time sense to help them understand that their parents would come tomorrow or the next day. They were overwhelmed. If a nurse stopped beside a silent toddler, he would usually burst into tears at the human contact and the nurse would be rebuked for 'making him unhappy'.

(Robertson and Robertson 1989: 11)

Although it seems hard to imagine now, it was the belief then that it was unsettling for children to be visited by parents and most hospitals confined parents' visits to a few hours at weekends. Robertson continued his observations, not only of short-stay wards, but also of long-stay hospitals and residential nurseries. He observed and described a pattern of response to separation which he called protest, despair and detachment. Children separated for short periods went through a period of active distress and searching; later on this gave way to an apathy, punctuated perhaps by crying, which was described by the hospital as 'he was upset at first but he's settled now'.

Robertson found that, if separation continued for longer, children entered a phase of detachment where they repressed the need for their parents and developed superficial, indiscriminate contacts with whatever adult was available. As Robertson pointed out, this type of indiscriminate behaviour would cause concern in a child at home but was accepted with relief by the institutions. Follow-up studies showed that even if children returned home these disturbances of behaviour and capacity to form relationships persisted for years to come.

However, to return to James Robertson in 1948, his problem was to convince sceptical medical authorities that it was the *absence* of parents rather than their presence which unsettled children. In 1951 with the aid of a borrowed cine camera he made the now famous film *A Two Year Old Goes to Hospital*. This is a study of a 2-year-old girl who goes into hospital for a routine operation, whose desperate attempts to manage her own distress were filmed at regular intervals to counter the accusation that she would be filmed only when upset.

Even after many years this film still makes distressing viewing. However, at the time, with the exception of a few enlightened doctors and nurses it was greeted with outrage, its accuracy repudiated and the film-maker accused of seeking publicity for his own gain. Using his psychoanalytic understanding Robertson suggested that the level of outrage suggested the fear of a breakdown of defences erected against an awareness of children's emotional pain. We defend ourselves against such awareness because this awareness resonates with painful experiences of our own. In fact Robertson's earliest allies were the parents of children in hospital who recognised the truth of his portrayal.

In fact, it took nearly ten years from the first showing of the film to the Platt Report of 1959 which recommended the extension of hospital visiting times, something which parents today accept as their right. It would be a mistake to think that these 'bad old days' were over; in fact, there continues to be an enormous resistance in our society to any attempt to draw attention to children's emotional needs or suffering, and this is something that we may be becoming less sensitive to, rather than more so. An interesting illustration of this, which echoes Robertson's experiences, was the film *For the Sake of the Children* transmitted by the BBC in 1994. This film was about the effects of divorce on children and based on research carried out in Exeter by a paediatrician and a researcher funded by the Rowntree Foundation. This research contradicted received wisdom that children are 'better off' if parents end an unhappy marriage. In fact, the researchers encountered very high levels of emotional distress and somatic illness in children affected by divorce and remarriage. The reality of this distress was communicated by a very tearful little boy and his parents undergoing a first assessment interview at a child guidance clinic.

Although much of the response to the film was positive, the film was also viciously criticised in the *Guardian* for exploiting a child's misery and those involved accused of seeking publicity for themselves, a response very similar to that which greeted James Robertson, and which encourages us to ignore the painful realities behind the film. A more concrete illustration of this type of denial was the recent revelation that premature babies have been subjected to painful medical interventions of a sort that would normally require an anaesthetic in an adult. Perhaps it is not a coincidence that many of the early psychoanalytic studies were carried out in hospital settings where suffering and the defences against it are particularly high.

## ANOTHER HOSPITAL STUDY: THE WORK OF
## ISABEL MENZIES LYTH

The emphasis in James Robertson's work is on the need for the institution to change for the good of the children. Isabel Menzies Lyth's work illustrates that certain models of institutional care are damaging for staff as well as those they care for. Like James Robertson's, her 'classic' study concerned a hospital, but in this case the situation was very different. The hospital themselves had asked her to examine certain aspects of the training of nurses. Using Kleinian theories of unconscious anxiety and defences, as well as the concepts of projective and introjective identification, Menzies Lyth was able to make an in-depth analysis of how the hospital functioned in certain key areas and make recommendations for change.

As in any other type of therapy the problem of nurse allocation was regarded as the 'presenting symptom' requiring a further understanding of what lay behind it. As the study progressed a different problem emerged, which was the high level of distress and anxiety among the nurses. This had very serious consequences: about a third of the nurses, including those who were very able, withdrew from training, senior staff changed jobs frequently and sickness rates were high. Menzies Lyth identified that this was due not just to the stress and anxiety of the job itself but *how the institution was structured to manage it.*

The anxiety and stress that nurses confront has a very strong objective basis. Nurses come into direct and intimate contact with injured, ill and dying people. Patients may view them with either hatred or resentment or may project into them feelings of anxiety and depression.

However, drawing on Melanie Klein's work on early anxiety situations, Menzies Lyth points out that these objective anxieties bear a close resemblance to unconscious phantasy situations that exist at the deepest levels of all our minds. These early anxiety situations relate to an inner world, whose origin lies in infancy, peopled by the infant and people who are deeply significant. These 'internal objects' exist in a form determined by the infant's phantasies. At this early stage these may be intensely cruel and aggressive and as a result the inner world is felt to be peopled by dead and dying objects.

For the small child these anxieties are allayed by encountering the objective world of people in a very much better state and these objective experiences modify the inner world of phantasy. The infant also makes reparation through love and achievements for the harm done in phantasy. This is not the situation of the nurse: the objective situation she encounters is like our worst phantasies. However, if she is able to see this external world as *symbolic* of her inner world, that is, representing it *but not the same*, then by successfully nursing patients the nurse can repair and make *reparation* to her own damaged objects and so obtain satisfaction at both a professional and a deeply personal level.

Unfortunately, the system under which the nurses worked prevented them from confronting these anxieties and operated like a primitive defence against anxiety which evades anxiety rather than confronting and overcoming it. The essence of this defence was that nurses were prevented from having any meaningful contact or attachment to patients. For example, patients were de-personalised as 'the pneumonia in bed 15', nursing was split into ritualised repetitive tasks carried out on a large number of patients by a number of nurses, rather than one nurse nursing a 'whole patient'. Nurses were expected to move wards frequently and were prevented from forming attachments to each other or the patients. Decisions were delegated upwards and there was little opportunity for personal initiative.

It is easy to see that being nursed in this fragmented and de-personalised way was bad for patients; however, Menzies Lyth points out that it is also bad for nurses. At an objective level nurses were denied the satisfaction of exercising their professional expertise and judgement fully. At an emotional level they were denied the satisfaction of encountering and mastering anxiety situations and gaining strength and confidence from doing so. The institution was composed of people, and it had incorporated the most primitive and unhelpful of defences against anxiety and therefore became an external constraint to the development of its members.

In Chapter 17 we reprint a later paper by Menzies Lyth in which she describes how a children's home became a more satisfactory model for both staff and children. Her work has enormous practical implications. Firstly we can see that, if we want to improve an institution, whether it is a hospital, a school or a day nursery, it is not enough to increase the skills or sensitivity of individual members; the organisation of the institution itself will need to change. However, because institutions frequently operate primitive defences against anxiety they are immensely resistant to any changes which threaten these defences. The enormous resistance of institutions to changes which are clearly helpful will be familiar to many people.

The last thirty years have seen a trend away from caring for young children in residential institutions to trying to keep them in their own families or in another family by fostering or adoption. This change has been very much influenced by the work of John Bowlby, a psychoanalyst who in turn was very influenced by ethology, anthropology and developmental psychology. As his work has considerable implications for how we care for children and support families, I shall summarise it in more detail here.

## THE WORK OF JOHN BOWLBY

Bowlby was a psychiatrist who also trained as a psychoanalyst and his work is based on two central psychoanalytic principles: firstly the enormous importance of the mother for a child's development and secondly the influence of early experience on later development. In its earliest form this was the concept of 'maternal deprivation'. In the period immediately after the Second World War Bowlby believed that if a child is separated from its mother during the first few years of life it will suffer lasting emotional damage. This extreme position was understandable in the light of the experiences of the Second World War when so many children had been separated from their parents, often under very unsatisfactory circumstances. Unfortunately, Bowlby based his theories on very unsatisfactory research evidence, and subsequent research has shown that, although the complete absence of a maternal figure is invariably damaging (privation), other types of loss and deprivation were not necessarily so damaging. Ironically, this difficulty arose in Bowlby's work because he omitted from his theory another key psychoanalytic idea, the concept of an internal world, which allows us to account for individual differences in response and experience. In fact, subsequent research has shown that children who have experienced a period of maternal care, even if it is fairly brief, may internalise a good enough internal object to see them through later adversity and keep alive the hope of finding something good in life. This is a very strong reason to offer mothers of young babies as much support as possible as this may make an enormous difference to a child even if other types of care are used later.

Bowlby's later concept of *attachment theory* has had lasting impact and usefulness. The basic tenets of this theory are that children need a stable attachment figure whom they will seek out in times of anxiety or danger. A secure attachment forms the basis from which a child can explore the world and underpins the capacity for forming relationships with other trusted people. Once having formed a secure attachment the individual is then capable, if the attachment is broken, of making further attachments. A necessary consequence of attachment is that *separation* from a loved person is painful and distressing. Prolonged separation leads to sadness and mourning, and an example of this is given by James Robertson earlier in this chapter (see p. 25). The implications of this for how we care for children are very far reaching but only very partially accepted. For example, it is widely recognised that a child who shows sadness and upset on first starting school is behaving 'normally'. However, it is far less widely recognised that a young child who separates from its mother without apparent concern on first starting a day nursery should be a source of concern; more commonly such a child will be said to 'separate well'.

Although Bowlby has been accused by some feminists of being responsible for the closure of day nurseries, the dangers of leaving very young children in day nurseries for as long as eight or ten hours a day for almost fifty-two weeks a year are rarely questioned. In fact, it is not uncommon for private and some council-run day nurseries to take babies as young as three months. This would be hard for children under any circumstances, but a programme broadcast by *Panorama* on 1 August 1994 claimed that half of Britain's day nurseries provide poor or mediocre standards of care. (The consequences of this and how they may be remedied are described in Chapter 19.)

Is this simply a conflict of interests? In the current economic climate many women need to work, and it is important that women have the opportunity to gain satisfaction from exercising their skills as well as benefiting from the social contacts at work. Ironically, the solution to this dilemma involves recognising the enormous importance that a mother has for a child's development. For those mothers who want to stay at home there needs to be far greater recognition and support, which I will discuss in more detail below. For those mothers who want to work there needs to be a more wholehearted awareness that good day care for young children involves providing something as near as possible to that which a mother does. The opportunity to form an attachment to a consistent substitute carer, who is emotionally receptive to the child and their needs. This secondary attachment can not only enable the child to cope with the absent mother, but also enrich the child's experience. This is not an impossible task. In Chapter 19 Lynn Barnett describes how a day nursery can be changed to provide a more satisfactory model of care. Yet, despite the extensive evidence that bad day care is emotionally and intellectually damaging for children, and the success of Barnett and Bain's work, there have been remarkably few attempts to build on these achievements and understanding. It seems unlikely that financial issues alone can explain this. To provide proper emotional care of small children is an enormously demanding task. In a professional context it requires both training and skilled support and it would also involve acknowledging how arduous and demanding being 'only a mother' actually is. It is not surprising therefore, given the financial pressures, isolation and lack of being valued many mothers suffer, that many feel unable to cope. There are remarkably few organisations in our society which offer support to mothers and fathers who want to care for their children themselves, unless there have been serious concerns about abuse.

In contrast to the huge sums of money which have been spent on research on the importance of mother/child relationships, many of the projects described in this book, even when operating in a statutory context, are run on a shoestring, dependent on grants or money from charities. Too often the only support available to a mother in difficulties is the offer of a day nursery place, which may temporarily alleviate the situation, but in the long run is likely to diminish her self-esteem and, unless the nursery can offer skilled support, is likely to exacerbate the situation. Bowlby was a powerful advocate of the need to support and value parents. This is not just a moral stance but a practical one, as he pointed out: 'Successful parenting is a principal key to the mental health of the next generation' (Bowlby 1993: 1). We hope this book will be a practical contribution to this principle.

# Individuals and families

*Marion Bower*

The purpose of these linking sections is to place the chapters in context as well as looking at some of the wider applications of the psychoanalytic concepts used (for descriptions of these, see Chapter 2).

There is remarkably little provision for practical and emotional support for parents and young children. The current emphasis on 'targeting' resources to families in need often means that where resources are scarce, as they often are, only families presenting extreme or easily identifiable problems, such as abuse or violence, will get help. For this reason we have included examples of work with families with more 'ordinary' problems.

Our first chapter on baby observation introduces two themes which recur over and over again in this book. The first is the very real difficulty we all have in allowing ourselves direct contact with and awareness of the raw and powerful emotions experienced and generated by young babies. It is the impact of these feelings which make parenthood such a stressful task, particularly if a mother is on her own or without adequate social support.

This introduces our second major theme. A well-supported mother (and fathers can often play a vital role here) can be receptive and responsive to her baby's feelings without being excessively anxious and by processing these feelings in her mind can make them more bearable and manageable for her baby (this is the concept of *containment* described in Chapter 2).

In the same way a professional who is well supported in the way illustrated by Trowell and Miles can be receptive to the emotional pain or suffering of their clients. This willingness to 'see' suffering or unhappiness, particularly in babies or small children, can be a life or death matter for social workers involved in cases of abuse, as many enquiries have illustrated. At the other extreme, support can enable workers to contain a problem in their minds without rushing into premature action.

This type of receptiveness and awareness of children's emotional needs and feelings lies at the heart of all good childcare practice, as some of our later chapters illustrate. There is a tendency to emphasise the need young children have for 'stimulation' at the expense of the need they also have for something more tender and reflective. In Chapter 19 Lynn Barnett describes the level of skilled support needed by nursery nurses to adopt this more receptive stance.

This raises the question of what happens to powerful emotions if they are ignored or neglected? Emanuel Lewis (1976) has discussed what happens if the need to mourn the loss of a miscarried or stillborn baby is ignored. Lewis draws attention to the distinction Freud made between normal *mourning*, which despite all its sadness releases us to get on with life, and mourning which is cut short or fails to take place, with its guilt, depression and identification with the lost object. This can impede enjoyment and progress in life. Lewis describes how siblings of stillborn children may fail to make progress at school because of this burden.

Here we see how important it is for the world of 'child mental health' and the world of 'education' to be more aware of each other's existence. Many 'child mental health problems' manifest themselves as learning or behaviour difficulties in school, and schools can be non-stigmatising settings in which help can be offered. In later chapters of the book we will be illustrating how children can be helped within a school setting.

In contrast to the experience of losing a baby, Rosalie Kerbekian describes the effects on parents and professionals when a baby arrives early and survives against all the odds. Kerbekian emphasises the importance of *containment* not only for parents and professionals but also for the babies themselves. Kerbekian movingly describes how their emotional and physical suffering can be alleviated to some extent by sensitive and receptive parents and medical staff.

Hospital settings provide particularly vivid illustrations of the power of *unconscious phantasy*. Birth, illness and death are all associated with phantasies which have meaning and significance beyond the objective experience. The chapter by Kerbekian replicates Isabel Menzies Lyth's findings (described in Chapter 17) that the stress on medical staff lies in the mixture of physical suffering and powerful unconscious anxieties that they deal with. As Kerbekian illustrates, supporting medical staff to be more emotionally receptive is not necessarily welcome because this disturbs the defences erected against pain and anxiety.

Dilys Daws describes the work of a child psychotherapist in a very different type of health care setting. Being physically located in a health centre has given her the opportunity to make brief and effective interactions with young children and families. This is true preventive work. Up until now health visitors have been particularly effective in identifying families needing help and finding it for them. However, with the many changes taking place in their role and organisation, it is important that new avenues are opened up to make contact with 'ordinary' young families in distress.

Daws's chapter also illustrates the difficult decisions and judgements which need to be made when working with families from other cultures. Her judgement that it was not 'natural' for a young woman to give her baby away, unless there were considerable pressures at work on her, is an important reminder that we need to keep sight of areas of common human experience and feeling at the same time as being aware of real cultural differences in experiences and expectation.

Later chapters in this book will illustrate how some of these similarities and differences can be kept in mind. At the end of this book there is also a brief discussion of some of the unconscious processes which underlie racism. It is interesting that the issue of class is often neglected. An example of this is found in the very different kinds of adjustments that need to be made by refugees from urban professional families and by those who come from poor rural communities.

Chapter 7 illustrates how psychoanalytic concepts of *projective identification, unconscious phantasy* and *containment* can be of value in working with families. An understanding of the unconscious meaning and communication involved in children's play can be enormously valuable in working with families with young or non-verbal children. This chapter also provides a particularly clear illustration of the value of *countertransference*. The worker's feelings of hopelessness about making contact with the mother provided an important clue as to what was going on in the family. Like *transference*, countertransference operates all the time, even if we do not plan to work with it; and many experienced and sensitive workers feel uncomfortable about powerful feelings of despair, rage or helplessness that clients can evoke in them. Rather than being seen as signs of professional 'weakness' these feelings need to be taken seriously.

Psychoanalytic ideas are unfashionable in social work at the moment. Stress is now laid very much on social and political factors, inequalities and oppressions, whether racial or otherwise. As we state in Chapter 1, we believe it is essential to keep these in mind. However, Anna Kerr's chapter suggests that there has been a loss of awareness of the importance of the inner world and unconscious forces. Kerr suggests that this loss can mean a loss of real empathy and compassion for clients struggling with powerful emotions and internal conflicts over which they have less control than we would like. We believe that the need to keep a balanced awareness between the external and internal unconscious factors influencing families is also a very practical one.

Child protection plans tend to emphasise the changes that need to take place in parents' behaviour. Trowell's research at the Monroe Centre (Chapter 11) suggests that changes in the parents' *internal* world and the development of insight are necessary for real growth and emotional healing to take place. The fact that such changes take time and considerable skill to achieve is not a reason for not aiming for them. We also have to accept the painful fact that for some families these changes are not possible, and difficult decisions need to be made.

Growth and development seem so obviously desirable that it is tempting to ignore the forces that operate against them. There are of course many external factors, such as poverty, unemployment and emotional damage, whose effects are hard to resist. However, there are also forces inside us which operate against change. Sue Kegerreis' chapter describes the operation of *envy*. This was first described by Melanie Klein, as an impulse to spoil or destroy the source of good things (to 'bite the hand that feeds us'). As Kegerreis points out, it is particularly striking in an educational setting, whose whole aim is growth or learning. Yet it is so common that few teachers have not experienced a child who has spoiled their own good work or the work of others or somehow 'mucked up' an exam they were expected to do well in.

There is controversy within psychoanalytic circles as to whether envy is constitutional or arises because of frustration and adverse experiences. Klein herself thought that the two interacted, that constitutional envy could be increased by adverse experiences.

Kegerreis also describes the phenomenon of the *negative thera-peutic reaction*, where a step forward is followed by one or even two steps back. Envy can be a factor in this, but Kegerreis also describes how an increase in depressive anxiety can also contribute to this.

Envy and other forces opposing change exist in many settings. Most of us have had an experience of inexplicably 'shooting ourselves in the foot' or making the worst of something potentially helpful. Dealing with clients, pupils or patients in the grip of these negative forces is frustrating, but awareness of what this is about can make it more tolerable.

## Chapter 4

# The contribution of observation training to professional development

## Judith Trowell and Gillian Miles

*The paper reprinted here was written specifically about an initiative to develop and encourage applications of observation training within social work training. It is reproduced here, as we feel the model and its applications remain a useful example which could be adapted for other professional trainings.*

## SUMMARY

The paper first describes a range of uses of observational training and the learning to which it can give rise. It goes on to describe in detail a specific project that was undertaken by the authors with a selected group of social work trainers. The range of observations undertaken by the participants is described and their own comments provide first-hand evaluations of the experience. Observation is seen by the authors as one of the most important foundation skills in professional development within the caring professions.

## INTRODUCTION

Throughout the three years of social work with the Beckfords, Ms Walstrom totally misconceived her role as the fieldworker enforcing care orders in respect of two very young children at risk. Her gaze focused on Beverly Lorrington and Morris Beckford; she averted her eyes from the children to be aware of them only as and when they were with their parents, hardly even to observe their development, and never to communicate with Jasmine on her own.

(Blom Cooper, London Borough of Brent, 1985)

Why is it so difficult to see what is going on in front of our eyes? In 1953 James and Joyce Robertson made the film *A Two Year Old Goes to Hospital* and, rather like the conversion of St Paul on the road to Damascus, we were all forced to see what really happens to a child during hospital admission. The Robertsons were not the first to be aware, but because of the power of their presentation on film the painful effects of hospitalisation could not be avoided. Spitz in 1945 described the destructive effects of long-term group care on infants, and Winnicott in 1941 described what is seen if babies are observed, but both of these accounts were written material that could be overlooked. The Robertsons in their series of films forced awareness of the child's world into the consciousness of professionals and the public. Others have looked at vulnerable groups in the population: for example, Irving Goffman (1958/61), in *Asylums*, focuses on mental patients. It seems that the only way in the first instance that anyone can see is by combining a determined and courageous stand, with a research passion to find out.

In the early 1950s the use of infant observation as a training tool began for those intending to work with troubled and disturbed children using a psychodynamic approach. A child analyst, Ester Bick, introduced the practice of systematic observation of the development of infants. This consisted of the student observing a baby, starting as soon after the birth as possible, and observing once a week for an hour over a year. Notes were not taken at the time, but students were expected to record in details afterwards the interaction they had observed, the emphasis being on what had been seen and felt rather than the student's own explanations or speculations on what might have been happening. This written account was brought for presentation to a small weekly seminar of three to six people where each student presented their material at least twice a term in the presence of a seminar leader. The task of the seminar was

> to explore, on the basis of the available evidence, the emotional events between infant and mother and the other members of the family present during observations. There may also be a babyminder or nanny sharing in the care of the baby and this might be part of what is directly observed. The aim is to describe the development of the relationships between infants and others, including the observer, and to try to understand the

unconscious aspects of behaviour and patterns of communication. Over time, a picture emerges which embraces a good deal
of knowledge of the characteristic dynamics of family interaction. Aspects of the inner world of the family members which
underline their personalities and relationships become manifest.
In particular, the creation of the infant's personality, the interaction between constitutional and temperamental factors in the
baby and the particular strengths and weaknesses of the holding
environment can be considered.

(Rustin in Miller *et al.* 1989: 7–8)

An early explanation of the method can be found in a paper by
Bick (1964). From Mrs Bick's start within the child psychoanalytic
field the use of infant observation spread geographically and
spread also in terms of its use. Young child observation developed
out of infant observation, firstly by extension for child psychotherapists of their observations, then other professional trainings
such as those for doctors, nurses and teachers found young child
observation a useful training tool. Family observation has since
developed, but is more difficult to manage. Institutional observation
has proved easier and highly productive, and students have observed
in a range of settings, such as supermarkets, offices, shops, hair-
dressers, schools, day nurseries and hospitals. The research study
by Bain and Barnett (1980) and the work of Menzies Lyth (1988)
describe examples of institutional observation in practice. A significant lead on institutional observation has been offered by Obholzer
and his colleagues at the Tavistock Clinic, although the work awaits
formal publication.

In the 1980s there has, however, been a blossoming of accounts
of infant and young child observations, including Stern (1985),
Piontelli (1986), Waddell (1987), Brafman (1988) and Miller *et al.*
(1989).

## THE USE OF OBSERVATION IN SOCIAL
## WORK TRAINING

The concept of observation is not new in social work training.
Some social work training courses have required students to carry
out some form of observation, usually of group care, and not
necessarily focusing on any one individual subject over time. Some
post-qualification social work courses, usually specifically in child

care, have had observation as a component module. An evaluation of five of these courses carried out by the DES shows that some students felt that the child observation module had been central to their learning on the course and 'the most useful thing they had ever done' (DES 1988).

Why has observation not developed in social work training, or lapsed where it had been used? This would seem to be for a number of reasons. First, finding a suitable subject to observe and setting up a contract can be very stressful. Then, students can become anxious because they are unclear about the observer role. The result of this is often that students appear to become bored. Again, the content can be very distressing and students who become upset may cease to attend.

The observation seminar depends on the skills of the seminar leader and, skilfully run, provides a setting where anxiety and distress can be safely discussed, thus enabling learning to take root at a deep level. The leader's knowledge from experience of the power and the usefulness of observation as a training experience is vital if the meaning of the task is to be sustained. All too easily observation can become a superficial, meaningless exercise.

What can social workers learn from observation? In their professional role they are required, bearing in mind issues of race and gender, to assess, monitor and make decisions and judgements about situations involving complex human relationships, which are often highly charged emotionally and where action may have far-reaching consequences. We would suggest that, prior to any action, social workers need to be capable of taking an observational stance to give themselves the possibility of objectivity in coming to their conclusions. The observational stance requires them to be aware of the environment, the verbal and non-verbal interaction; to be aware of their own responses as a source of invaluable data, provided they are aware of what comes from them and what from their clients; and to develop the capacity to integrate these and give themselves time to think before arriving at a judgement or making a decision.

By the very nature of their task, social workers are constantly asked to work with acutely painful situations. As we will be describing, all the members of our course found aspects of their observations extremely painful: for example, to watch a child's needs being ignored or to follow the cumulative trauma of constantly disrupted placements for a small child. It is extremely difficult to bear such pain or the associated feelings that might be stirred by what is seen from the worker's own past experience. Action can so easily take over as a way of avoiding the impact of what is seen, if it can be seen at all. Observation training, with its supporting seminars, gives the opportunity to reflect on the experience, and to understand and tolerate the emotional impact.

The mind of the trained observer needs to include several simultaneous functioning perspectives (see Fig. 1). In addition a range of other aspects of learning can follow from observing (Fig. 2). Observing can provide the student with an opportunity to become familiar with the individual's internal and external world (including issues of race, culture and gender), as a precursor to learning the skills of communications, e.g. a young child's observations lead to communication with other children.

We and our colleagues have used observation in social work training in the following ways in post-qualification courses.

1 *Child protection course.* Young child observation – 10 weekly observations with 10 weekly seminars.
2 *Post-qualification child care course over 2 years.* Nine months weekly observation of an infant and 9 months weekly observation of a young child with weekly seminar for 2 academic years.
3 *Social work tutor's course to become observation seminar leaders.* Nine months weekly observation, mix of observations of infants and young children. Weekly seminar throughout.
4 *Multi-disciplinary group working with severely disturbed adults.* Nine months weekly observation of infant, with weekly seminar.
5 *Course on organization and institutional process.* Two terms of weekly observation of an institution.
6 *Post-qualification specialist child care course.* Five fortnightly observations of young child with fortnightly seminar.

## A SPECIFIC PROJECT

The Report of the Inquiry into Child Abuse in Cleveland, 1987 (Butler-Sloss 1988) was one in a long line of child abuse enquiries to point out the ease with which the child is lost sight of when there are very needy families and the difficulties, in these highly charged situations, of carrying out careful, thoughtful, thorough assessments.

The Central Council for Education and Training in Social Work, UK (CCETSW), in response to this concern about social work

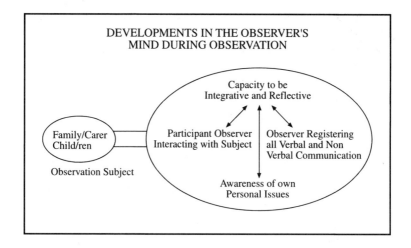

*Figure 1* Developments in the observer's mind during observation

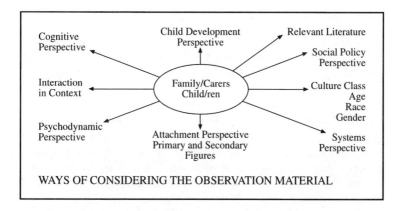

*Figure 2* Ways of considering the observation material

training, sponsored as one of its projects a Training in Observation for social work tutors who, it was hoped, would then become able to teach observation skills on their own courses. The hope was that over time this would create a growing number of teachers in the field. It was recognised from the start that the first priority was to train these seminar leaders and that the quality of the teaching observation skills would depend on the skill of the leaders.

Ten social work tutors from across the country joined this course for an academic year. They observed children ranging in age from newborn to 4 years, for one hour weekly. The children were a mix of boys and girls, cared for in their natural families, by a single parent, in care, in substitute families and in day nurseries. The children had a range of racial and cultural backgrounds; some were only children, some had older siblings and others had become the older sibling when a new baby arrived.

The participants attended a weekly seminar to consider their detailed recording of their observations. In addition, there were theory days to discuss various theoretical perspectives both on family relationships, child development and current research, race and gender, and on the application of observation to social work training. To conclude the training and to enable the participants to make sense of the experience, each member wrote a paper on an aspect of the observation, centred on a particular area of interest that had been sparked off for them.

**Examples of some of the observations**

*Case history 1.* A black child in an inner city day nursery 8.30 – 5.30, five days a week, where the first impression was of a bright, colourful, relaxed environment. What emerged was a picture of limited mechanistic play activities and the need to conform to such an extent that when a child, who for weeks remained silent, isolated, masturbating or sucking his thumb, joined in a nursery rhyme song he was told not to shout and to be quiet. The carers were, bar one, all white and their preoccupation was in gaining support from each other, e.g. at lunch time talking to each other, leaving the children to feed themselves, remaining unaware of the children's difficulties.

*Case history 2.* A child moved through five placements in the year. The number of adults and children in this child's experience became hard to remember, just as it was not easy for the observer to see the particular child because of the need repeatedly to establish a relationship with the adults and children in the new environment. When visible, the child's distress and withdrawal were painful, but only noticeable because of the comparisons possible over time, the child having been seen consistently in the different contexts. The child's resilience was impressive; when at last given permanence, her developmental progress was a delight.

*Case history 3.* A new baby in a middle-class natural family aroused concern because of lack of responsiveness. Developmental delay was a real worry. Over time the mother's depression and exhaustion became apparent. The father was absent for long periods on business and the older child repeatedly woke afraid at night. A few weeks after father's return the baby showed marked progress in development and seemed to come alive. Anxiety about developmental delay evaporated.

*Case history 4.* In a middle-class suburb the central issue of the observation became whether this was a safe environment for a young child. The observer was constantly concerned as dangerous moments were perceived or recounted. The mother's state of mind was a worry, but there was always her accompanying explanation that what took place fitted with her own or her husband's cultural background (between the two all eventualities could be 'normalised').

The impact of observation was powerful and unexpected to the participants. Finding a subject to observe was more difficult than they expected and this seemed to be linked to the problem of shedding their professional roles and feelings of vulnerability in a student role. It was not easy to find a comfortable way of being because the situation of observer was an untried role which was neither a professional nor a social relationship. They all became aware of the painful position of dependent small children, and the inadequate and inappropriate provision for them, and also aware of how powerless and hopeless the adults could feel. Most striking, however, was the ease with which they became concerned for the adults and on the occasion lost sight of the child.

### Examples of particular problems

In case history 1 a black observer struggling with issues of racism and deprivation.

In case history 2 the recognition by the observer that she had become the most consistent figure in the child's life, who at times seemed to know more about the child than anyone else. She felt the pain of knowing what impact the constant moves made on the child and the lack of support for a single teenage father.

In case history 3 the overwhelming boredom of the observer only made sense when the depression and exhaustion of the mother were ameliorated and the unresponsive blob of a baby became a human being.

In case history 4 the anxiety for the observer and the seminar group was invasive. Setting limits and boundaries was seen to be a problem for the mother not only in relation to her children, but also in relation to the observer, whose home and mind were invaded by it. This was mirrored by the ease with which the observation took over and invaded the seminar.

In none of the observations were the observers untouched by raw personal issues brought to the surface by what they were seeing. Another issue was the extent to which any crossing of social contact lines between the observer and the observed inevitably led to difficulties.

## COMMENTS FROM THE COURSE MEMBERS THEMSELVES ON THE OBSERVATION

### Finding the observer role

At our introductory meeting the little boy took me to see his bedroom and pointed to a map of the world on the wall, indicating Great Britain, saying that was the island where he lived. He pointed to a dot on the Southern Hemisphere and wondered what it was – I suggested a tiny island with which he agreed and then said that all that blue was the sea. As I struggled hard to identify an observer role, especially with a child this age (3½ years) from whom pro-social interactions were so important, we were both children with maps beyond our comprehension.

### The emergence of personal issues

As well as being an observer observing a family, I was provided with a further opportunity in the seminar to reflect about the observation process, both about what was recorded of what was seen and about the nature of the perceiver. The seminar experience heightened awareness of myself as a participant in the group, as an observer of a child and as an individual. Increased self-awareness is not always a comfortable process, but the group was a reasonably safe place to explore boundaries.

### Parenting issues and child development

I have listed a number of the tactics used by the mother to shape her son's behaviour. I find this interesting as many of the requests for me to help from parents when I was a social worker focused on bringing up their children to behave 'acceptably' according to parents' standards. The repertoire of my suggestions to help parents become effective were less subtle, more generalised, less specific, creative or contextual, lacking in responsiveness to the nuances of the child's emotional needs than are evidenced by this mother's range of methods . . . it provides justification for the observation of children in their own families by social workers.

## Issues for assessment

I am still uncertain about the reasons for the baby's slow development; was this a response to the mother's depression in the early months or simply his innate temperament? Insofar as his passivity was a response to her depression one could suggest that he became more active as the mother became less isolated and more able to express some of her frustrations with her husband. I am also uncertain how far the judgement of slow development was arrived at because of the middle-class expectations of the parents and the observer. Thinking about possible applications to social work assessments, I am sure that an assessment cannot be made on the basis of one visit; my view of the baby in the sixth month was certainly skewed by my own anxiety and I also failed to take sufficient account of the child's recent illnesses. Finally, I have been depressed by the social isolation and the process of gender construction which I saw in this family; I feel this reflects the social position of women.

## Staying with uncertainty, not rushing to make judgements

If I had met this woman as myself, with my own personality, tending to be controlling, we might well have clashed. If I had gone in as the social worker with an agenda I might well have missed an important dynamic, and provoked a different response. As an observer, I was under no pressure to do, and so I could watch and wait. That absolution from doing made the space to see the observed, as well as to become aware of my own traits and feelings. . . . It was the *dissonance* between what I wanted spontaneously to do but contained that was the key to my understanding.

## The pain of observing

I had anticipated a struggle with home observation in terms of maintaining my role. I had thought a good deal about detachment, rather less about attachment and the echoes of my childhood experience, and very little about the experience of counter-transference. Frequently there are references in the observations to 'distractions', to very powerful unexpected feelings and even, though not often, to the desire to escape.

## The difficulty in seeing the child

I can well appreciate why social workers, when working with much more demanding and needy mothers than this mother, are unable to withstand being taken over by the parents' needs. The easiest observations were those where she and the child operated as a unit because then I didn't need to split my attention; by focusing on Mum I was of necessity focusing on the child. In those cases where the parent/child dyad does not even function as a dyad, it could be impossible to see the child unless you consciously impose that on the person (against probable resistance). Thus, the need to reinforce that awareness in social work training is crucial, and perhaps there could be no better way to experience it than to come to it through being an observer.

## THE PLACE OF OBSERVATION SKILLS TRAINING IN SOCIAL WORK TRAINING

The following outline refers to the different levels of the career continuum of social work in the UK.

### Basic training (Diploma in Social Work)

We would argue that the capacity to observe is central to social work practice whatever the specialism. Before any judgements and decisions can be made, the worker, in assessing a situation, needs to be able to observe from a boundary position, not totally engulfed, but appropriately involved. However skilled and talented they are, students entering the social work profession usually need to learn this skill. This is at the core of social work and, therefore, should be considered as part of the core social work skills learnt early in the course.

In discussion with the social work tutors we became aware of the enormous pressures on the curriculum. Another alternative might, therefore, be to place the observation and the seminar within the remit of the practice placement. Wherever placed, the module would enrich the teaching of both Human Growth and Development and Practice Skills sequences, but centrally it is about learning to adopt the observer role.

However tightly packed the social work curriculum, this can be taught only in an absolute minimum of five observation sessions, if the professional is to have confidence and competence in the observer role. This means five hour-long observations, weekly or fortnightly, with five seminars alongside, preferably in small groups so that each student can present a detailed recording twice. (For further details concerning setting up observations and the role of the seminar leader see CCETSW (1990) Diploma in Social Work guidelines and an unpublished CCETSW paper.)

Where students have chosen to specialise in child care we would strongly urge that the observation module be extended to a minimum of ten observations and ten seminars and, if possible, the observation subject should be a child under 5 years. This module could be extended to other specialities, such as the elderly, the mentally ill and those with learning difficulties.

**Post-qualification phase**

For those who have not had an observation skills module as part of their basic training we would strongly urge local authority training departments to consider organising one for their newly qualified workers. Hopefully, it should consist of a minimum of ten observations with twenty supporting seminars. As we have suggested for basic training we would suggest that observing a young child (under 5 years) makes an excellent introduction to observation skills. Some social workers in the post-qualification phase should be encouraged to consider undertaking an observation course for an academic year. This would enable them not only to acquire an observational stance, but also to gain some of the other range of learning referred to in Fig. 2.

**Advanced award in social work**

Observational skills should definitely be a module in any advanced training. The subject should be specifically relevant to the speciality.

Alongside the specific skills acquired it needs to be stated that professionals gain from this experience both in their professional development and in their job satisfaction.

For anyone wishing to specialise in child care or child protection we would see an observation module as essential, preferably for an academic year (Pietroni 1991).

## Multi-disciplinary training

From our experience of running observation seminars on a specialist course we have found the training was enriched for participants by a mix of professionals, e.g. social workers, teachers, nurses, psychologists, doctors. As far as we are aware, however, no systematic work in this area has yet taken place, although serious interest in it has been expressed.

## Seminar leaders

As with other specialities where the teaching is dependent on the knowledge and skill of the lecturer, observation skills training depends crucially on the atmosphere of the seminar and the competence of the seminar leader (Pietroni 1991). Training, consultation and supervision will be required until there are sufficient numbers of trained leaders to cover training needs. Social work courses and local authority training officers could be encouraged to employ members of their staff who have done a post-qualification or advanced award observation as seminar leaders with consultation. As more people undertake these courses, resources will increase. Members of other disciplines, predominantly from the mental health field, could also be used as seminar leaders; at the moment child observation is perhaps more widely taught in other professions, so there is a resource that could be used.

## UPDATE ON TRAINING DEVELOPMENTS

### a) Social work training

Since this paper was first written there has been a considerable expansion of the social work training which we describe for trainers and supervisors. Small group trainings have taken place across the country: in Birmingham, Manchester, Leeds, Newcastle, Newark,

Brighton and Southampton. These have shown the benefits of small group training for the participants, facilitating the development of teaching networks and opportunities, and enabling personal learning and the prevention of professional burnout. Course participants have gone on to use their training experience imaginatively in setting up trainings designed to meet the needs of the locality; for example, in day care, within local area teams and in multi-professional groups. An example of a particular application has been in child protection work, where training groups have brought together all the involved professionals, including social workers, health visitors and the police. It is hoped to extend the training to guardians ad litem, with a particular emphasis on observation as part of assessment work for the courts.

## b) Further training applications

Within the community setting, we have become increasingly aware of the value of brief observation as part of assessment. Where professionals have not been able to undertake a formal observation training, however brief, undertaking one or two observations, with the opportunity for supporting discussion, can create an awareness of the importance of using observational skills in day to day work before going on to make recommendations.

Within the training sphere for primary care workers, we have become aware of a link between the way trainees have been able to use the observation experience, including the reflection on their learning and experience in the written paper, and their potential development as professional workers. It has been possible to identify those with a particular aptitude on the one hand, and on the other those who are likely to experience difficulties in professional training. In other words, the observation training is a useful part of assessment of a trainee's capacity to grow and develop professionally.

## c) Multi-disciplinary issues

The project described in this paper arose out of concerns in the field of child protection. It set out to address the issues for social work training, but at the time the Department of Health found it necessary to emphasise the need for multi-professional work, and revised and strengthened their document *Working Together* (issued by the Department of Health, DES and the Home Office). Since then there have been major policy changes within Health and Social Services following the NHS and Community Care Act. This legislation has led to radical changes in the care of the mentally ill and those with learning difficulties, with large institutions being closed and the move towards the care of these patients in the community. Within the NHS the use of hospital provision is being reduced dramatically, whilst primary health care is expanded, to enable health needs to be met in the community. These developments have increased the demands and pressures on the whole range of workers in the community. At the same time, there has also been a proliferation of voluntary organisations. Working together is now more crucial, not only in child protection, but in all aspects of provision of services for physical and mental health and social care. Locally based observation training has proved to be an effective way of increasing professional skill, confidence and self-esteem, and has had the additional benefit of bringing diverse professionals together, and hence increasing their understanding of each others' perspectives and skills.

### d) Theoretical developments

Over the past few years there has been a burgeoning literature around the understanding of observation, and its development as a method of understanding human behaviour and relationships. In the field of attachment there has been an explosion of literature, in which observation has played a part, for example the writings of Gaddine, Wright, Piontelli, Fonagy and Vygotsky.

## CONCLUSION

We return to the comments of the social work tutors who have done our observation course and who vividly convey the advantages and problems if observation skills are to be taught in a meaningful way:

This account reflects both the privilege I feel at being part of this learning experience and also the privilege of the life experience of this child. The features of the seminar which feel privileged are the time, the size of the group and the style of the learning environment, each of which contrast markedly with the constraints of the educational framework in which initial social work training operates.

All this leads back to my final task, which was to connect this experience to the consideration of observation in social work training. In many ways the effect of the course was a reaffirmation of what I knew already, the validity and crucial role of observation in social work ... the social worker, due to the prescriptions of his/her very role, has to impose on situations. But imposition without observation is skewed at best, and managing at worst.

## ACKNOWLEDGEMENTS

The authors gratefully acknowledge the contributions of Elizabeth Oliver Bellasis to the teaching on this course.

Robin Soloman, Ivis Lasson, Lynda Ellis and Gill Bridge were all members of the original seminar groups, as were Janet Gill, Christie Vigars, Veronica Calder, Rusty Livock and Cathy Aymer. Our thanks to them for the enthusiasm with which they have contributed to the development of social work trainings in observation.

*This paper was written in 1990 and published in 1991, under the title 'The contribution of observation training to professional development in social work'. Since then the recognition of the importance of observation training has continued to grow and develop across a wide spectrum of trainings for the caring professions, both at introductory and advanced levels. We are ourselves aware of such developments within nursing, general practice, day and nursery care, and we have heard of wider applications. Not only does observation play a significant part in professional training and development, but, additionally, there are now higher degrees which address observation in its own right. Alongside these training developments, there has been an expansion in the literature: see, for example, articles by Wilson and Briggs in the* Journal of Social Work Practice *1991: Trowell and Rustin in the* Journal of Infant Mental Health *1991; and McFadyen in the* Bulletin of the Journal of Psychiatry. *In press, a detailed manual on the teaching of observation on social work courses by Soloman, Lasson and Ellis, and the publication by CCETSW of a group of essays from the course which we describe, edited by Bridge and Miles.*

# Chapter 5

# Consulting to premature baby units

*Rosalie Kerbekian*

For the person and for the species,
love is the form of behaviour
having the highest survival value
                              Ashley Montague

## INTRODUCTION

As Brazelton (1992) says, the birth of a premature baby is a shock.
It is a shock which begins with the parents and the baby and
then reverberates through the family and the staff of the Special
Care Baby Unit (SCBU) or Neonatal Intensive Care Baby Unit
(NICU). The shock can give rise to feelings of hopelessness,
despair and pain which can feel intolerable to all those concerned.
For the baby it is a shock because she (for simplicity, I refer to the
babies in general as 'she') is having to be born before her body is
fully developed and probably before she feels psychologically
ready to be born. It is important therefore that someone is available who has the capacity to contain these feelings.

Ordinarily, the mother is a container for the infant's projected
feelings, needs and unwanted parts. This implies a particular state
of mind in which the mother is open and ready to take in and
reflect upon what the baby projects and convey back to her a sense
that her anxieties and communications are bearable and have
meaning. It may be that with the shock of having given birth to a
premature baby the mother is not able to contain the feelings of
the baby, or even her own. Ideally, her husband, her mother and
other members of the family would then be able to take on this
function. However, it is often more than can be expected for any
family to bear, hence the need for someone who can provide

containment for the baby, parents, siblings and the staff of the unit, i.e. a psychological consultant who would act as a facilitator in helping to establish a caring setting for the babies and their families by supporting them and the staff of the units.

Some units have recognised the need for psychological support for staff. Experience has shown that, where a request for this type of support does not come from staff, they may be actively resistant and unwilling to accept this if it is offered, possibly because this undermines their defences against the anxieties aroused (see Chapter 3) by the events surrounding a premature birth. This chapter is based on experience as a member of a multi-disciplinary staff group in a special care baby unit. I will start with a vignette of work with parents and staff.

Whenever I hear a baby crying in the unit, I investigate the reason for it. On this occasion I found that the Sister was having to apply new dressings to a baby suffering from epidermosis bullosa – a severe skin disease requiring constant renewal of the dressings. It helped him a little to have a dummy in his mouth and to have the Sister and me talk soothingly to him, but he was clearly in pain every time she had to touch the lesion. The Sister, as she had seen me do on previous occasions, was telling the baby how sorry she was to be hurting him, but that unfortunately it was necessary. Somehow he seemed to recognise that we were with him in his agony even though he could not, of course, understand what we were saying. Later on I was asked by the Registrar to accompany him in taking the baby to his mother in the maternity ward. I was impressed by how in touch the Registrar was with what the baby was going through physically and what both the mother and baby were going through psychologically. Afterwards the mother and I talked about how long she had waited to have the baby. She was now 37 and this was her first baby, who had also been eagerly awaited by the grandmother and the rest of her large family. It felt that the Sister, the Registrar and I were working together to contain this mother who was feeling so distressed at having given birth to such an ill premature baby.

## WORK WITH THE PARENTS

Very often the parents are not only physically unprepared for the birth, especially of a first baby – they may not have a place prepared for the baby in their homes or in their minds. Like Brazelton, I find that the mother may well blame herself that she has been unable to carry her baby full-term, afraid that something is wrong with her or with her care of the baby during pregnancy. She is usually distressed as soon as she knows that she will have to give birth prematurely. She may feel helpless and angry, taking out her anger on her husband or other caregivers such as the staff of the unit.

These accusations against others for not caring well enough for her baby are probably a mask for her feelings of inadequacy or of being in some way deficient. There are a host of other ways in which the mother and her partner may try to deal with this sudden and overwhelming shock, e.g. by denial or emotional and physical withdrawal. Once the parents know that their baby will survive they may begin to worry about whether the baby will be normal or not. I think it particularly important that they have a person to talk to who is professionally trained to understand and help them cope with these feelings.

Parents who have been through the trauma of the birth of a premature baby may well label their infant as vulnerable and this may be the way they relate to the child for years to come. Not surprisingly, parents who themselves feel vulnerable find it difficult to contain their vulnerable premature baby. I have found that immigrant parents from Third World countries, who seem to give birth to premature babies more than parents in the West, are particularly vulnerable themselves especially if they have no family nearby to give them support.

If the mother or any member of her family of origin has suffered a previous miscarriage, stillbirth or death of a baby, the parents usually feel more anxious. The staff also need support and under-standing of the parents' state so as not to retaliate when being blamed or accused of giving inadequate care. The more the staff can take time to keep the parents informed, the more they will reduce the parents' anxieties as well as forming an alliance in the care of their baby.

The following illustrates the work with parents who have a premature baby in special or intensive care:

First I introduce myself to the parents – or, more usually, the mother is there on her own – by saying that I come to the unit regularly to talk to parents because I know that having a baby in special care is a very stressful situation. Then I encourage her/them to tell me about their worries and concerns.

Mrs Ngomo talked of the shock of seeing her baby for the first time in an incubator and her anger with her husband for going back to their native Nigeria on a business trip when the birth was imminent. As a result he was not there to support her during and after the birth. She went on to talk about how lonely she felt at night without her baby by her, and seeing the other mothers with theirs. She was able to use me to unload her feelings of frustration with her husband and her hopelessness, despair and guilt that she had been the cause of her baby's prematurity, which then freed her to respond better to her baby who needed her to contain him.

## OTHER WORRIES THE PARENTS HAVE SHARED WITH ME

A mother sometimes finds out only at a routine prenatal examination that she will have to give birth to her baby prematurely. For example, some mothers I saw recounted having had to have an immediate Caesarean section because they were suffering from pre-eclampsia. The shock takes some time to get over so that years later, in child guidance clinics, I have worked with mothers who were still feeling traumatised by the shock of having had their baby prematurely and by Caesarean section, not having been able to hold and care for the baby straight after the birth. Indeed, it was experiences such as these that led me to do the preventative work I am describing here.

One father, whose wife was in the maternity unit far away from her baby in the SCBU (special care baby unit) recovering from her Caesarean section, asked me how he could help his wife. I suggested that it would be useful for her to hear about how the baby looked and what he was doing – in other words, to make observations of the baby and relay these back to the mother (cf. Elkan 1981). I also suggested that, until the baby was able to be with the mother, he could perhaps ask that she be brought to the baby in a wheelchair, in order to establish the bonding between mother and baby as soon as possible.

It is painful for a mother who has to be left in the maternity ward while her baby has been taken to the SCBU to see the other mothers having their babies by their side. One mother described how she cried all night when this happened to her.

When they see the unit, parents are invariably shocked at the technology – i.e. seeing their baby in an incubator with a respirator and wires taped to her from bleeping machines monitoring vital functions.

One single parent, a mother of 22 who produced triplets, worried that she would lose her children because home help was no longer available from the council. She was afraid that social services would take her children from her because it would be so difficult for her to look after triplets. Other single mothers are often worried about whether they will be able to look after the baby on their own when they get home. In order to help them get over this fear, it was the policy in one of the units where I worked to have the mother stay in the mothers' room the night before she would be taking her baby home, in order that she look after the baby on her own, knowing that the nursing staff were there to act as a backup if she felt at all worried. Ideally I think it would be better if more rooms were provided, and with double or twin beds – as in some hospitals – where *both* parents could stay with the baby as long as they felt the need, rather than restricting it to only the mother and the one night.

The provision of rooms would also obviate the pain of parents who want to stay with their baby in the unit but who at present must return home at night. Nevertheless, it is quite common for parents to feel that the baby is not really theirs until they are able to take her home (cf. Klaus and Kennell 1979).

Some mothers become very worried about whether they will manage to take care of their baby. They have described to me the pain of seeing their baby feed better with the sisters than with them. I try to reassure a mother that it is not unusual for it to be difficult to feed her baby at first until they get used to each other. Most parents feel in competition and others feel inadequate, if not intimidated, as they observe the nurses who appear so confident in their care of the baby.

It is particularly difficult for parents who, having once got over the fear that their baby would die and as a result feeling confident enough to buy baby clothes, etc., then to have to face a set-back when the baby gets very ill again. This scenario may be repeated several times. It is also difficult for parents to come to terms with the birth of their baby if either of them has recently suffered any form of bereavement.

Occasionally it is known that a baby will die. In such cases I will have the opportunity to help the mother or parents work through the process of acceptance of this sad fact as the baby will be in the unit for a more extended period of time. It is a particularly poignant situation when one of a pair of twins dies. One mother and father talked about how they felt their surviving baby was also depressed when her twin died. They felt evidence of this was the fact that for a time the surviving baby hardly moved and was generally lifeless.

It was often not until the baby was over the worst that the parents could talk about the anxieties they had been through, which would then come pouring out.

## PROBLEMS OF THE INSTITUTION

The administrative and physical separation of maternity care (obstetrics) and baby care (paediatrics) can give rise to a lack of liaison which can create problems in the care of premature babies and their mothers. These include the provision of separate staff for the two units, so that, for example, instead of one health visitor working in both departments to see the mother through both pre-natal and perinatal phases, there may be a different health visitor in each department.

In one unit where I worked, an ill mother had to stay in the maternity ward whilst the baby had to be taken to the SCBU some distance away: thus the essential bonding of mother and baby which should begin immediately, or at least within the first few minutes after the birth, is impossible if staff cannot bring the baby and mother together. Some babies could remain with an ill mother on the maternity ward if staff were available to help in the care of not too seriously ill babies and thus render unnecessary the baby's transfer to the unit. However, if the baby must remain in the unit, a mother who is unable to walk, e.g. if she has had a Caesarean, could be wheeled in to her baby in a wheelchair or even on her bed as I have seen done.

In one hospital I attempted to make a link between the maternity ward and the SCBU, at the same time hoping to provide support to the maternity unit by offering to see any mother who had a baby and wanted to discuss her experiences with me. The accounts of the mothers included one or two incidents which caused me alarm because the birth experience had seemed to be so badly mishandled. I approached the new Director of

Midwifery, thinking that she would be as sympathetic as her predecessor, in a spirit of hoping that we could sort out some of the difficulties for future mothers and babies. Unfortunately, she reacted very angrily, misinterpreting this as an attack on her department, and I was given written notice not to see mothers except those who had a baby in the SCBU because I 'might carry germs from the SCBU to the Maternity ward'.

## HELPING A UNIT TO SUPPORT CONTACT WITH BABIES BY PARENTS AND STAFF

Once the baby arrives in a unit, usually carried bundled up in the arms of medical personnel, the nursing staff must hurriedly go through procedures to ensure the life of the newborn premature baby. It is understandable if under that pressure they may not always appreciate that the baby is going through the momentous experience of trying to adjust to being born with a body unprepared for the task.

For that reason, the babies need an environment resembling more closely the intra-uterine environment with the minimum disturbance from essential interventions. The following are some of the procedures which might be implemented:

Instead of babies being weighed naked on thin paper towels on cold metal baby scales, with the result that the baby flails about, crying in an uncontained way, how much nicer it would be if the baby could be weighed in the arms of one of its parents or a nurse on the type of machine which subtracts their weight from the result (Urquhart 1980).

On a recent visit to Winnipeg, Canada, I was impressed to see how very quiet and homely was the atmosphere of the unit. Great care had been taken to soundproof the rooms and to create subdued lighting with individual lights for the section where each baby's cot was placed. In addition, there were rocking chairs for the parents in which they could sit and rock their babies, whom they held in skin to skin contact (Kerbekian 1987). I was impressed to see that each baby was helped to feel 'held' in her cot or incubator by having a rolled-up towel placed firmly around her to contain her in a womb-like way. Some units use bean-bags, a water-mattress or sheepskins for the babies to lie on to simulate the womb as closely as possible.

There are units which have found it helpful to produce a tape of the mother's voice, whilst others have had the parents produce a tape of whatever they would like the baby to hear, be it family conversation or their favourite music (Negri pers. comm.).

Nurses may not realise the enormous anxiety of mothers of premature babies, who often conceal their true feelings under a superficial manner. In this context, a seemingly innocuous action on their part can cause great distress to a mother, e.g. some mothers told me that they feared their baby had died when, returning to visit her in the unit, they found a blank space where the baby had been.

A warm and supportive environment can do much to reduce parents' levels of anxiety: this could include a kitchen and sitting area where parents can feel at home and support each other in their anxiety about their babies. A drinking fountain would also be useful for parents, staff and visitors in these very hot and humid units. Visits might be further encouraged by posters with encouraging messages such as 'Dear Parents, your baby needs not only the medical and nursing care which we provide, but the love and attention that only you can provide. Signed:- The Doctors and Nurses of the Neonatal Unit' (Fletcher 1983).

Mothers have told me how helpful it is to have a library of suitable reading material on premature babies as well as general reading material. It would be best if the prospective parents could see the unit in an early enough phase of the antenatal classes, so that if they do have a premature baby they will have seen the unit, which will lessen the shock of seeing their baby surrounded by all the technology. Of course, for parents who do not speak English, interpreters are essential so that they too can understand what is going on and express their joy, their fears and their anxieties.

As I have stated, the parents are the best people to look after their baby, but if for a variety of reasons they do not visit their baby very often, or not at all, it would help the baby and the nursing staff for there to be volunteers assigned to care emotionally for that baby as 'honorary foster-mothers': these could be caring mothers and grandmothers whose own children have grown up and left home.

The staff need to feel appreciated for the very high level of strain under which they have to work, which will be increased if they are to respond fully to the needs of the babies and their often distraught parents; and they should be encouraged to meet in support groups to share their difficulties and get support. This would also help them to identify with the babies and their parents, and to come up with further ideas on their care.

## CONCLUSION

In terms of human suffering, the cost can be considerable if the quality of the birth and immediate emotional care of the premature baby and mother – the bedrock of mental health – is deficient. For example, it has been shown (Frodi l981; Macy *et al.* 1987) that the prematurely born have been found to be at risk of abuse and neglect, particularly if the parents lack social support from the extended family and the community. The financial cost of trying to repair the damage in later life can be considerable, in addition to the vast and unnecessary cost in human suffering.

# Chapter 6

# Consultation in General Practice

*Dilys Daws*

Most of the week, I work in a grey, concrete, flat-roofed, five-storey 'Ivory-Tower', the Tavistock Centre in London. In spite of its ugly 1960s look, I love this building. I am surprised and hurt on its behalf when I am told by patients, or even colleagues from elsewhere, that they find it intimidating, inaccessible or depressing. I suppose that I love it for the work that I am a part of, and for the people that I work with, patients, students and colleagues alike. I think that many patients, having first braved it, come to feel affection for the building, as the shape of the institution which may be a crucial part of their lives for a time.

For half a day a week, I also work in a health centre in Kentish Town, a very mixed socio-economic district only two miles away. This building is two-storey, also flat-roofed and no more beautiful than the Tavistock Centre. However, it contains two General Practices and many ancillary services and, in the heart of a crowded inner-city area, it is viewed with affection, and experienced as totally accessible; in some ways perhaps too much so for the well-being of the staff there. Unhappy, disturbed people, with nowhere else to go, especially since the closure of mental hospitals, haunt the building, using it almost as a day centre, and take out their frustrations on the always visible reception staff. But the crucial fact is that, although owned by the NHS, the building does belong in a very real way to the local community.

It makes sense, for me as a child psychotherapist, to be part of this most accessible aspect of the NHS, for some of the week. I work in one General Practice, the 'Wigg' attached to the baby clinic, and have been visiting there for nearly twenty years. There are also psychotherapists working with adults and older children and other counsellors attached to the practice.

I introduced this chapter on consultation in General Practice, by referring to my main work place of the Tavistock Clinic. This was intentional; I believe that I function at the practice from the strength of this base at the Tavistock. My relationship to the other workers, to the health visitors and GPs, whose practice this is, is very different as a visitor from another clinic than if I were directly attached to the practice.

Being an outsider can either make for difficulties or help to solve them. I have elsewhere (Daws 1985) made the analogy of the outsider to a group being like an anthropologist living in a primitive culture. Elenore Smith Bowen (1954) describes how lonely this can be. When night draws in and the anthropologist hears laughter from nearby huts, she feels excluded and wonders if she is the subject of the laughter. She might wish to belong, but she remains useful only if she continues to study the culture, not if she settles in to become a part of it.

My role at the baby clinic is not to study it. In fact I do belong when I join in with clinical work. It is however also my role to bring in from outside ideas that are not part of the usual culture of a primary health care team. My aim, in fact, is to help make some psychoanalytic ideas part of the ordinary language of the GPs and health visitors that I work with. For some, in an enlightened practice, this is already so. However, ideas about people in disturbed or stressful states are always difficult to have, and difficult to hold on to. Often, when patients are discussed, I am grateful that I have a 'team', back at the clinic, who I can feel fairly sure would agree with me, when I am being challenged, or worse, ignored, for my views at the practice.

What do I do at the baby clinic? I go there for one morning a week, at a time when a baby clinic is actually being held. I can see, and to some extent be part of, the routine of the clinic and be available to talk about families that doctors and health visitors have on their minds. I think of my role as being for the staff in this way, and equally to work directly with parents and their babies. I first thought of doing this work when I had babies myself, and wondered where I would have gone to talk about the turmoil of feelings stirred up by giving birth and being responsible for the life of a small baby, if I had not happened to have sympathetic friends and a professional network close at hand. Now I try to be the sort of person available to talk with mothers and fathers about their own feelings, and about their concerns over the development of their babies. The aim in working in a baby clinic is that, by seeing families about problems of their infant's development as early as possible, later difficulties in the relationship between parents and child may be prevented. Problems in, for example, sleeping, feeding or behaviour are presented urgently. Parents may also quite openly describe difficulties in 'bonding', in getting established with their baby. Whatever the presenting problem I hope to be able to look at the underlying emotions and relationships between members of the family. Although this work is brief, often one or two meetings only, the method is psychoanalytically based.

Problems are thought of as connected with emotions and in the context of the baby's and its parents' history. I tell the parents that in order to understand problems in the present I need to know what has happened in the past. I ask for memories of the pregnancy and birth, for details of how the parents established their own relationship, and how they get on with each other now. I also ask for what they feel is relevant about their own childhoods and their relationship with their parents now. In describing all this, links between the ideas often emerge and parents seem strikingly relieved to make these connections. Advice is rarely given: it seems to me that most parents have access to much advice from family or friends, from books or the professionals they have already consulted. They often come preoccupied with specific advice they feel unable to take. 'Don't tell me to leave her to cry', they tell me about a sleepless infant. My task often seems to be to think with them about what the advice represents for them. I assure them that I agree that 'leaving a baby to cry' could be a cruel and neglectful act, but that 'allowing' a baby to protest as she settles need not be. Crucially, I look at the personal trauma that underlies this dilemma. When asking parents if *they* were left to cry, surprisingly often some painful history of separations or abandonment in the parents' own history comes up. It may be in their childhood, it may be a recent bereavement such as the death of their parent, or a miscarriage, or stillbirth. But where commonsense action by the parents to deal with a problem in their child's development seems to be impossible, one almost always finds some unbearable event in the family. Discovering and understanding all this strengthens parents' ability to change things in the present. Using this reflective approach I observe the baby carefully and tell the parents what I notice. The meetings are packed with emotion and action. I take in and think about what the family tells me and shows me, so that an understanding and integrative process that begins in my mind can then take over in theirs. Solutions are as much the province of parents as myself; my task is to restore their ability to think effectively so they can provide the answers for their child.

In order to do both these kinds of work, to get referrals, and to be available for consultation, it is necessary for me to be visible, and I have learnt how to stand next to the weighing scales at free moments (Daws 1985). This is the focal point of the baby clinic, near the reception desk, where parents, clinic clerk, health visitors, clinic nurse and doctors congregate. Bringing the baby to be weighed can be the rationale for coming to the clinic and parents can visit with no other ostensible reason. This alone validates the visit, while enabling the mother or father to make use of a contact with the health visitor or make friends with other parents. Standing by the weighing scales can be an effective way for me of eavesdropping on the progress of some of the babies who attend the clinic. By casually watching, I am able to see a whole range of parents and babies interact: wonderful information about normal development, or sometimes, miserably, seeing things begin to go wrong. At the end of the baby clinic, a meeting reviews each attendance, and any worries about a baby and its family are noted. These meetings are a necessary exchange of information; they are also an opportunity to share the experience of the anxieties that have accumulated during the two hours or more of the baby clinic. I can be part of the process where anxieties are picked up and highlighted, or where the group reassures itself that all can be left and thought about again next week.

One of the problems for a psychotherapist offering consultative work in such a setting is to decide when it is appropriate to help raise the anxiety level in colleagues and when to help settle it. In General Practice, and in the primary health care team of a baby clinic, doctors and health visitors are seeing the whole range of the population. In the main they are supporting normality and healthy development. In order for such a clinic to survive there must be a basic assumption that the anxieties brought constantly are being met and dealt with by the routine activities of the clinic.

Parents who have just had a baby are *normally* in a heightened state of emotion; life and death feelings are part of the ordinary stuff of a baby clinic. Doctors and health visitors have to stand the stress of this, and evaluate when some of it is out of the ordinary and needs special attention. The professionals also have to stand the feelings stirred up in themselves by patients. This brings me to what may be the most helpful contribution that a psychoanalytically trained worker can bring to a primary health care team. This is in helping the team to learn to distinguish the feelings aroused in them by patients, to help them manage these feelings and indeed to use them as a valuable source of information about feelings the patient might have and be unable to deal with. For example, I meet with all the health visitors once a month for one hour. This is of course, in addition to many short informal meetings during baby clinics. We sometimes talk about cases they might wish to refer to me. More often, we will talk about a case that is perplexing them or, even more likely, irritating or angering them. We talk about where these feelings come from, about how some people provoke anger and rejection as they go through life. In particular, vulnerable new parents may elicit in a receptive health visitor feelings that really belong within unresolved relationships with the parents' own parents. Spotting this process may help health visitors to manage it. Wryly seeing that their feeling that they have somehow 'got it wrong' for the mother connects with the mother's experience of not being supported by her own mother can make a big difference to their tolerance of it. Because the health visitor then does not snap back at her, the mother may start to feel understood and supported at a crucial emotional moment in her life. She might even be experiencing this for the first time. Feeling supported herself, the mother in turn manages her own baby's feelings better. When this happens, there is a wonderful chain of people getting things just a bit better than they have been done previously, with a better start in life for a baby.

Similarly, I meet once a month with the trainee doctors. They are in the practice for a year, a training year in which they decide whether to throw their life into General Practice. Highly motivated for the most part, they may be meeting the population at large for the first time. One of the skills of a GP is in assessing how much or how little is behind a patient's request for attention to a particular symptom or condition. An awesome task. The *Health of the Nation Consultative Document* (Department of Health 1991) tells us that 23 per cent of the population consult their GP each year with symptoms of mental illness. In addition, there are the subtle connections between body and mind that any illness or symptom implies. There are also the patients who come about a specific symptom but are longing to be asked how they are, or about the trouble at home. In this practice the trainee GPs are well supported by their trainers, but cumulative experience of patients' undefined needs can be overwhelming. One trainee doctor said to me recently that the meetings were a chance to 'let off steam'. This in itself must be useful for a profession that has a high sickness rate. In an inner-city practice there are patients who seem to bring generations of social, relationship and personal problems to any consultation. When small children from such a family are brought to the surgery, it feels like the opportunity for a 'fresh start' in helping this cycle to change. Young idealistic doctors bring energy to this. They also wish to be realistic. It seems to me that the balance of expectation of what is possible needs talking about over and over again. Airing the feelings of hope, of therapeutic zeal and of disappointment makes it possible to keep on trying. Doctors need to learn to entrust such feelings to each other; on occasion the visiting psycho-therapist 'outsider' can be the useful recipient of the 'let-off steam' for trainees and experienced practitioners alike.

Perhaps much of my own usefulness in this consultative way is because I also do hands-on work seeing patients. I am therefore as vulnerable myself to all the feelings engendered by working with either ordinary people who are at the moment in a highly emotional state or with the more frankly disturbed. I too am 'living dangerously', working with chaotic, suspicious, traumatised people. I too can be drained after a morning's clinic, or find myself in tears after hearing a family's story of loss and despair. I experience all this directly, so that my ability to think with an over-view is continually refreshed, and also challenged. We should note here that patients referred for psychotherapy have been found to make considerably fewer demands on their GP. Also very relevant is the comparison of the use of psychotherapists within a practice and the use of psychotherapeutic skills by the GP him or herself (Launer 1994).

The shared interest in the psychodynamic aspects of work with patients is discussed in a weekly lunch-time meeting at the practice. Several of the 'attached' workers attend this meeting at various times. It must be said that papers such as this one are 'tried out' first at these meetings. It seems essential to be able to say *to* the practice what I say in public and write about of my work with them.

## CLINICAL WORK

Getting to the specifics of the therapy setting, the room where I work is in itself significant; it is just off the baby clinic area. I close the door for privacy when seeing families, and open it to be visible in between. Yesterday, I had a 'dropper-in' while the door was open – a mother with her 3-year-old son, Peter, whom I had previously seen about his eating problems. Mother, father and son had come a few times some months ago. The mother told me that Peter had asked to come to my room, and indeed he went straight towards the toys. It was clear that she had some pressing problems to talk about herself. I said that I thought Peter was looking after her, by bringing her to my room. She agreed and accepted an offer of an appointment. This is one of the pleasures of a long-term connection with a health centre, and of being physically present in a place where families routinely turn up, that families can slip back into work at an appropriate time. I am always careful, however, not to confuse the friendly greeting of previous patients with a need for more work. Possibly even more useful is the chance to bump into people with complex problems, where the work between us did *not* go so well. Sometimes, I think a benign process can start belatedly just because I continue to be around the place, looking interested but not demanding. On *many* occasions such patients have asked their health visitor or doctor if I would see them again and the second time around their ability to think with me has been greater.

The physical attributes of the room I work in are also worth comment. The usual bare serviceable NHS room has one property which is unexpectedly brilliant as a diagnostic feature in working with families. Namely, there is an electric socket bang in the middle of the wall, at toddler height! Most small children are irresistibly drawn to it, and prepare to put their fingers into it. What the parents then do - whether they think it is their responsibility as parents, or mine as the authority, the person in charge of the room, to stop him or her from doing this, to save the child's life so to speak, is really illuminating.

In the actual clinical work that I do, referrals come from doctors and health visitors. Whichever one actually makes the referral, I try to check that it has been done with the knowledge and agreement of the other worker involved with the family. Usually this happens smoothly, and is part of a shared idea of what might be useful. In other cases, a referral arbitrarily coming from one discipline may express bitterly held differences of opinion about the needs of the family. It may further express a family well practised in dividing professionals and spreading their own disarray into their would-be helpers. When the process goes well, I expect to discuss with the referrer some of the issues about emotions and relationships that the family and I have discovered. I also sometimes see a family together with the referring professional.

From recent referrals, I picked out some interesting ones to give a flavour of the work. In a quick over-view there is a strong multi-cultural element in these cases. Several families came with feeding and sleeping difficulties, opening up emotional issues within the family. Feeding problems may reveal relationship difficulties between parents and infants. Sleeping problems often connect with losses and separations in the parents' own lives (Daws 1989, 1993). Several, sadly, deal with the effects of divorce or separation between parents on their children. Symptoms of bed-wetting, nightmares or general upset may be part of children's distress. Helping very small children to put their feelings into words can be a great relief to them, and enable them to communicate better with their parents. This may in turn help estranged parents manage better their dealings with each other about arrangements for the children.

I now give two cases at opposite ends of the range of seriousness of problem. In one very ordinary situation a pregnant mother came with her 15-month-old son who was biting other children. He was no longer invited anywhere to play. We talked about his feelings of jealousy of the coming baby. Perhaps when he bites these relatively robust children he is sparing his mother the brunt of his feelings, and also being selective in not biting any babies. We explore further that mother herself might have some aggressive feelings that do not seem to have an outlet. Although happily married she is bringing up her family far from her own home and parents. Is her little boy doing some biting for her? She is intrigued and amused by this idea. Next week she reports that the biting has almost stopped. While obviously preoccupied with the imminent birth, she is more able to manage her little boy's aggressiveness and appreciate the vigour underlying it. Father is not able to attend our meetings but she tells him of the ideas that we discuss. The family seems less at odds with each other.

At any one time there is usually a complex case which particularly interests me, and involves me with colleagues. My second case is particularly dramatic. A young oriental couple were referred by their GP and health visitor together. These two professionals were themselves in a state of distress about the couple. It appeared that their 5-month-old son had been taken back to their own country by his grandmother. When I met the parents it took a long time to decipher what had happened. It seemed that the grandmother had come to help at the birth and the following few months. She was very good at looking after the baby; the more competent she was, the more useless her daughter felt herself to be. When grandmother's visa expired, she offered to take the baby home with her. Neither parent felt able to protest and grandmother and baby departed. This mother then told me in flat repetitive phrases 'I miss my baby'. She did not mention his name, and I had to ask what it was. I was told 'Cyril'. She continued to repeat her sad complaint. The next week she had a different indignant story, of injustice in her job. I wondered, and discussed with her doctor and her health visitor, as to whether this was an injured woman, numbed with the shock of losing her baby, or did she always feel herself to be badly wronged, was she even psychotic? Perhaps she had felt persecuted by her baby, so that her mother might have felt impelled to rescue the baby. There seemed no way to tell. Justice called for helping her to reclaim the baby. For several weeks I worked with her on how to feel stronger in relation to her mother, and on how to ask to have her baby back. Her husband seemed warm and supportive, aware of his mother-in-law's dominance, but not able to challenge her outright. The mother finally managed the phone call asking for the baby to be returned, and with some compromise a date a few weeks later was set. She seemed transformed, and started to look longingly at other babies in the clinic. Previously she had kept her gaze away from them.

The week after the baby was returned home, the whole family visited me at the baby clinic. Grandmother, the two parents and Cyril, now aged 11 months, came into my room. I realised that I had a difficult task, how to show sufficient respect to grandmother, while treating mother as the one in charge. Cyril solved it for us. On a small table, I had put a plastic box of bricks. Cyril took one and threw it on the table. The family gasped. I held my hand out and he handed the next one to me. I thanked him and we smiled at each other. He turned towards his father. I said 'give it to Daddy'. I asked his father what Cyril called him. He said 'Papa', then smiled and said 'he usually calls me "Mamma"'. I said that I thought Cyril had a lot of sorting out to do of who was his 'Mamma'. It was obvious that Cyril was torn between his two 'Mammas'. I talked sympathetically of his dilemma. I said to Grandmother how much she would miss him when she left.

Grandmother kept an iron hand on Cyril's behaviour. When too many bricks came out of the box, grandmother put them back. When he tentatively threw them he was sternly told not to, and he briefly cried. Much of the time he smiled at the roomful of attentive adults, and his father perceptively remarked that Cyril was being nice to everyone. I said that he had a lot of people to please.

Next time the parents came with Cyril. The grandmother had stayed at home 'for a rest'. I actively talked about how upset I thought Cyril would be when grandmother left – that they would have to expect him to be miserable or angry with them. When Cyril tipped the box of bricks over, his parents asked him to tidy it up. I said that they had not been used to the mess a baby makes – they had had to manage without him and had got used to no untidiness, nothing out of place. Father warmed and talked about the freedom of his own childhood in the country. Cyril pulled himself up holding on to the little table. He seemed nearly ready to walk. I said how good it was that he had come back to them before he could walk – that they had seen the last stages of his babyhood even though they had missed a lot. Cyril pulled himself round by the table towards me, and touched my brightly coloured beads. I smiled and talked to him. The parents told me that they had found a childminder for when grandmother leaves, so that mother can go back to work. It seemed crucial that this mother does return to work – as well as economic necessity, the emotional strain of being with Cyril all day might well be too much for her. The childminder is an older woman from their own country. I congratulated them on finding someone who might make Cyril feel as well looked after as his grandmother does. I also thought that the childminder would be a mother figure for mother herself. In addition I perhaps represented for this family, an English grandmother, who had helped them after a gravely false start become a family in their adopted country. As they left father lifted Cyril up to kiss me goodbye.

In this case, where the reunion between Cyril and his parents is still uncertain, we see the different facets of a complicated piece of work. Firstly, doctor, health visitor and I struggled to try to understand whether the mother had lost her baby through her mother's domination, or whether her mother had recognised that she was unable to care for the baby properly. It seemed most likely that she had suffered from severe post-natal depression, not been able to 'bond' with her baby, and then been robbed of the chance to do so gradually. The work I did was an attempt to confirm both parents as the 'real' parents of Cyril, by watching their interactions with him, and putting into words the steps they were taking in getting to know each other. I also tried to help them tolerate the disturbance a baby implies. When Cyril overturned the box of bricks the 'mess' created symbolised the emotional havoc of having him back with them. We were able to discuss, frankly, the different cultural expectations that this family held from my own. They expected to obey the grandmother, as an elder, and they expected Cyril to obey them, and keep things tidy. My inclination was for more freedom of action, letting him have a mind of his own. Having got this straight between us, we were able to explore their conflicts in such matters, of wanting to hold on to what they had got from their own upbringing, and also to make use of some ideas from the culture in which they are bringing up their baby now. I had the difficult task of speculating to myself on the degree to which a state of mental illness in the mother had affected her perceptions of how much to be obedient to her mother. It seemed to me not 'normal' to give up a baby at a grandmother's request. I in some ways counter-balanced this as an authoritative English professional 'grandmother', who allowed the parents to have their baby back. When grandmother did leave, there were some weeks of upset and illness for all the family. Things settled down and mother went back to work. She felt very supported by the childminder, who cooked dinner for her when she went to collect Cyril.

I will end with a vignette from our latest meeting showing how the attachment between mother and Cyril has belatedly come into being. Mother told me that Cyril loves the childminder, but he runs to *her* when she arrives after work. She touchingly said, 'When we get back to the house, he looks up at our flat. He knows it is his home.'

# Chapter 7

# Psychodynamic family therapy with parents and under-5s

*Marion Bower*

## INTRODUCTION

It is now widely recognised that problems in pre-school children need to be taken seriously and attended to promptly. The range of difficulties which worry parents and professionals is very wide. These include sleeplessness, feeding difficulties, disobedience, aggression, temper tantrums, restlessness and speech delay.

Although there is agreement on the need to offer help, there are many different ideas of how help should be offered. Parents themselves often want help managing different aspects of a child's behaviour and professionals working with children and families are often asked to give advice about this. Recently there has also been the development of more systematic parent education programmes.

This raises the issue of what we are trying to achieve when we offer help to families with young children. In Chapter 11, Judith Trowell makes a distinction between changes in parental behaviour and management skills and changes in meta-cognitions: that is, the capacity to understand and think about what the difficulties are about and how parents' own past experiences may be influencing the present. Although the parents' behaviour may change fairly readily, changing feelings and developing insight into a problem usually takes considerably longer. As this is a chapter on how we can help parents develop insight and understanding, it is worth considering why we should opt for this more troublesome approach.

There are two practical reasons for this. Firstly, research has shown that childhood emotional disturbance (and often developmental delay) is closely related to parental states of mind and attitudes towards children. For example, maternal depression has been linked to behaviour problems, speech delay and later reading difficulties. Maternal criticism and lack of warmth has also been shown to be an important predictive factor for childhood disturbance (Pound *et al.* 1989). Secondly, it is more difficult for changes based on learning particular techniques to spread into other areas or persist in the face of adversity. For example, Carole Sutton found that improvements produced by an eight-week parent education programme fell away somewhat over the next eighteen months as parents slipped back into old patterns of behaviour (Sutton 1994: 14).

The third reason is based on an experience which I think will be familiar to most professionals. A desperate parent asks for advice on how to manage a child. Practical, sensible advice is offered. The parent goes away and either makes no attempt to act on the advice, or returns to say 'I tried it out, but it didn't work'. This, I think, illustrates the enormous influence which parents' own emotions and childhood experiences have on their capacity to cope with their children. When parents come to child guidance or similar services, it is absolutely routine to find that the problem they are having with their child is one which they share themselves. For example, a parent who experienced intense jealousy of their siblings, which was denied or badly managed by *their* parents, is likely to find jealousy between their *own* children difficult to cope with.

Here we run into a difficulty which Freud also encountered. Although these links between the parents' past and current difficulties may be easy to see, it is not enough simply to inform them of this. Although they may accept the understanding intellectually, there is no emotional change. However, without an emotional change the knowledge is unlikely to be effective. Unless a parent can get in touch with a painful memory or experience at an emotional level, it cannot be used as the basis for an empathetic understanding of their child.

For some time Freud struggled with the difficulty of trying to make patients aware of emotions and memories so painful they were subjected to *repression* (see Chapter 2). However, he discovered there was a process whereby these repressed emotions were brought into the therapy whether the patient wished it or not. This is the phenomenon he called *transference* (see Chapter 2). By this process the patient 'transfers' onto the therapist emotions and experiences that originally belonged to loved and hated people in their past, usually their own parents, so that painful emotions and memories are re-activated and can be examined and thought about. (This process runs through all relationships although it is mostly not acknowledged.)

When a parent approaches a professional for help, the process of transference is activated, whether or not the professional chooses to work with it, and the worker is experienced as if they are the parents' own parents. If a parent has been emotionally deprived or neglected as a child, they are likely to approach a professional with very intense feelings of need and little hope that these will be met. In this situation they are likely to experience their own children as if they were brothers and sisters competing with them for parental attention. I think this explains another experience which many of us have had. In this case a parent comes with their children and pours out their concerns in a way which commands our attention, and we have the uncomfortable feeling that the children are being neglected. Yet at the same time we know if we try to get the parent to pay attention to the children *they* will feel neglected.

The intense needs of emotionally deprived or disturbed parents can be a reason for seeing parents and children separately (and most of the chapters in the next section describe work of this sort). However, this chapter describes an approach which I think allows us to work with parents and children together, by looking at the *meaning* the child's behaviour has for the parents and how this is enacted in the transference. Having children present is also helpful because however young they are they can contribute to our understanding of the problem by their play and behaviour, and also have the experience themselves of being understood.

## A THEORETICAL FRAMEWORK

I shall start by examining the psychological processes whereby a child can come to represent something difficult for the parents. This is based on Freud's idea that we develop *defences* against painful feelings. Many people will be familiar with the idea that unwanted feelings or attributes can be 'projected' onto a family member (the scapegoat or black sheep) who then becomes the object of attack or criticism. Melanie Klein developed Freud's concept of 'projection' into the more complex concept of 'projective identification'. This is an *unconscious* phantasy that a part of the self can be split off and located elsewhere. However, we do not actually rid ourselves of this unwanted part, but remain in relationship (identification) with it in the other person in whom it is located. I think this often accounts for the sort of angry preoccupation that parents often have with a difficult child. As one woman said to me about her son, 'He's in my head all the time, even when he's at school I can't get away from him.' (I have emphasised *unconscious* because this is a deep-rooted defence and is likely to be slow to change, however obvious it may be to the outsider.)

Projective identification is part of the web of relationships that bind a family together. It is not only a negative process, 'good' parts of the self can be projected and this is part of the basis of love. For example, in 1834 Mrs Gaskell wrote of her baby daughter Marianne: 'I had no idea the journal of my own disposition and feelings was so intimately connected with that of my little baby, whose regular gentle breathing has been the music of my thought all the time I have been writing' (Uglow 1993: 94). The nature of projective identification itself can change, from its earlier form which is aimed at ridding the self of unwanted feelings, to something more positive, as Betty Joseph has said:

> Although projective identification is probably never entirely given up, it will no longer involve the complete splitting off and disowning of parts of the self, but will be less absolute, more temporary, and more able to be drawn back into the individual's personality – *and thus be the basis of empathy.*
>
> (Joseph 1989: 169, my emphasis)

I think this type of shift is a very important goal to aim for in family therapy and I shall return to this in a moment. Through projective identification a child may come to represent an aspect of the parent, or to play a part in a pattern of relationships which has great significance for the parent. (This does not mean that the child is a blank sheet. Unless a parent is very disturbed, projections usually 'hook on' to real aspects of the child.)

For example in the D family, whom I describe below, there was a repeating pattern whereby the need for love and affection was misunderstood or confused with sexuality. Through the action of transference I was also drawn into the pattern. I found myself acting like a mother who does not understand. My experience of the family (my *countertransference)* was of feeling unable to 'get through' or of being misunderstood.

Where do these patterns come from? I believe they come

from the parents' *internal object world* which in turn is based on their own childhood experiences and relationships. We may be unconscious of this world, but its power is immense and at times it may be more real to us than the external world. Joan Riviere has summarised this world and its significance very beautifully: 'It is a world of figures formed on the pattern of the persons we first loved and hated in life, who also represent aspects of ourselves' (Riviere 1952: 302). Becoming aware of these very deep roots of family patterns makes it easier to understand how very difficult they are to change, however unpleasant and unsatisfying they may be for the family. How then can we bring about change?

In the introductory section we touched on the idea that problems are caused not just by painful experiences but by how these experiences are *managed* for us as children. Bion suggested that the earliest form of this is a mother's capacity to respond to the intense feelings, needs and unwanted parts projected into her by the baby. The mother does this by 'processing' these feelings in her own mind and returning them to the baby in a more bearable and meaningful form. This is an intuitive process in a mother but the therapist has to make a conscious effort to make sense of the powerful emotions projected into them, emotions which are often carried by the child for the parent. By putting these feelings into words and surviving the experience, the therapist helps the parent take a step towards re-owning these feelings. If this happens then the parent's projective identification with the child can begin to change in the way described by Joseph (see above) from its split off form to a basis for empathy. I have tried to describe such a step in more detail in my account of the work with Miss D and her children later in this chapter. This change does not happen once and for always. Many shifts need to be made before the position is consolidated. However, once it begins then parents are usually more able to manage a child more sensitively and effectively. As this change comes from within the parents themselves, it can raise their confidence in themselves as parents far more effectively than if they had acted on advice from outside. The child then becomes a source of satisfaction and a benign circle can begin.

## THE D FAMILY

This is an extract from work with a single mother, who at times experienced her two sons as rival younger siblings, and at other times as unbearable aspects of herself and her own experiences as a child.

## THE PROCESS OF ENGAGEMENT

The family were referred to the Child Guidance Unit where I work by their health visitor. She told us that Miss D was a young single parent with two sons, Edward aged 3½ years and Christian aged 14 months. The health visitor felt that Miss D had difficulty in coping with both boys, but was particularly concerned about the effects on Edward. After Christian's birth Miss D had persuaded social services to offer Edward a day nursery place. Staff at the day nursery said they had never heard him speak and he often cried without apparent reason. His mother said that he spoke a little at home but was very disobedient. Edward was due to start school in six months and everyone was anxious about how he would manage.

My first sight of the family in the waiting area gave me a vivid impression of their difficulties. Miss D was an attractive young woman with very long hair and a very short leather skirt. She was engrossed in a magazine, apparently oblivious to the fact that Christian had wandered away out of sight. Edward sat hunched in a chair, his anorak hood over his head. Despite their smart clothes there was an indefinably grubby and neglected air about the family. Once in my room Edward sat immobile in a chair, his anorak hood still up. During the session I made several attempts to talk to him, but it was like speaking to someone who was deaf. Christian buzzed rather aimlessly round the room; occasionally he handed me a toy. Miss D continued to ignore both boys completely. In a flat monotone she complained about Edward. He hardly talks at all although his hearing has been tested and it is normal. At home she thought he was naughty to annoy her, she added contemptuously that 'he cries, even when he is asked to do simple things'. As Miss D was French I asked her if she spoke French to the boys at home. She said that she spoke only English. She went on to tell me that she had originally come to England as an au pair to escape from her family. She had met the boys' father here and they had lived together until Christian was 6 months old, when they split up. 'He was more interested in his rock band than me.' Miss D said that she was the eldest of three children all born within a year of each other. She said that her mother was a cold religious person, 'but I had her attention because I was always ill'. Miss D said that she thought she was her father's favourite 'but he was more like a boyfriend than a father'. Miss D's manner was so remote and indifferent that I felt it was quite hopeless to try and engage her to think about the boys. With hindsight I think my despair about getting through to Miss D and my experience of Edward turning a deaf ear to me should have given me a clue about the experience the family were communicating to me. Instead, I behaved like a mother who is insensitive to her children's needs and suggested to Miss D that perhaps she might like to come to a group I ran for mothers and children. Miss D was outraged. 'They would all have problems and everybody would be wanting to talk, it would be like being with my sisters again.' Miss D was very late for her next appointment. This time she told me that she had been thinking, and what she thought she really needed was individual psychotherapy for herself. She told me she had made a suicide attempt in her teens and had seen a 'psychologist', now she was feeling depressed, could I help her find someone? At face value this seemed reasonable, her flat manner certainly suggested depression, but I felt uneasy. As she was thinking of changing her GP I gave her the name of a practice with a psychotherapist, but suggested that she came back once more to see me. Miss D was very late again, and this time she had brought only Christian. She said that she had not brought Edward because he is tired of hearing her talk about him, although friends say he is depressed. There was no mention this time of psychotherapy. Miss D said that what she thought would be really helpful would be to go back to college, perhaps to study psychology, could I recommend her a good course? Christian had been occupying himself very well up until now. Then he seemed to become rather tired and fretful. He tried to engage his mother's attention by banging against her knee and smiling at her. Miss D picked him up and offered him her breast in a detached manner. Christian turned away and slid off, in fact my impression was that he had wanted comfort rather than food. This time I felt more confident that I understood what was happening. I told Miss D that I thought that she was trying to leave the depressed part of herself (Edward) behind, and that she was trying to get me to behave towards her as she was towards Christian, to offer her career advice when she really needs help and understanding. Miss D smiled and said that she would think about it.

Although my attempts to really understand and respond to Miss D's needs did not get an immediate response, she did return to see me and it seemed that her capacity to think about and respond to Edward in particular had increased. Miss D missed the next two appointments, but a month later her health visitor rang and said that Miss D would like to come and see me again. I wrote to Miss D offering a prompt appointment and made it clear that I was prepared to offer regular appointments if she wanted them. This time Miss D arrived early with both the boys. She said that Christian had been offered a place at Edward's nursery, she was worried that he was too young to tell her if he was unhappy, at least Edward could do this. Meanwhile Edward, for the first time, got out of his chair, and went and sat at the table I have with toys and began tentatively to pick them up. From time to time Christian joined him and brought toys to me, giving me a very winning smile as he did so. I commented how much more involved both the boys seemed. Miss D said she wished they would play more together but this usually led to fights. She added that Christian was friendly with everyone, 'But Edward is more like me, he's suspicious; he doesn't want to come here.' I said that it seemed that Miss D was wondering if she could bring the part of her that was like Edward suspicious and uncertain of being understood. Miss D agreed. Miss D said that Christian was happier than Edward although Edward had known his father better. At this point Edward began banging the table loudly with one of the toys. I said that it sounded as if the talk about his Dad made him angry. Miss D said that she wanted the boys to stay with their father over the weekend. I said that it seemed hard to think the boys would prefer to be with their mother, and perhaps hard for her to be with them. Miss D looked relieved. She said, 'I'm often too wrapped up in myself to pay attention'. I said that I wondered if that had been her experience of her mother, and that perhaps she wondered if I was really going to pay attention to her needs. Miss D said that she was very relieved that I had responded quickly to her wish to see me.

In this session Miss D is more able to think about the boys even though it makes her guilty. Instead of being contemptous of Edward she sees him as 'like me'. Once Miss D felt that her needy depressed self had been 'heard' by me then she could 'hear' Edward who represented that part of herself and he could find his voice. During this session I offered the family regular fortnightly appointments, which Miss D accepted.

## EDWARD SPEAKS

The next session Miss D again arrived early with both the boys. Edward looked much more cheerful and came eagerly in and sat down at the table with the toys. Miss D and Christian came in more slowly and reluctantly. Edward caught my eye and gave several ostentatious coughs. Miss D said she was worried because the nursery fees were going up. Could I support her in keeping Edward's place? Miss D added that Edward likes the nursery and had wanted to go there instead of coming to see me today. I asked Edward if he would rather be at the nursery than here. Edward said, 'I have a cough, I'm not well, I want to go home.' Miss D was astonished. She said, 'But when I put him to bed he says "I want Daddy".' I said maybe that was because he was angry with her for sending him to bed. (It was also interesting that Edward, like Miss D, has to be 'ill' to get his mother's attention.)

A little later Miss D said that Edward was due to have grommets fitted in his ears. She was worried that this would not make things better, and that his speech problem was connected to her. She seemed depressed. In this session we had begun with the usual pattern of projection and misunderstanding. Miss D seemed reluctant to come and attributed this feeling to Edward. However, this time it was possible to sort out which feelings belonged to Edward and which feelings belonged to his mother. Edward was able to speak for the first time in a session because he felt his true feelings could be 'heard'. Miss D was able to accept some responsibility for the situation. It also seemed that as Miss D 'owned' some of her depression Edward had become less depressed. From then on Edward was able to both speak and play in his sessions, which was satisfying and reassuring to his mother. The nursery also reported that Edward was also speaking there and was showing quite a talent for making models. Of course things were not changed overnight. Although Miss D was much more able to think about the boys and their real needs, this tended to deteriorate if I was away on holiday when she would visit on the boys her experience of being sent away and abandoned by sending them away to their father.

I have not described another strand of the work which was the way Christian represented another aspect of his mother in his attempts to gain affection through rather seductive behaviour. In Miss D's case this took the form of casual sexual encounters which left her depressed. I think this had its roots in Miss D's rather sexualised relationship with her father, and this was re-enacted in her concern that my interest in her was really an attempt at seduction. As these confusions between sexuality and affection were explored, Miss D was more able to give and accept physical affection from both the boys.

Although for the sake of simplicity I have described work with a single parent family, this approach also works well in families where both parents are present. It is also equally applicable to families with older children.

## CONCLUSION

The central point I have tried to make in this chapter is that the nature of the parents' internal world and the emotional meaning that their children have for them are crucial factors in determining their capacity to care for their children sensitively and effectively. To improve a difficult parent/child relationship an emotional shift in the parent is essential. This can be achieved in the sophisticated way I have described above, but there are many different ways of using this understanding.

Simply offering a parent a regular appointment to talk can make an enormous difference. This was illustrated by the experience of one of my colleagues. She was interviewing a mother who had a very irritable and aggressive manner. While this woman talked her 3-year-old son ran in a frantic manner around the room. At the point where my colleague offered to see this mother and child once a week, the mother scooped up the little boy into her arms and settled him on her lap.

Identifying the emotional meaning a child has for the parents can be useful in deciding whether or not to include a child or children in sessions. For example, if a child represents something the parent feels is unbearable then just including the child in a session can be a potent message that the worker can bear what the child represents and may help the parent to do so too. In more extreme situations the emotional meaning a child has for the parents can be a helpful contribution to an assessment of whether a child is safe at home. Understanding the nature of projective identification makes apparently inconsistent or rejecting behaviour by parents more understandable. For example the mother of a mildly handicapped girl frequently requested respite care for her but at the last minute always turned it down. This girl represented an aspect of the mother which she felt was damaged. She could not bear to be with her daughter, but could not part with her either.

Working in this way places considerable demands on the therapist, but it has advantages for both workers and families. For the worker it enables realistic expectations to be formulated. Parents and children have an experience of being understood, and parents have the experience of their *own* growing self-awareness leading to a more successful relationship with their children.

# Chapter 8

# A psychoanalytic approach to the work of the guardian ad litem

*Anna Kerr*

Home is where one starts from. As we grow older
The world becomes stranger, the pattern more complicated
Of dead and living.

T.S. Eliot
'East Coker', *Four Quartets*

## SUMMARY

This chapter is written by a practising guardian ad litem and psychotherapist. Its aim is simple: to comment on trends in child care practice and policy and, in particular, to lament the loss of a perspective on parents' and children's histories and pasts. Guardians have a privileged position in the child protection framework. The task, in care and adoption proceedings, 'to safeguard the child's best interests until he achieves adulthood', (DOH 1992: 3), requires guardians 'to investigate all circumstances relevant to the proceedings ... regard as the first and paramount consideration the need to safeguard and promote the infant's best interests until he achieves adulthood and ... take into account the wishes and feelings of the infant, having regard to his age and understanding, and ... ensure that those wishes and feelings are made known to the court' (DHSS 1984: paras 34–8).

This role, new in opposed care proceedings since 1984 and constantly evolving, is both responsible and engrossing. 'In attempting to comply with their statutory responsibility to give paramount importance to the best interests of the child the guardian ad litem is entering an ideological minefield in which notions of protection and welfare jostle for position with those of natural justice and children's rights' (Kerr *et al.* 1990: 7).

# THE ROLE OF THE GUARDIAN AD LITEM IN CHILD CARE CASES: AN ILLUSTRATION

## Case history 1

Ray, aged 5, a large, serious, over-sexualised black boy, lived with his Jamaican mother, Edna, aged 33. Her local authority social worker had supported her since pregnancy to help her care for Ray. Edna was lost, deprived, rather mad and self-centred. She earned regularly by casual prostitution, bringing the men home where Ray was in the same room, sometimes the same bed, with them. Edna adored her son and did not see him as separate from her. She was angry when told about his individual and childish needs; to her he was part of herself. She believed his father was a bus driver and she and Ray spent days on the tops of buses, riding to the end of the line, searching for the lost bus driver. At 5, Ray's speech was seriously delayed, he was missing two-thirds of his schooling, could not relate to other children, worried about his mother when parted from her and approached all adults in a sexy, provocative fashion. The social worker could not bear to contemplate his removal although aware of his emotional damage. Care proceedings were commenced and the guardian's job was to make an assessment and recommendation as to Ray's long-term interests.

A typical case involves a guardian in eighty or ninety hours' work spread over four to five months and culminates in the final court hearing, for which the guardian must prepare the child, submit a thorough report and be ready to give evidence and react spontaneously in court. In many ways the guardian is a detective like Agatha Christie's Hercule Poirot.

> the GAL has to pursue the investigatory duty without being influenced by the pressure of people's wishes and hopes. It is a general experience for guardians as they go along, meeting those involved, hearing their stories, to be affected by each in turn, feeling sympathy now for the child, now for the parent, now for the foster parent. Each time there is a sense that this one deserves the greatest sympathy and understanding. The skill of the job, learned by experience, is to allow oneself these feelings, let them accumulate as one progresses, see how they stand up as the whole picture starts to show through, and what is left when one sits down to write the report.
>
> (Kerr *et al.* 1990: 11)

Very importantly, the introduction of the guardian calms down the action and hopefully some of the panic; the court process and the investigation give a structure, a container, to events and a sense that there is time enough to take a thorough look at the child and his/her family.

## PURPOSE OF THE CHAPTER

In this chapter, I will use my guardian ad litem experience to look at some areas in child care thinking and practice which I believe are crucial. These are:

1 The social worker's professional and personal attitude towards the client/s. The social worker's professional and personal child care philosophy.
2 The loss of psychodynamic thinking in social work.
3 The importance of recognising and remembering the child's past and history, whatever it may be.
4 The decision about whether the home is a 'going concern' for the child.
5 The myth of permanence.
6 The question of time and a time scale in child care planning.
7 Is the social work task now impossible?

## THE SOCIAL WORKER'S ATTITUDE AND PHILOSOPHY TOWARDS CHILD CARE WORK AND CLIENTS

This is likely to be a complex configuration of individual familial, life and social experience, political influence and departmental and area office orientation. The worker will be affected by the level of resources and staffing and the state of morale in the team. These bear significantly upon the quality of hope and compassion a worker can feel and communicate about a client or a case.

For example, two similar cases evoked quite different responses from the same department.

### Case history 2

A single, white mother, Lois, whose mother and grandmother died before she was 4 and who was sexually abused by her father, in care from 5 to 15, always running away to father, a drinker, who always sent her back; she lived in a crowded, damp flat with her three half-black children. For thirteen years the family held together, partly maintained by a succession of social workers and students, more or less compassionate and effective. The oldest girl failed to attend secondary school and began a steady process towards an anti-social street life, mother and authorities powerless to contain her and turn around her life. The two boys got themselves to primary school and ran somewhat wild in the holidays. The mother, deeply attached to them, cleaned the home, washed their clothes and fed them well. Sometimes, overcome by her own loss and despair, she drank; many of her friends were desperate, lost characters. All three children were devoted to their mother. The youngest became the family bad object. At school he fell asleep over his books, at home he exploded into temper tantrums, flinging furniture around, the smallest member of the family, expressing much of the family anger.

When the guardian became involved, the local authority had decided the mother could not change, could not be worked with and the children needed long-term alternative homes. There was an embattled relationship between family and social workers, increased by the unaddressed racial issues in the case, between the workers (black woman and white man) and between workers and mother (white woman who slept with black men). The mother was regarded with suspicion, at times with disgust. The professionals had run out of hope and compassion.

**Case history 3**

Clara, aged 7, was removed at midnight by the police from her mother, Mary, a 42-year-old white drug abuser for the past twenty-five years. The police found the flat in a filthy condition, full of illegal drugs and uncared for animals, child and mother asleep together. Mary had lost two older children; Clara was her last chance. Clara was placed with local foster parents who encouraged contact with mother; the local authority began to assess rehabilitation. A guardian ad litem was appointed. What was striking and moving about this case was the humane and positive social work approach to the mother. She was given real encouragement to keep contact with Clara, to see if she could improve her life style and do some emotional work on her past.

In the event, after support and preparation, Clara went home to her mother, a violent and chaotic boyfriend came on the scene and severely frightened the child and she asked to come back into care. Thereafter, she refused to see her mother and attached herself vigorously to her foster parents. The local authority social worker continued to support the mother in her sense of failure and loss.

The idea of working with a family, what would be called treatment in a medical or psychotherapeutic setting, can lose its meaning in local authority departments. Instead, they get swept into operating a crisis service alongside programmes of assessment and monitoring, which are frequently confused with working with or treatment. Many local authority social workers say they no longer have time to consider and work with children and family difficulties. They rush at the case, made anxious by the idea of risk and the spectre of failure, and start immediately on a tough, investigatory programme which fails to hold or understand the family. This comes from lack of support, increased bureaucratic demand, larger decision-making systems, less emphasis on caring for staff or clients in training and in practice, combined with a serious withdrawal of resources and the lurking horror of publicity and humiliation.

The shift in approach towards child care problems seems to be linked to the loss of a psychodynamic perspective. By this I mean the ability and inclination to consider individual and family history, to work with issues of loss and separation and, most importantly, to make use of the ideas of ambivalence and the unconscious. It has also led to a more judgemental, punitive attitude towards poor, borderline parents.

I, and other guardians, feel passionately about these issues; they affect poor, underprivileged families, often from backgrounds of emotional and economic poverty. They do discredit to the profession of social work, whose origins were philanthropic and political. They deny the importance of psychodynamic factors in family functioning and social work understanding. They run the risk of leading to the destruction of families who could, with help, be viable. Finally, they involve a loss for local authority social workers: the loss of opportunity to undertake what used to be known as preventive work, work with a family towards helping them stay together, using strengths, and facing pain and loss in the past and present.

## THE LOSS OF PSYCHODYNAMIC THINKING IN SOCIAL WORK

The influence of psychoanalysis on the developing social work profession has been well documented (Pearson *et al.* 1988); it was undoubtedly one of the more significant inspirations of social work theory and growth through the 1950s and 1960s. It is now largely neglected by mainstream social work, and its ideas seem to have been lost within local authority thinking. Briefly, this change can be attributed to the increased politicisation of social work in the later 1960s and 1970s, the development of more community orientated methods of working, the development of alternative strategies such as family therapy and behaviour therapy, the development of feminism and feminist-orientated social work, the great increase of pressure on local authorities from changes in child care legislation unmatched by increases in funding, and, finally, the impact of materialistic, client-condemning Thatcherite philosophy.

In my view, this privation has had two major damaging effects on local authority social work. Firstly, it has become harder for social workers and social carers to employ a tender, optimistic stance towards their work and clients. Since there is less emphasis on understanding clients' histories, it is more difficult to feel hopeful and forgiving. The emphasis is on mistaken notions of efficiency and testing.

Terry Bamford, in his address to the 1990 BASW conference in Northern Ireland finished by an eloquent description of prolonged, careful, devoted social care at its best:

> Thirty years ago, a child of seven was found living in a henhouse in the north of Ireland. His mother had kept him there with the hens feeding him scraps morning and evening. He was severely mentally handicapped and was without speech, having taken on some of the characteristics of the hens with whom he had spent most of his life. . . . Slowly, painstakingly caring staff, first within education and then within social services, have helped him towards a more normal existence, rebuilding trust and confidence. Those early years cannot be eradicated but what staff have given him through their care is in the words of a poem by Seamus Heaney about the episode 'wordless proof of lunar distances travelled beyond love.' Each of you could provide examples maybe less dramatic of the influence of good practice. It is underpinned by a belief in the worth of each individual and

their right to self-fulfilment. Those are the values for which we stand and for which we must continue to fight.

'Lunar distances travelled beyond love' evokes the passionate, involved response to human predicaments social work can contain.

Secondly, I consider some key psychoanalytic concepts have been forgotten: in particular, those of ambivalence, the unconscious and transference. These indispensable concepts need to be included in all social workers' induction courses. They are not at all esoteric or obscure. It is commonplace to hear workers talk about, for example, an adolescent child, as follows: 'Last week she said she was interested in foster care. This week she's gone off the idea and wants to stay at home. I don't know what she does want. She'll probably just abscond anyway.' Clearly the girl felt considerable ambivalence about a decision as major as leaving her mother and going to a foster home. The idea that she could feel just one thing, and then stick to it, seems to me naive. Ambivalence is the stuff of life and should be recognised and accepted.

Similarly, it is rare for social workers to give any attention to the idea of unconscious feelings and unconsciously determined actions. They carry on as though all their clients' actions were rational and under control. For example, 'If she really loved her children, she'd visit them regularly in care.' This ignores the likelihood that the mother is feeling ambivalent and beset by difficult conscious and unconscious feelings. Visiting children who have been removed because of failure in parenting and given to someone else deemed to be a more successful parent (and who is paid for the job) is daunting and painful and bound to stir up feelings, some bitter, sorrowful and submerged from the past.

The theory of transference, too, should, I think be reintroduced into mainstream social work understanding. It is such a simple and helpful contribution to our view of our own and our clients' reactions to people. It also helps workers to depersonalise their responses to their clients. For example, in case history 2, described earlier, the two workers felt repulsed and rejected by the mother who would not open the door or speak to them. It could have helped them to see that she was not reacting to them personally, to the people they felt themselves to be, but to them as representing a harsh, judgemental authority, such as she had known all her life. The relationship was further compounded by the departure of the previous social worker, who had been seen as caring. This loss, insufficiently mourned, provided the new workers with a further handicap in getting through the mother's defences. Unfortunately, within the rather brisk, 'monitoring' sub-culture of this local authority team, the mother's resistance rendered her 'uncooperative', therefore 'unworkable'. The use of some psychodynamic concepts like transference and ambivalence would, I think, have cleared the scene considerably.

## THE IMPORTANCE OF RECOGNISING AND REMEMBERING THE CHILD'S PAST AND HISTORY, WHATEVER IT MAY BE

All the children guardians ad litem and local authority social workers encounter have, by definition, suffered in the past. Indeed, suffering in childhood is inescapable; its quality and quantity, however, have become the concern of the modern state. I think a crucial task of workers with hurt and damaged children, especially when they are uprooted into the care system, is to help them face the past. Another contribution of psychoanalysis is the idea that the personal past cannot be buried, and that good therapeutic work entails bringing the past out of hiding.

Yevtushenko (1987) writes of the danger of submerging the past in his poem 'The Unexpressed':

The unexpressed,

the unarticulated
are frightening,

when as fragments
they burn

beneath the skin,
with no way at all

to be scratched out,
plucked out,

or brought to reason.
Events

bricked up inside
cry out in despair.

'We've been forgotten
We'll be eliminated

from history.
Let us out!

Let us out!'

Suffering rises up
> like a lump in the throat:

'We are
> like stifled sobs.

We long so
> for our liberation:

Express us!
> Express us!

I would like to see a much greater emphasis in social work training and child care policy and in-service training on teaching and supporting students and workers to do this vital work. I believe the tendency for child care workers to brush away children's unpleasant histories illustrates the common human wish to forget about distress and difficulty and move on to a trouble-free future. In case history 3, after rehabilitation failed for Clara and she returned to her foster mother, she was adamant she never wanted to see her mother again, and the workers did not think this should be forced. Nevertheless, it was agreed and recorded that, as soon as possible, Clara would need help with dealing with her experiences with her mother and the idea of her mother as a person. This was a piece of work as important to her future development and mental health as choosing the right family placement for her.

## THE DECISION AS TO WHETHER THE HOME IS A GOING CONCERN FOR THE CHILD

This is the one of the finest judgements the social worker and guardian ad litem have to make. Is the home a going concern? Does it work well enough for this particular child or could it work well enough, given definable and available resources and therapeutic work? I agree with Winnicott:

> in the great majority of cases we manage to help the child in the setting which already exists. This is of course our aim, not only because it is economical but also because when the home is good enough the home is the proper place for the child to grow up in. . . . We must see that we never interfere with a home that is a going concern, not even for its own good.
>
> (Winnicott 1985: 133)

The commitment to keep children within their birth families as a first priority is written into national and local child care policy. For example, the Department of Health publication *The Care of Children* (DOH 1989: 7–15) offers forty 'principles in relation to individual children and young people and their families', the fifth of which is: 'There are unique advantages for children in experiencing normal family life in their own birth family and every effort should be made to preserve the child's home and family links.'

Two case examples illustrate the dilemmas:

**Case history 4**

The guardian was involved after 10-year-old Peter was taken into care. He was living with his father, stepmother, stepsiblings and baby half-brother. Father and stepmother were at loggerheads over Peter; father finally took him to social services, saying he feared he would kill him if he were not removed. Peter spent the first year of life with mother and father, mother left, he lived with father and paternal grandmother until she died when he was 4. Father was living with stepmother and her two children and took Peter in. Stepmother could not accept him, and he was sent to Germany to mother (whom he hadn't seen since a baby) and her new army husband. This went well until the birth of a half sister. Apparently great jealousy transpired and Peter was sent back, aged 8, to father. A year and a half later this broke down, resulting in the current situation. How should the court decide for Peter's future?

**Case history 5**

A 6-month-old baby was removed from a young, unmarried couple, living with her parents, because of a fractured arm. They gave no account of the injury and were hostile to their social worker, but were desperate for the baby's return. They visited daily, getting on well with the foster parents, who spoke highly of them. The local authority wanted to place the child in a permanent, alternative family, regarding the home as unsafe and the parents as unworkable.

In case history 4 Peter's home with his father and stepmother was not a going concern for him. It just about hung together well enough for the other children; for Peter, it did not work. The stepmother's personality, the long history, Peter's high intelligence and insecurity about siblings, and the stresses in the family weighed against this being a good enough home for him. The task was then to look at the other possible home, with his mother and stepfather, to explore substitute alternatives and to keep the question of access and contact with both parents in the forefront of the picture.

In case history 5, the child's home had little history. The guardian eventually decided that it had potential, was worth supporting and had a better than average chance of succeeding. It was a finely balanced decision, especially with a young baby, potentially more easily placeable in a substitute home.

In case history 1, the home was not a home for a child, nor was he thriving. However, he was bonded to his mother, and the social worker was enmeshed in their symbiosis. In addition, the social worker was white and felt particularly unable to make the removal decision about a black child and mother. A black guardian was useful in quickly forming a more confident assessment of the mother's mental health and the boy's needs. He decided that foster care, with contact, had to be tried. In care, Ray thrived, began to speak more fluently, looked outwards and showed the first signs of a sense of humour.

In case history 2, the guardian believed the home was a going concern. Sitting round the kitchen table with Lois and children, there was a strong sense of family. At the family centre for an 'observed access visit', the mother froze, unable to be natural. The conclusion drawn was of an impoverished, shallow relationship. The next day, in the court waiting room, mother and boys were united, Lois equipped with drinks and crisps and board games. They were together naturally for hours, squabbling and affectionate, full of feeling. The social workers stayed closeted next door and missed seeing a family in operation.

It seems to me there is a first consideration: what is the child getting in the home? and a second, equally vital: what else needs putting in and is on offer? It is only when the conclusion is mainly negative in both areas that permanent separation should be contemplated.

## THE MYTH OF PERMANENCE

The move of the 1970s towards 'permanent alternative placement', the boom in fostering and adoption departments, and fostering placements, the closure or conversion of the large old children's homes and residential nurseries: the dangerous end of all of this, I consider, is the deep fantasy it generates that each child from a deprived, problem-beset family can be offered a better, more life-enhancing permanent alternative.

This kind of naturally seductive thinking needs challenging, particularly in individual cases. There is increasing research evidence that some permanent placements do not work for children (DHSS 1985; Thoburn 1985). They may break down or they may produce children with serious later difficulties in achieving their potential and sustaining relationships. A major cause of placement break-down or adult maladjustment is now seen to be the absence of contact with the birth family, and of work with child (and new carers) aimed to help them recognise and incorporate the past.

## TIME AND TIMESCALES

Local authority social workers have lost assurance in having time or space to attend to their clients. Being rushed, under pressure, not having enough time: these are major impediments to good practice. I think the lack of time operates in the short and the long term: day to day, with workers forever feeling hassled, rushing from one thing to the next, responding to crises, constantly chasing deadlines. As Martin Ruddock, Greenwich team leader, claimed in his written statement to the team enquiring into the death of Kimberley Carlile, quoted in the *Guardian* (12 December 1987): 'Social work is about thinking, assessing and planning. Undiluted and uncontrollable pressure is incompatible with thoughtful work.' The first sentence leaves something to be desired. Social work is also about living, on-going work with clients. The second sentence, however, expresses the impossible awareness of perpetual pressure which weighed down on Martin Ruddock.

In the long term, there is a terrible pressure operating now, born out of an anxiety about the drift of the past, the 'children who wait', the bad old days when children grew up in emotionally sub-standard homes or waited for years in unsatisfactory institutions while rehabilitation was halfheartedly attempted. There is constant reference to 'the child's time scale'. This is neatly expressed in the DOH *Principles & Practice in Regulations & Guidance*.

Time is a crucial element in child care and should be reckoned in days and months rather than years. Immature children cannot wait but need what they need when they need it. Providing it 'later' is often too late and the younger the child, the greater the urgency. For some adolescents, learning to wait for 'later' is part of growing up but the wait should be based on the young person's need and not on the social worker's convenience or the bureaucracy's time scale. The Children Act 1989 specifically requires courts to avoid delay in child care cases.

(DOH 1989: 10)

Of course it is sometimes crucial for workers to act fast; there is a need for confident crisis work. But there is also a need for discrimination about the nature of a crisis, about children and families, and, most critically, about time itself (DOH 1989: 10).

## IS THE SOCIAL WORK TASK NOW IMPOSSIBLE?

Bill Jordan observes in *Invitation to Social Work*:

But since the mid 1970s the purpose of state intervention has been shifting. It has been much more explicitly concerned with monitoring family life, and stepping in to protect vulnerable individuals from cruel or neglectful families. The notion of support or supplementation or family care has weakened, as the social services have come to be seen as expensive and a potential drain on national prosperity. But the need for more controlling measures by the state in the family's sphere of influence has been increasingly emphasized.

(Jordan 1984: 95)

The theme of local authority social work today is predominantly child rescue. Many social workers have lost the time, the inclination, the training or the institutional support to undertake the delicate, skilled task of unravelling the child's past, the family's history, the parent's story. This should be part of the treatment of the disturbance that has come to their attention. Winnicott's writings have much to offer social workers: his descriptions of the relief obtained by the child and family when an unrealised and un-expressed preoccupation is brought into the light make compulsive reading.

Instead of spending time listening and attending, once the spectre of risk (meaning possible failure and shame for the worker) has been raised, a process of hounding the family, known as assessment and monitoring, begins.

Guardian ad litem and social worker should be detectives like the psychoanalyst or the poet, mining for the crucial hidden factors, conscious or unconscious, which need to emerge and be heard.

This is not an attack on workers as individuals. It is much more about the coming together of a number of factors: increased statutory responsibility, increased public attack on social work and reduced public expenditure. Social workers have to be super vigilant, they are not allowed to make mistakes (Kimberley Carlile: Greenwich 1987); every child in care must be protected from injury or neglect (Tyra Henry: Lambeth 1987); and no child over-zealously removed from home (Cleveland: Butler-Sloss 1988). This has all to be achieved as central funding is withdrawn and local funding is in jeopardy and dispute.

I agree with A.C. Woodmansey, in the *Journal of Social Work Practice*:

> While it must be accepted that the social workers' task is inherently difficult, what cannot be accepted is the imposition of conditions making it impossible. Not only are social workers unjustly held responsible for children's deaths, but the procedures they have to follow ensure that the deaths will continue. It is utterly unfair to them and their clients that they are rewarded by continual fear of retribution instead of receive the preparation and support necessary for their work to succeed.
>
> (Woodmansey 1990: 20)

The welfare climate in this country after fifteen years of Conservative government is influenced by the notions of 'You have to get it right. There must be no mistakes; if there are, don't admit them', and 'Social work clients are inferior and should be able to sort out their own lives.' I believe this has contributed to an unspoken belief creeping over social services departments that clients have something wrong with them, and do not deserve treating as adults worthy of respect and self-determination. Recent moves to include parents in case conferences perhaps represent the beginnings of greater respect and openness.

## FACING THE PAIN OF FAMILY BREAK-UP

It may be very hard for social workers to recognise pain and anxiety about loss and separation and deal with it. The DHSS document *Social Work Decisions in Child Care* says:

> It seems very apparent that the deep emotional problems generated by separation/care experience receive insufficient attention (parents feel ignored and direct work with children is minimal). It is not clear whether the pain and grief goes unrecognised or whether it is recognised but social workers shut their eyes to it because, lacking support themselves, they cannot tolerate the pain of getting involved and working with feelings.
>
> (DHSS 1985: 21)

I think myself that the task of removing children, breaking up old families and creating new families, is experienced as intolerable and that the unconscious defence is to dispose of all the uncomfortable, ambivalent feelings onto the 'bad' parent. Then it becomes more tolerable. Encouraging and enabling the vital business of contact between parents and children in care is one of the more painful, ambivalent duties of the social worker. If discouraged or rendered impossible (as in the observed contact in case history 3 described above), all parties manage to avoid the distress and sense of ambiguity it creates. This is likely to be to the disadvantage of children whose relationship with their parents begins to wither.

Local authority social work is a possible and gratifying task if workers are supported as individuals and within their teams to meet their own and their clients' feelings; if they expect their work to be full of ambivalence, unconscious feeling and transference, it is much simpler to keep on a professional path.

## IN CONCLUSION

As a guardian working in inner London, I have been saddened to observe a decline in the personal support offered to families in need, aimed at helping them stay together and come to terms with their history. Instead, there may be a hasty and panicky attempt to assess and monitor the family, likely to lead to a worsening in family functioning and the expected outcome – removal of the children. Once removed, unless contact is actively encouraged, it is probable that children and parents will lose one another in the service of the myths of family permanence and perfection.

There is a loss of psychoanalytic inspiration in the social work task and ethos linked to a harsher, more judgemental approach to clients. The notions of ambivalence, the unconscious and transference need reintroducing into social work. There is no longer the time available to work with parents and children. The social work task has become unrewarding and difficult; support and understanding and a spelling out of basic principles are needed to withstand the pain of the job.

The 1989 Children Act, implemented in 1991, has provided a possible framework for a more supportive and sensitive role for social services. By enjoining them to provide resources and counselling to help families stay together, and by introducing contact as an issue for consideration at the first hearing by all parties, the Act looks for a greater commitment to working with parents and keeping children living with or in touch with their past and their birth families. The return, in many local authorities, to specialisation of practice and task may foreshadow a return to an approach rather more oriented towards clients' emotional lives and needs.

# Chapter 9

# Getting better makes it worse
## Obstacles to improvement in children with emotional and behavioural difficulties

*Sue Kegerreis*

Every teacher has at some stage faced the frustration of seeing a child who has been showing great improvement suddenly relapse or a child who is doing good work deliberately spoil it. This paper is an exploration of some of the difficulties children face when 'getting better' in an attempt to understand why this happens. To open, I would first like to give some illustrative vignettes from a school for children with emotional and behavioural difficulties. Much of the material in this chapter comes from work in such a school although similar problems could well have occurred in mainstream schools.

1 Peter, 13, had been really successful and much liked at special school, rarely in trouble. Plans were made for him to return to mainstream school. One week before he was due to start, he was caught shop-lifting, apparently a first offence.
2 Wayne, 14, had been working up to starting a trial period in mainstream school, but after only a short while he gave up, saying it was 'too much for him' although nothing had really gone wrong.
3 On a smaller scale, Carol, 15, was congratulated effusively by the headteacher for having had a really good morning. At lunch-time she 'flipped', and had one of the worst confrontations with her teacher that he could remember. She later complained to the head that he had 'jinxed' her.

## THE PROBLEM

What is it that makes change for the better such a desperately difficult challenge for these children? As reasonably mature adults, we tend to assume that improvement is simply improvement, clearly visible as such to the children, and as clearly desirable to them as it looks to us. We can become baffled by the resistances that the children bring up to thwart our best efforts to help them to change, and often despair in the face of self-destructive behaviour of the sort illustrated in the examples given above.

## NEGATIVE THERAPEUTIC REACTION

One term for this kind of problem is 'negative therapeutic reaction'. This is a useful formulation as it underlines that this is a negative response to something helpful, part of getting better that causes a destructive reaction. This is familiar to all of us, both as therapists and teachers (in any setting) and also as individuals. We all know how hard grievances can be to give up, even when we experience a longed for change, and we all know how complicated our reactions can be when a problem disappears. For children negotiating all the stresses of growing up, in mainstream as well as special schools, each bit of progress calls for a complex letting go, and can bring into play some of the difficulties described in this paper.

Children in special schools have to face the fact that improving probably implies leaving to return to mainstream school, which carries with it all the problems familiar to primary school children on secondary transfer magnified many times. From being a special, cared-for success they have to become an odd and threatening newcomer, managing all the ordinary problems of school life with far less support. They also have to deal with complex feelings about leaving a place which simultaneously symbolises both their problems and the kind of nurturing they needed. They also have a great deal more to lose now. It is far worse to fail a second time around. Whether in special or mainstream school, children who make a move away from their 'problem' status have to wrestle with the burden of having real hope for their own future. They are leaving behind their dreadful but safe despondency and are now newly in a position to let themselves and others down. Carole in the opening vignettes illustrates how doing well can create such anxiety over 'keeping it up' that it feels better to 'blow it' straightaway. A public schoolboy I saw recently had very nearly been expelled. Once he got in touch with how much he did not want to fail, he found it tremendously hard to fight an impulse to push himself over the brink, to get away from the terrible new feeling of responsibility.

## AVOIDING THE FEAR OF LOSS AND DAMAGE

Many children with emotional and behaviourial difficulties can be understood as being caught up in a psychic state dominated by persecutory anxieties. By this I mean anxieties of such a primitive and basic nature that the children feel their very existence is under threat. This is in contrast to depressive anxieties caused by internal conflicts between loving and hating feelings. If persecutory anxieties predominate a child will tend to deny any bad parts of himself, projecting them into others and so experiencing himself primarily as the victim of outside maltreatment. He has no secure sense of self-nurturing, internalised from a sustained sense of being nurtured. The idea of something stable and good, whether inside or outside himself, is constantly under threat and often quite absent. He may feel that his inner world is irretrievably in ruins, and may do his utmost to reduce his outside world to an equally devastated state.

There may seem from this description no possible incentive to stay in this state of mind. Yet the children so often cling to it despite its so apparent self-destructiveness. What could it be that is so much worse?

If one leaves this state behind, in the jargon if one begins to establish a good internal object, one has to encounter the fear of losing it. If you live in an entirely loveless world, you have nothing to lose in your destructive rages, but once you allow yourself to care, then you have to bear the fear of spoiling something worthwhile. Thus a child I see repeatedly said, 'But I don't care. I don't want to care. If I did I'd have to MIND.'

For many children it is more comfortable to be engrossed in a fight than suddenly to wonder what one is fighting about and face sadness instead of anger. Thus Rod, seen for individual psychotherapy, after spending half the session physically threatening and attacking me, finally stopped and had a miserable, depressed second half, saying with an air of discovery, 'It's silly, isn't it, hitting you'. He was having to face the painful, dawning realisation that he had both with me and elsewhere in his life been fighting something helpful.

From this, we can see why one possible reason for the children resisting the transition to what, in our eyes, looks so obviously a better way of being is that they simply cannot afford to. To do so puts them in so painful a position that it sends them rebounding back into the 'sicker' yet, in a sense, less immediately agonising state from which the healthy part of themselves is struggling to escape.

## INTERNAL ENVY: THE ENVIOUS VOICE WITHIN

One powerful cause of negative therapeutic reactions of the kind described here is the presence within of an envious internal figure who cannot allow the child to break free. We all have within us a 'cast' of internal figures, with whom we unconsciously relate and who influence both our actions and how we feel. These might include an internal judge, who makes us feel guilty and watches us critically, the internal good parent, who helps us take care of ourselves, or the voice inside which undermines our confidence by always stressing our shortcomings. Each of us will have our own distinctive collections of these 'internal objects' depending on our experiences and what we have made of them. If there exists in a troubled child a vocal envious internal object then improvement will be fraught indeed. One girl I see is plagued by anxious, guilty feelings whenever she feels she is making progress or even having ordinary good luck. For her, it seems, the world is populated by deprived, fiercely envious people who are only waiting for her downfall. The more her life improves the more anxious she feels as she waits for what feels like the inevitable crash.

As another example, a boy who recently left special school for mainstream school spent a good deal of his time telling me how he despised the children who remained behind. He claimed he wanted to be like a computer tape that could be wiped clean of any association with the school and with them. In one session he climbed onto the very highest bit of furniture in the room, balancing on a chair up there very precariously. He then told me that the chair was an aeroplane and that he was shooting down all the 'special school kids' who were themselves desperately trying to shoot him down and topple him. They would, he said, be so pleased to see him fall. Here he is externalising his problem onto the other children, but we can see how precarious his progress is if he is embroiled in a battle with an internal envious figure who cannot allow him to succeed.

The problems for this boy of being the envied one are acute, but do not completely preclude progress. Some others have an even more powerful voice in their minds telling them: 'It won't last, what right have you to put yourself forward, you're too bad to do well, who do you think you are?' This can lead to total paralysis, or to the all too familiar pattern of progress followed by self-sabotage, as illustrated by the introductory examples.

## ENVY: DIFFICULTIES OVER FORGIVENESS AND GRATITUDE

Another problem is illustrated by an adolescent I see. She had apparently developed well and happily until puberty, at which she suddenly fell prey to a series of phobias and fears that led her to retreat almost totally from normal adolescent life, being unable to leave her mother. In treatment, when in fact a good deal of improvement was taking place, she told me that *if* she was getting better, and she didn't say that she was, but *if* she was, then she certainly wouldn't tell me, because then I would think that I had done it and she didn't want me to have that pleasure! In saying this, she was giving me a clear indication of what had been part of the cause of her failure to develop smoothly into a successful young lady. To grow successfully was to give her parents the great gift of taking pleasure in her, in the fruit of their creativity. Such was her anger and envy of her parents that she could not allow this. They, like me, were not to feel that they were able to be really fruitful, so she would punish them and me by being an unrewarding baby/patient.

'Getting better' is also giving pleasure, affirming the creativeness of those who have tried to help. For some the unconscious rage against the parents makes such a gift impossible to make. Their only weapon is the spoiling of their own lives. In a sense, getting better implies forgiving. In an unpublished talk, Dr Robert Hale, who has done a great deal of work with drug-addicts, emphasises this as a reason for the addicts' persistent refusal to save their own lives. Underlying much self-destructive behaviour is this refusal to forgive what seem to be unrightable wrongs, unrelievable grievances, over what has gone on in the child's past. Indeed, many of the children have much to forgive, and it is unsurprising that this is difficult.

'Getting better' not only implies forgiveness, it also implies grati-tude. This in its turn necessitates an acceptance of vulnerability and neediness. It is against the psychic pain of this vulnerability and dependence that so many of our children's symptoms have been developed as defences, especially when such states are rendered infinitely worse by parental unreliability and failure. But the poten- tially terrifying state of dependence has to be accepted before the gratitude, the feeling of having received something good from outside themselves, can be felt. Often, the children would rather maintain their far from splendid isolation than face the reality of their position and needs, with the ever-present possibility that they will again feel let down. The apparently simple psychic manoeuvre of feeling grateful involves many of the areas of most acute difficulty for the children and can add to the load holding them down in their illness.

## EXTERNAL FACTORS INHIBITING PROGRESS

It has to be acknowledged that some parents may in reality be ambivalent or even destructive towards their child's progress, which may put extra pressure on him/her at the point of possible success. For example Wayne (no. 2 in the opening illustrations) is the 'baby' of his family and his mother has consistently treated him as being much younger than he really is. Her fear of what his growing up will bring has led her to reinforce his own fears with statements that he was not yet ready to return to ordinary school and to meet his anxieties with encouragement to give up, rather than reassurance to continue.

So 'getting better' can bring additional burdens in terms of the child's relationship with parents and peer group. In the extreme cases, if his milieu is a very disturbed one, then improvement can often mean isolation for the child. For Martin (14) who is struggling to keep in touch with the softer, more caring side of himself, when violent 'macho' behaviour is the hallmark of his family, to be different implies a determined breaking out of their mould and maybe out of their world.

It is to be hoped that greater mental health in a child would improve relationships at home, but it also has to be acknowledged that in some households the child may be the only one well enough to break out of a destructive family system. There can be terrific conflicts of loyalty for a child in this position.

Improvement can also be a family 'minefield' for children whose progress arouses envy in the parents towards the people who have helped him. The parents of the children have their own guilt and feelings of inadequacy to face, and it can be full of conflict to see one's child being helped out of difficulties that one has been unable to help them with and maybe partially caused. The parents therefore may have their own problems in allowing the child to get better, even if these are entirely unconscious and at odds with all their love and concern. They, as well as the children themselves, may be unable to allow the teacher or therapist that amount of potency.

Children can also be held back in their progress by a fear of being of less concern to parents and teachers if they give up their attention-getting troubled behaviour. It can seem to them that their parents are only really mobilised as forces in their lives in activities centred around their difficulties. So, despite the fact that they know that they provoke much negative feeling in their parents and teachers, they do at least feel that they exist for them, and this can seem better than what feels like being quite forgotten.

## CONCLUDING REMARKS

When there is the possibility of improvement, all these motivations to self-destructiveness are potentially activated. Before this, when the child seems stuck, it may not be apparent quite how powerful they are. One's attention is often on the more striking features of the child's difficulties, such as his inability to share or his hatred of anyone challenging his omnipotence. But when hope begins to dawn, the child can be thrown into a most painful state. Mental health is not the absence of psychic pain, far from it. It is the ability to encounter it, tolerate it and develop through it. The children's difficulties are not caused solely by the overload of such pain, but rather by the attempt, for whatever reason, to avoid it.

In a very real sense, getting better does, some of the time, make it worse. We need to be aware of what we are asking of the children when we offer them the chance of improvement. We are setting them no easy task, and the pain on the way may be enough to drive many a child back into the comparative safety of his illness. Understanding what they are going through should help us deal better with the despair and frustration engendered by their resistances, to contain their anxieties and therefore to steer a straighter course ourselves. It can help us more meaningfully to talk to the children about their fears, thereby making them more comprehensible and less uncontrollable. One hopes that we would be better able to avoid unrealistic expectations or over-enthusiasm in the face of progress if we can always hold in mind the anxieties aroused and the probability of there being set-backs. This will strengthen us and help us strengthen the children against giving up hope when things get difficult. It will perhaps take many periods of progress followed by failure before the necessary inner strength can be built up. There is no escaping the pain of this process, but an understanding of what is at stake will help us help the children negotiate the difficult path through the worst, on to a state where being 'better' brings its rewards of stability, creativity and peace of mind.

# Groups

*Judith Trowell*

This section contains papers that describe how children and families can be helped in groups. Understanding group process and the dynamic of groups has been developed by two psycho-analysts, Bion and Foulkes. Bion understood groups to be using very early mechanisms to cope with anxiety and conflict such as splitting, denial, projection and projective identification. He saw groups as either working groups that were attending to the task or anti-task basic assumption groups. Where the latter occurred, what could be observed was 'fight/flight' behaviour or 'pairings' or a 'dependency' group. By this he meant that members of the group might engage in fights, arguments, might try and avoid issues, perhaps by not attending (flight); or they might make intense relationships in pairs, or they might become very dependent on the group leader.

Foulkes saw groups rather differently, with the 'leader' joining the group and co-working with the group membership rather than staying on the boundary and commenting from there on the process. He also saw the dynamics rather differently: the whole life and activity of the group repeated what occurs in the member's outside world and could be usefully understood in this way. This way of working is illustrated by Maggie Mills and Christine Puckering's chapter on Newpin. It is particularly well suited to groups run by trained volunteers, as working in this way can avoid confronting the more destructive aspects of these groups.

Working with the very emotionally deprived and vulnerable populations described in other chapters the authors are mainly referring to levels of functioning more easily understood in terms of Bion's work: that is, where very early mechanisms dominate and these processes are worked with by the group leaders.

Where the group leader is clearly identifiable they will be particularly liable to envious and denigrating attacks on their functioning. This is very stressful for the workers, as the chapters by Marion Bower and Michael Morice indicate. However, the survival of the group leader is immensely important for the members of the group.

In the mothers' group described by Bower, the leader represents a robust maternal figure who can be internalised by members of the group. This process makes an important contribution to the improved capacity of the group members to care for their children.

A similar process is described in the chapter by Zelinda Adam. She also illustrates clearly how important it is for mothers to develop a more tolerant and sympathetic attitude towards themselves by which they can extend this type of support to their children.

Most of the children and families described in this section are suffering from maternal deprivation. All of them are suffering from emotional deprivation which is by no means confined only to poor families. Emotional deprivation has a variety of forms, it may simply be a lack of warmth and understanding. However, in many of the families where there is maternal depression it is not simply a matter of an absence of something. Adam describes how many depressed women are preoccupied with a chilling inner figure creating an atmosphere of deadness and despair. They may also project unbearable aspects of their own experience onto their children. (This is described in relation to one particular family in Chapter 7 in the previous section.) The 'hyperactive' behaviour of the children of depressed mothers is often an attempt to liven up a deadly atmosphere.

This type of emotional deprivation and suffering in its more extreme forms becomes emotional abuse. Many of the children described in this section have also suffered physical or sexual abuse, or come from families where violence and perverse sexuality are a part of life. In families such as this the usual processes for dealing with vulnerability and psychic pain are absent or distorted and there may be a culture in which destructiveness is idealised.

Rosenfeld (1971) has described a process in individual patients which is very helpful for understanding families such as this. This is the creation of a psychological 'mafia' where a destructive and narcissistic part of the personality offers 'protection' and freedom from pain to more needy aspects of the personality. Membership of the gang is maintained by intimidation and coercion and real dependency needs cannot be met.

Michael Morrice uses this model to understand why the children in the group gang up to attack the group leader who represents (at that moment) hope and change. This type of 'gang family' will be familiar to those who work in social services and the model makes it clear why it is so difficult to offer such families effective help.

Another difficult aspect of working with very disturbed families is their tendency to defend themselves against the emotional pain characteristics of the paranoid-schizoid position (see Chapter 2). Unbearable emotions and conflicts are split off and projected into people outside the family. Unless this process is identified professional networks can find themselves re-enacting a family's problem rather than working with them. The value of a consultant to help workers contain these processes is illustrated in Judith Trowell's chapter on the Monroe Centre (Chapter 11).

# Chapter 10

# White City Toy Library

## A therapeutic group for mothers and under-5s

*Marion Bower*

There is a paradox in the way a generation sees the mother as uniquely powerful and responsible yet puts its young mothers in such isolated and dishonoured social positions that they are particularly prone to depressive breakdowns.

(J. Temperley 1984)

## DEPRESSED MOTHERS

Depression among women with young children is a huge, yet intensely private and neglected problem. Women who are depressed rarely come to the attention of social services or receive psychiatric or psychotherapeutic help. Yet the cost in human misery for such women and their children is enormous.

Curiously, although there is so little help available, the problem is very well studied. The effects of maternal depression on children are well known to psychologists, child psychotherapists and psychoanalysts. We know that it is not only the child's emotional development which is affected, but also cognitive, speech and language development. These effects may persist right through late childhood and adulthood if untreated.

This paper is an account of a group which attempts to help such women and children, and is psychoanalytic in its orientation. It is based in the Child Guidance Unit where I work as a psychiatric social worker.

The White City Child Guidance Unit is in a health centre in the middle of a huge post-war council estate. There are many single parents, ethnic minority families and families where there are mentally ill members. There is also a huge population of under-5s.

The flats with their stone stairs and balconies are inconvenient for families with small children. Despite the provision of good facilities, the area has an air of deprivation and neglect that is not simply due to poverty.

These are precisely the conditions under which depression flourishes and, although a high proportion of referrals to the Child Guidance Unit are families with children under 5, it seemed certain that there were many more who could use our help – the question was: how could we identify the families and how could we provide the help?

I wanted to provide a setting that not only offered help to mothers and children, but also provided mothers with an opportunity to form friendships to break the cycle of isolation and depression. A group was the obvious answer, although there is already a 'One O'Clock Club', a mother and toddler club and a playgroup in the area, and I did not want to duplicate their work. Talking to other under-5s workers in the area, it was obvious that women who most needed these groups were least likely to use them. The groups were too large and socially intimidating, and this problem would be even worse for a woman who spoke poor English or had a child whose behaviour was embarrassing.

Colleagues in other London Child Guidance Units had found it was possible to build a group for mothers and small children around a toy library. Families felt they were being given something concretely 'good' and the title 'Toy Library' is less intimidating than 'Child Guidance'.

## SETTING UP THE GROUP

I would like to say a bit about this, partly to help others thinking of setting up a similar group, partly because it highlights some difficulties in working in this area. One problem I am particularly aware of myself is the vast number of different professionals working with under-5s, and the nature of the relationships between them. Although each profession tends to be quite sensitive of their own area of expertise being encroached upon, there is considerable vagueness about what other people do.

After some informal exploration I called an initial meeting of everyone in the area who was involved with under-5s: health visitors, speech therapists, the community medical officer, the heads of local day nurseries and nursery schools, school nurses, etc.

There was some discussion as to whether what I was proposing duplicated any of the existing groups; however, most people could think of families with the kinds of needs I had in mind – depressed, isolated mothers with children who were showing signs of emotional difficulty and very often developmental delay. The biggest difficulty was felt to be getting such women and children to attend a group. It was suggested that we would need to visit at home and possibly bring them to the library. (Interestingly, we found that in practice this rarely proved necessary even if a woman had never been to a group before.) The workers in the group have varied but the core is a psychiatric social worker (originally myself), a nursery nurse (employed by the Education Department, my own employers), and an occupational therapist (from Riverside Mental Health Trust). We have also had students from a variety of trainings. I was also able to persuade the senior nursing officer (responsible for the district health visitors), the community medical officer and the speech therapists to form an advisory working party, which still exists and meets every three months.

Getting money for toys was an initial (and continuing) problem. We joined the Toy Libraries Association and, using their charitable status, obtained a first grant from the Department of Social Security. We have now developed the filling in of grant application forms to a fine art!

## THE FORM OF THE GROUP

The group meets once a week for just under two hours. There are, in fact, two parallel groups, one for mothers and one for children, which are held in two rooms on opposite sides of a corridor. The mothers' room has comfortable chairs and an electric kettle for coffee. The children's room has toys and play materials such as sand and water. Drinks are provided at a communal sitting. At the end of the morning mothers can borrow a toy for each child. After the families leave there is a period of discussion among the workers. Although the two groups are separately run, each with their own workers, in practice there is not a rigid division between them. Children may come in to join their mothers and mothers may go into the children's room – particularly if their child is new to the group. Small babies stay with their mothers. Mothers may be asked to comfort a child or take them to the lavatory, otherwise they and the children are completely 'looked after' for the duration of the group.

I chose to have separate groups for mothers and children because I believe it is impossible for a mother/child relationship to improve unless the mother's own personal and infantile needs are also recognised and attended to. This conflict of interests is one of the most difficult aspects of mothering; it is a time when enormous demands are made on a woman's personal resources, yet there is least opportunity to have her own needs met. As one woman interviewed by Dana Breen puts it: 'And I've got this very strong feeling now, that I just would like time to myself, not somebody's mother, not necessarily to be anybody's wife, just for half a day' (Breen 1989: 186).

Schamess (1987) describes an American group run on very similar lines for teenage mothers and their small children. Like Schamess, I think the separate mothers' group provides opportunities for regression. As a result the mothers' group comes to represent certain aspects of family life which is further reinforced by the small size of the group – not more than ten. I shall discuss below how these issues are dealt with.

Working with the children separately is not simply a means of giving mothers a break. At its crudest it gives children who may be very aggressive or withdrawn a new experience of socialisation, as well as of play and stimulation.

## THEORETICAL APPROACH

When I say the group is psychoanalytical in its orientation, I mean we concentrate on the development of understanding and change *from within*. We provide a constant setting, and take account of unconscious factors and infantile needs and experiences. However, the dynamics of a group like this are so complex that it is impossible to have the neutrality and precision of individual or even group therapy, although I find my own experience as a psychoanalytical family therapist particularly helpful in this work.

In practice we tend to intervene in the way which seems most helpful at any given moment – either with an individual or with the group. Interventions also depend on the particular skill and orientation of each worker. I shall try to illustrate this process with clinical material later on. Here, I will just mention some aspects of psychoanalytical theories that I have found particularly helpful (an introduction to these concepts will be found in Chapter 2).

My own work is particularly influenced by Melanie Klein's ideas and subsequent development of her work by Bion. Klein's work concentrates on the very early stages of mother/infant interaction. From the beginning this interaction is suffused with intense love and intense destructive feelings. In the early paranoid-schizoid phase the child deals with these contradictory feelings by splitting the mother inside into different fantasy figures. In the later more integrated, depressive phase there is a realisation that the mother who is hated and attacked in fantasy is also the mother who is loved. Guilt and depression ensue and hopefully reparation to the attacked internal mother may take place. (It is important in this respect that the child feels he or she is a source of pleasure to the real external mother – many children who come to us do not feel this.)

Klein's theory of envy is fundamental to her view of the developing mind of the infant and aspects of our adult mental functioning. Putting it simply, Klein sees constitutional envy as a powerful destructive force. Its prototype is the baby's envy of the mother's breast; the breast's capacity to give and sustain life arouses a primitive hatred, and a wish to destroy and spoil its goodness. These envious feelings can be mitigated by the infant's care and gratitude for what is received and by the quality of the mother's response to it.

I think Klein's concept of envy can be used to understand some particularly difficult aspects of working with groups like this. Envy can interfere with a mother or child's capacity to take what might be called 'help food' from the group. (One example of this is the refusal of some mothers to acknowledge obvious improvements in themselves or their child and give us the satisfaction of helping.) More uncomfortably, we as workers have to struggle with our own envy of mothering. We see some happy moments between mothers and children, and the envy it arouses in us can lead us to concentrate only on the difficulties and lose sight of the good points of a difficult mother/child relationship. (This is a problem which is not often acknowledged. It is easy for us to accept that our clients may envy us, but not comfortable to see that we may envy them.)

According to Klein, object relations begin in the first days of life, through a complex interaction of projection and introjection. The first object relationship internalised in this way is the relationship with the breast and then later that with the mother as a whole person. The so-called internal mother is, therefore, a complex and composite figure – partly based on the actual mother and partly based on the infant's fantasies and feelings – which in turn colour perceptions. This internal mother will later be the source of a woman's own strengths and weaknesses when she becomes a mother herself.

I think this conceptualisation enables us to understand how some of the women who come to the Toy Library have survived even very bad experiences with a good capacity to care for their children. However, with most of the women one gets the impression of an 'internal mother' in a very bad way – weak, damaged and depressed, often harshly critical and reproachful. The relationship with the internal mother can be witnessed and experienced through the type of transference.

Schamess suggests that the group as *a whole* 'unconsciously comes to represent a nurturant maternal figure for the individual members' (Schamess 1987: 38). He refers to a transference to the workers only in its positive aspects.

My own experience is that a marked parental transference develops between adult or child members and the workers. There is certainly a particularly marked maternal transference towards myself in the mothers' group. I suspect the reluctance to recognise and work with this transference derives from the fact that it is often very unpleasant and negative in nature, as will be illustrated.

Bion (1961) has developed Klein's concepts of projective identification (a fantasy that a good or bad part of the self can be split off and concretely enter the body and/or mind of someone else) to understand certain aspects of group functioning. The concept of projective identification has undergone various refinements and redefinitions since its introduction in 1946 by Melanie Klein. In the mothers' group in particular there are times when it is clear that different members of the group are expressing different aspects of a shared feeling and a group interpretation can be made.

Although the activities of the workers are very varied, from interpretation to wiping noses, I think our role can be summarised by Bion's concept of containment. In origin this is the mother's capacity to receive and tolerate the infant's projections and return them in modified form. In adult terms the group is a place where such primitive interaction can be born, thought about and in some instances responded to with appropriate action or words so that a kind of detoxification can take place.

## HOW THE MOTHER'S GROUP IS RUN

The boundaries of the group are set by the time limits, we start and stop on time. Mothers come in and leave their children in the children's room if they are able to separate. I make people tea and coffee as they arrive. I leave the conversation to take its course; if someone wants to discuss the weather I accept this, in fact it can often tell me quite a lot about members' internal 'weather': for example, 'I don't believe the rain is ever going to stop.' However, I do encourage members to pursue topics which are important. Where it seems helpful, I try to make an interpretation but try to relate it to the concerns of the group. (There is an example in the section below when I discuss Alice.) Where there are practical issues being discussed I try to encourage people to draw on each others' skills and experiences. In summary, I try to strike a balance between 'support' and therapy. As I explained earlier I think the group leader functions in the transference as a mother, and my task is to be a supportive and containing figure for the group members to internalise.

## CLINICAL MATERIAL

I am presenting material separately from the mothers' and children's groups. As I said earlier, the boundaries are blurred and children come into the mothers' group and vice versa. My own perception is influenced by the fact that I have always worked with the mothers' group. The two groups certainly function rather differently.

### Case history 1

Alice, an Afro-Caribbean woman and her daughter Yvonne, aged 2 years, were referred to the Toy Library by the Community Medical Officer. Yvonne was very clinging and shy. She spoke only a few words and showed no interest in toys. Alice was married and had an older son, Tony, aged 4, at school.

When they first came to the Toy Library we were very struck by their appearance. Both mother and daughter looked grubby and bedraggled. Yvonne had a permanently runny nose. Alice seemed offhand and unconcerned about Yvonne.

In the mothers' group Alice always sat as far away as possible from me and usually managed to inch her chair out of the circle.

When she spoke it was usually to complain about 'the children'. She came every week and I often wondered why. After six months Alice was, unusually, absent for several weeks and I wrote her a note asking how things were. Her response to this was very striking. She arrived promptly the next week, and said how pleased she was to get a letter and was surprised that anyone had noticed she was not there.

I think Alice's behaviour in the group can be understood very much as a repetition of her own family experiences. She was born in the West Indies and when she was 2 her mother left her to come to England (Alice did not rejoin her mother until she was 10). Alice was left with her maternal grandmother who had many other relatives living with her. She felt no-one cared or took any notice of her. It was interesting, of course, how much she herself perpetuated the situation in the group. The letter was something of a turning point and after one year Alice is now a very vocal, enthusiastic member of the group. She now usually marches in and sits very close to me.

I think the transference Alice brings to the relationship with me is typical of a number of other mothers. She sees me as a rather feeble and depressed person with few resources.

She often says 'you're looking a bit tired today'. Sometimes this concern is directed towards the large plant I sit next to. 'It's very droopy, it must be our noxious fumes.' I would say that this is a projection into me of the mother inside her, who is in a poor state. She feels damaged, and hopes that her anger and pain about this damage can be healed by my understanding and surviving her projection. Her persecutory relationship with the mother inside her is, therefore, combined with a depressive concern about her and its accompanying wish for reparation.

Recently, Alice has acquired a new hairstyle and some smart new clothes suggesting that she (and her 'internal mother') are feeling in a better state. I think the neglected child in Alice is also feeling better which is reflected in her increased interest in Yvonne and her new found pride in Yvonne's achievements.

## Case history 2

Jenny and her daughter Lucy, aged 2, were referred by her health visitor who was concerned that Lucy was restless and aggressive, whilst her mother seemed to have little ability to control her.

Jenny is a white single mother. She comes from a middle-class family. Her parents have recently retired to the country. Jenny quickly took over the mothers' group, dispensing advice to the other mothers, making a lot of complaints about Lucy, but not really listening to what anyone else said. Lucy could not settle in the children's group and soon invaded the mothers' group, climbing on the chairs, imitating our talk and fiddling with the tea and coffee. This was in line with Jenny's complaints that Lucy was always 'into my things'. I think Jenny was unable to stop Lucy because she was so identified with Lucy's wish to 'be Mummy'. After a while I took to removing Lucy from the chairs, saying 'This is Mummy's room and the Mummies' chairs', and one of the children's workers would take her back in a kindly fashion into the children's room. Although Jenny is identified with her daughter she did not take offence and began to identify with a new 'mother' who was prepared to set generational boundaries. For example, she soon moved Lucy out from her bed into a little bed of her own.

**Case history 3**

Elizabeth is a Nigerian woman who was referred with Albert, aged 2. Elizabeth was so depressed she never spoke. Albert ran frantically about, he had no speech and could not play. At intervals he would erupt with rage and hit his mother and other mothers. Initially, Elizabeth dragged him away when this happened, but I was able to persuade her we wanted them to stay and we would help. From this time on things began to improve. Elizabeth now talks freely; she told us she was abandoned by her mother when she was Albert's age. Albert can settle for as long as half-an-hour to play, his speech has improved and his mother can cope with his tantrums. I think it was important to Elizabeth that, unlike her real mother, we did not abandon her at this difficult time in her life.

**THE CHILDREN'S GROUP**

The children's room is laid out with a variety of toys including material for sand and water play. The same lay-out is kept from week to week so the workers can follow a child's relationship to the toys and how it changes.

Although we do not do 'psychotherapy in public', from time to time one worker will follow a particular child that we are concerned about.

The following section on Anthony was written by Claudio Rotenberg.

## Case history 4

Anthony started coming to the Toy Library when he was 2. His family are Roman Catholic from Sri Lanka. Anthony refused to leave his mother's side, but was also very aggressive towards her. Anthony's mother had been severely depressed after his birth, and was briefly in a psychiatric hospital. We decided that our male worker would try and form a 'special' relationship with him, although it could not be hurried or forced. At first he did this by communicating with Anthony at a distance through smiling, waving and eye contact. Later, he was able to encourage Anthony to play with toys while remaining near his mother. After a while Anthony developed enough confidence to follow the worker into the children's room. At first he showed fear of other children and was violently possessive of any toy he had been using. However, after many months of focused work, Anthony began to play co-operatively with other children.

Although the children's group does not develop the sort of 'group atmosphere' that the adults' group does, at times children seem to react to the group in ways which reflect their family situation.

## Case history 5

Marie is 3½. Like Anthony she has had difficulty relating to other children and sharing things. She is an only child who had just started nursery school in the afternoon, but, during the transition, she was continuing to come to the group. When she arrived early one day there were a male and a female worker and a 1-year-old boy in the children's room. Marie began throwing dolls and animals into the waste bin in an angry way. The workers talked to Marie about her worry that now she had started school she would be thrown away and replaced by a new baby. After a few weeks Marie settled well into the nursery school class.

## THE DYNAMICS OF THE GROUPS

The dynamics of a group like this are obviously very complex and it is not possible to understand everything that goes on. However, I would like to pick out a few areas which I think are important and likely to be repeated in similar groups.

First, the relationship between the mothers' and children's groups changes from session to session. It is common for the workers in each group to have periods of feeling rivalrous or envious of each other's roles. It is important to be able to air and examine these feelings between ourselves, as they can be a useful guide to what is going on between the mothers and children.

As I mentioned earlier, I think the mothers' group is often experienced by its members as a family with myself as 'Mother' or, if children are present, 'Grandmother'. The response of current group members to the arrival of a new member is a good example. It may arouse memories of their own younger siblings being born, and a fear I will lose interest in them and transfer it to the new 'baby'. Discussion of mothers' own childhood feelings of jealousy sometimes helps them respond more sympathetically to this sort of behaviour in their own children. Crucially, it provides a model whereby unpleasant, envious or jealous feelings can be understood and taken in rather than punished, judged and kept at bay. Such rivalrous feelings arise from a positive maternal transference towards me.

However, there is another quite different process which seems to operate in parallel, which is a quiet denigration of the group and, in particular, my maternal function within it. I have already given some examples, but at times the process is very subtle, with members arriving late and an atmosphere of boredom and ennui. Other times there are complaints that the group does not help things and the children are as bad as before. Of course, there may be legitimate criticisms being voiced, but very often this sort of group follows from a session which has been particularly fruitful and lively, with mothers reporting improvements in themselves and their children. This sequence is common and has its parallels with the idea of negative therapeutic reaction in actual clinical work.

I try, when possible, to encourage the group members to think why they or others are absent, or frequently late or particularly negative. One woman said, 'If I come here I feel I'm giving something to you, making you important, if I stay at home I can look after my own house.'

I think this summarises very nicely the feelings of rivalry and envy which lie behind the behaviour described and the state of mind that promotes. The process is, however, difficult to deal with, but it is important to address it. I think a denigrated 'internal mother' is often at the heart of many women's difficulties in mothering. Hopefully, by understanding and withstanding this projection I provide a safer, more robust mother to internalise.

## OBSERVED CHANGES

I have tried to illustrate some of the changes observed in the clinical vignettes. These include improved self-esteem and mothering skills in the mothers, and improved speech and play in the children. However, I think the most important change lies in the internalised aspects of the mother/child relationship inside. The sort of change I am thinking of is exemplified by one mother who described her 2-year-old son as 'the destructive one'. By the time she left the group, she referred to him as 'my most affectionate child'.

In psychoanalytical terms this example illustrates the withdrawal of negative projections and crippling identifications. The importance of this inner shift is borne out in research by Richman. She found that the single most predictive factor for child disturbance was maternal criticism closely followed by lack of warmth (quoted in Pound *et al.* 1989: 240).

## WHO CAN WE WORK WITH?

I think the Toy Library has fulfilled our hope that we would reach families who would not otherwise make use of the child guidance service. We have been particularly successful in working with ethnic minority women and a majority of our members are of Afro-Caribbean or Asian origin. I think one reason for this is that the 'extended family' style of the group has a familiar feel and is particularly welcomed by women separated or estranged from their families and cultures of origin. A group where practical aspects of caring for children are incorporated is also easier than a purely verbal group for women whose English is poor as it gives a sense of shared experience even if this cannot be communicated in words.

## CONCLUSIONS

I hope I have demonstrated that a group like this can help mothers and children from a wide range of backgrounds and personal difficulties. I believe a network of groups such as this in every borough could make a real contribution to the happiness and mental health of a significant number of mothers and children.

Support for mothers who want to stay at home with their children is tremendously rare, despite all that is known about the need for it (e.g. Pound *et al.* 1989). I think this reflects the deeply ambivalent attitude society has towards mothers and children.

However, we have to remember that many of the mothers we want to help share in society's devaluation and denigration of the maternal role. There needs to be at least one worker who can understand and tolerate the denigration with which the workers in a group like this are often treated, and can support the others in dealing with it without retaliation. This process is very important because it provides group members with a more robust and sympathetic maternal figure to internalise, which becomes the basis of real improvements in their own mothering capacities.

# Chapter 11

# The Monroe Young Family Centre

*Judith Trowell*

Four years since it was set up, what lessons thoughts and ideas can be learnt from this project? The initial phase has been described elsewhere (Trowell and Huffington 1992) including the complex problems associated with trying to build in audit and evaluation from the start. Here the issues that have emerged will be explored. These are some of the things we have learned working in a multi-disciplinary team on a regular, on-going basis.

The centre was set up to offer assessment and treatment to families where there was known abuse or where there was serious risk of abuse – families who caused serious worry and concern, for whom the centre would be the last hope of treatment, where decisions might even have to be made that change was not possible within a time frame suitable for the children's needs. Because the centre is located in a small prefabricated hut the service was limited to families with children of 5 years and under.

The centre offers an assessment programme of six days, i.e. one day per week for six weeks, and a treatment programme, i.e. two days per week for up to one year. The expectation was that most of the families would have severe problems involving sexual abuse. This has proved to be wrong: many of the families have the possibility of sexual abuse as one of the issues but most of the referrals have involved neglect, assessment of parenting capacity and physical abuse in the context of family violence or parental mental illness. One of the significant questions is very frequently whether the mental health problems of one or other parent mean that they are unable to parent.

It seemed likely that this particular issue – mental health problems – was involved in many referrals because the centre is part of the child and family department of the Tavistock Clinic which is a mental health clinic. It was thought that the presence of a consultant psychiatrist and also a senior registrar in child and adolescent psychiatry also contributed significantly to this. However, there is increasing evidence that indicates mental health problems are not infrequently a feature of families with a child on the child protection register. This is likely to be an increasing area of concern as more families involve individuals who were previously in mental institutions and as there seems to be a general rise in mental health problems in the community.

The team therefore has had to cope with a rather different range of stresses than expected and the powerful issues which sweep through the families, the team and the case discussion meetings are often to do with sanity and madness, life and death, as well as the violence and sexuality frequently associated with abusing families. The families are very often coming because they must, sent by Social Services because they are on the child protection register and or sent by the courts. A few families come as Health Service referrals. It is generally important there be an allocated social worker to support the families' attendance; where this is not available families frequently drop out, finding work at the centre itself and the journey difficult. If a social worker is visiting regularly to support and encourage attendance, families feel they have not been dumped, the interest and commitment of the social worker then enables them to sustain a commitment to attend.

Whole families, if possible, come for the day and have a range of experiences. The families take part in family group activities as a large group; there are centre meetings, key worker sessions, adults' groups, children's groups, individual therapy sessions for the adults and children, family sessions and parent–child sessions. Network meetings are held and workers attend case conferences and go to court.

Many of the families have lone female parents. Afro-Caribbean families have been represented but only one Asian family. Most of the families are white European. The centre's work is based on psychoanalytical principles and uses attachment theory and systems theory in working with these very complex, disturbing multiproblem families.

## ISSUES

### Working together in partnership

*a) In running the centre*

The centre was set up to try to work very closely with all the other agencies involved; it was set up as a partnership between different agencies or stakeholders. The agencies involved in the Monroe Young Family Centre are the NHS Tavistock Clinic (now a Trust), the Marilyn Monroe Children's Fund, National Children's Homes (now NCH Action for Children) and the American Junior League of London. There have been difficulties and conflicts as well as the benefits of collaboration and cross-fertilisation. Inevitably there has been rivalry and competitiveness; there have also been problems of communication, of language, of management structure, of different systems of accountability and responsibility and also of the different personalities. It has been an enormous help to have a good understanding of group process and dynamics (Bion 1961) in order to make sense of what was going on and to be able to intervene. Very often the meetings have felt bogged down in feelings that have been difficult to name but that have felt very powerful. Using consultative skills and a knowledge of groups has made it possible to steer the focus away from inter-agency fights, who was to blame, who had done what to whom, to move the discussion so that the emphasis is on how we can work together to solve this problem in order to provide a better service for the children and families. It has been very painful and stressful sometimes to let go of procedures or beliefs about the best way to do something built up in one's own organisation, but the shared learning has been rewarding and the benefit to the service has been apparent.

One of the important lessons has been that good inter-agency collaboration is not static. However well resolved issues have been, it is vital to keep working at the relationship, and keep communicating because new questions arise and can open up old conflicts and present new differences. The inter-agency partnership needs constant work.

*b) With outside agencies*

As well as working in partnership with the stakeholders, there are outside professional agencies, the local authority social service departments, health authorities and trusts, GPs and voluntary sector groups. Again, there is the need to spend time building relationships, communicating, listening to their needs. Once families are attending the centre the splits and conflicts in the families are all too easily repeated in the professional network and this can sabotage the work. What happens is that positions are taken up, different agencies identifying with different members of the family. Decision making can then be biased by these identifications: for example, a social services social worker very involved with and supporting the mother and the centre speaking for the child can provoke a confrontation and this can lead to a breakdown in the network relationship. This occurs most often when a decision must be made about whether a child can be rehabilitated back to live with mother or perhaps sadly deciding that the needs of the child mean the parent has to let the child go.

### c) Partnership with parents

This need to work together in partnership with parents is part of the Children Act and part of the change in legal climate in child care. Parents need to be encouraged and supported to take seriously their parental responsibilities. This means involving the parents in considering their children's best interest. There has been confusion about partnership but it now has become clear that it means as much openness and honesty as possible but above all respect for the person. It does not mean all the partners are equal. Partners have views and opinions which need to be heard; they need help to secure the best they can for themselves (empowerment) but they may not have equal say in what will happen. Professionals have to exercise their professional responsibility and say what they think and why. Parents may well disagree but deserve to have a full discussion of the professional opinions and reasons for it.

One of the difficulties we find is that some of the centre workers become very involved and identified with the mother or parents and other centre workers feel very strongly about the children and their needs. This conflict in the family over whose needs, whose interests have primacy is mirrored in the centre staff. Most of these families comprise a group of very needy, deprived individuals, some of whom happen to be adult (parents) and some who are chronologically children. Family members project their neediness and vulnerability and different centre workers become identified with the different individuals in the family.

A mother with three small children, whose partner was detained by the Home Office, cared about her children. But she was often preoccupied, missing her partner a great deal. When she was down and the children irritated her she either became angry and threw things or switched off and was unavailable and the children, who had no sense of danger, did very risky things, climbing, playing with matches, roaming the estate where they lived. The children were adequately fed and reasonably clean but they were not able to learn at nursery and, in the nursery class, they had problems behaving appropriately with friends and they were terrified to speak to anyone about what had gone on at home. The children were developmentally delayed and showed signs of emotional and behavioural disturbance. Some members of the centre team and the outside social worker and GP felt very concerned for the mother and her struggle to survive as a single parent. Most of the centre team felt enormous concerns for these three young children. Meetings provoked very violent feelings with some professionals unable to speak to others. It was a tremendous effort to insist on further discussions with each participant being given space to present their views and be heard. During this process the intensity of the identifications lessened and the extent of the mother's ambivalence to her children became more evident. The mother's splits and conflict could be addressed, the meeting could then move on to consider whether additional support could improve matters sufficiently or whether we needed to say enough is enough. In this case carefully planned support work for mother in her own right and therapy for the children seemed to be the right outcome.

All this professional work depended on an understanding of the many splits, identifications and projections which re-enact the conflicts in the family.

### d) Partnership with the child

Most of the children are 5 years and under so this partnership is worked with on the basis of respect for the child, honesty and an explanation to the child that what they are able to share with staff is taken seriously. The most difficult aspect of work with the children is, sadly, trying to make space for the child's voice to be heard. Despite constant effort, it is frequently overlooked and the children are 'forgotten'.

## Therapy versus child protection

Another issue that often arises from this same process is a serious split in the centre staff team. Because the team is multi-disciplinary the split very often repeats and reinforces rivalries between disciplines: responsibility for child protection is held by social workers and the individual, family and group workers carry the belief and commitment to the importance of therapy. In reality 'child protection' workers must consider therapeutic needs and the 'therapy' workers have to take on some of the responsibility for child protection. As well as the real ideological difference, these conflicts can be exacerbated by the conflict in the family. Different members of a family engage differently with team members and reveal different aspects of themselves. Professionals working therapeutically with a child are expected to concentrate on the internal world and also remember external world issues, but they do not want to have to think about the material arising with a view to a report and a court hearing. It is a repeated issue to struggle to help all the workers acknowledge they must be helpful and therapeutic and they have a responsibility to protect. All parenting involves using both these aspects, authority and caring, and working professionally does as well. But the risk of becoming too punitive with a 'protection' hat on or too permissive and 'blind' with a therapeutic hat is very real. The resulting polarisation is unprofessional, anti-therapeutic or abusive. A family of mother, stepfather and two boys attended because of physical abuse and neglect. One of the boys in his individual sessions gave material suggestive of sexual abuse. The therapy worker ignored it, then shared it with the team; she didn't want to explore it further or for social services to be informed. 'Child protection' workers became enraged and declared the team unworkable, the centre dangerous for children. When, the situation calmed down the distress of the child was apparent, as were the despair of the family and the enormous anxiety in both the 'therapy' workers and the 'child protection' workers. This was a family everyone had felt were using the centre well and making good progress. Facing the pain, the betrayal and the awfulness of what had been going on for this boy at the hands of his stepfather was hard. Only when the centre team would talk together and share their views and feelings was it possible to decide how best to proceed. The children needed to be removed if the stepfather would not leave. Their mother, just pregnant again, could not tolerate this and the boys were removed for a further period of work and reassessment.

## Race and gender

The storms in the staff team dealing with very powerful feelings by splitting, denial, projection and identifications are manifest not only in the discipline differences. The team comprises a fair balance of male and female workers and a number of ethnic minority staff. The male staff seem to have made it possible to engage fathers and stepfathers but inevitably the issues when dealing with male abusers can focus on them. The female staff can be accusing or rejecting, the male staff apologetic and unassertive, or the male staff become defiant and mildly delinquent. In the case discussion the team may split along gender lines. Very often the ethnic minority staff are ignored, diminished or overlooked. They find it hard to have a voice or are invited for a token 'cultural view' of the issues. The centre has no disabled staff and the only disabled patients so far have had learning difficulties. Constant attempts are made to keep us all aware of these issues. An active equal opportunities policy is in place, but over and over again the black workers or the female workers are silenced.

There are some shared reasons for this, as well as some specific reasons. In our early development in order to deal with conflict and unbearable feelings we use mechanisms such as splitting, denial, manic flight, projection and projective identification. This means that certain internal states are so distressing that they are split off from awareness (conscious or unconscious). These split-off parts can either disappear into some inaccessible part of the mind or can be pushed out, externalised, known as projection. These projected parts of the self can then be relocated in others, the individual involved may be unaware and find themselves acting on these feelings. A good enough mother when aware of these uncomfortable and distressing feelings may be able to think about them, when she can put them into words and respond in an appropriate caring way. A troubled mother may feel persecuted and respond in a hostile and critical way because she is unable to tolerate distressing feelings or uncertainty.

As well as individuals functioning in this way, groups also use these mechanisms: in different situations, women, people from ethnic minorities or disabled people can be the recipients of these projections. 'Bad' feelings – hate, rage, anger, shame – are projected on to them when these feelings are active. From early on in their lives women and people from ethnic minorities become used to being the recipients of these projections, identify with them and see themselves as no good, useless and remain silent. In addition, there are particular conflicts around gender: boys and girls, men and women have an awareness of mother/woman as the powerful one. She has the womb, the babies (the foetus) inside her and she is the source of life. Little boys and little girls fear this mother who is so powerful, they fear her and envy her. If at the same time they feel angry and hateful feelings which they deal with by projecting these into mother, they are then left very anxious that, in addition to her envy, she will retaliate because she will be aware of their hatred. This perhaps gives us a way of understanding why men and women are fearful of women, because they are aware of the inner strength, the value of women.

Not surprisingly, power issues also play a part; men's reaction leads them to assert their power and domination over women. Another way this appears is in the power issues in racial discrimination and the long period, until late in this century, of white people assuming power over other ethnic groups. Identification can lead to women and people from ethnic minorities accepting their powerless positions, as they have done for so long.

### Patients/clients/users/consumers

How to view the families is a dilemma: are they patients, people in a state of 'disease', vulnerable, dependent and in need of health care? Or are they clients in need of a service but able to shop around and take their business elsewhere? Perhaps they are users who come to avail themselves of the service but have no or little choice. Or are they really consumers using up resources for which they are paying indirectly? Does it matter? It is significant because the uncertainty leads to confusion. This confusion then provides fertile ground for misunderstanding, miscommunications and the use of unconscious process – mainly denial and splitting. Different workers see the families differently, different agencies in the network view them differently and the different centre stakeholders view them differently. Inevitably these differences become caught up in conflicts. It is not possible to reconcile these differences completely but discussion that makes clear where everyone stands can avoid unnecessary conflicts.

The NHS has for many years seen the people it helps and assists as patients. Increasingly however, the NHS is seeing them as clients or users, people who need a service and who may have a choice. Social Services have for some time seen the people they assist as clients for whom they provide a service. The voluntary sector has also referred to them as 'their clients'. The complexity of this work is that, because the families are obliged to come by the court or because they are on the child protection register, they are in many ways none of the above but 'involuntary patients', people who can have a view on what is to happen but who know only too well their view may be overridden. Patients at times do want doctors to make decisions for them (they cannot know all about each disease, medication or investigation) but they do want to be consulted appropriately. Families on the child protection register cannot decide, they are not consulted, they have information shared with them, they have the right to express their opinion and correct misunderstandings, but often decisions taken do not go along with their wishes.

These families do seem then to be in an in-between state, in part patients, in part clients and users and certainly consumers in the sense that they need a great deal of time, energy and commitment. It is little wonder professionals inside and outside the centre have problems agreeing how to describe and view the families.

**Staff turnover**

This is high: in the four-year period staff have had only six-month spells where there has been stability. This in part explains the constant need to re-work issues. It is the constant feeling of being overwhelmed by the awfulness of the work that is so painful and makes it difficult to stay. Supervision is provided, hopefully of good quality, and the team meeting plus daily time to reflect, although never enough, is also available. Life events sometimes seem as frequent for staff as for the families. All too easily these factors can compound the splits and projections and the denial that is provoked by the families. It is always important to sort out what conflicts are coming from the families and what is to do with the pain and difficulties between staff. These may be added to or be caused by yet another departure.

**Evaluation**

To audit and evaluate the work of the centre was built in from the start. Collecting the information in a systematic way has encountered considerable difficulties. The questionnaires have been seen as unhelpful, not asking useful questions, as preventing the establishment of good working relationships with referrer and parents, and as time consuming and too much on top of other tasks. The need to audit and evaluate has been denied, forgotten.

Just as families resist anyone looking at what is going on for them so the workers have found it unbearable to look at what they have been doing. In spite of this, some information is available and this is of interest. Families on the assessment programme change, their problems are reduced, so the assessment is 'therapeutic' and not simply an appraisal. The families that do not change have not been offered a place on the treatment programme and may not have their children back or may have children removed and this indicates that the assessment is also considering 'treatability'. The problems that change most are those relating to poor practical parenting. The parents become more aware of their children's needs for protection, for reliability, regularity and consistency, and this results in an improvement in management of meal times, bed times and conflict resolution. What does not seem to change in the six-week block is the meta-cognitions: that is, the capacity for insight, to understand and think about what the difficulties are about, how past experiences maybe influencing the present difficulties, whether there may be difficulties in the parents' past that link with the problems being experienced by the children. This seems to indicate that meta-cognitions need further work to change, that changing how we think can follow changes in behaviour. This does seem to be a challenge that a psychoanalytical way of working needs to continue to explore, to try to understand the process of change better. What we now understand as the task is to help these very traumatised families with decisions about their capacity to parent and then to prepare them for some form of therapy, which will enable them to work on the problems in their past experiences and help them to look at their current relationships, their choices and to make sense of their situation.

**Thinking, understanding versus mindlessness**

So perhaps the fundamental issue is to do with the need to think, to understand. This involves understanding each other's different agencies and different disciplines. It also involves trying to understand the families and to help them to think, make sense of events and experiences. But most of all it involves developing frameworks of thought, developing concepts that can take forward the work with these very worrying families.

The ease with which thinking is attacked, links are broken and conflictual violent feelings erupt are well known: the way mindlessness sweeps through groups of workers. Psychoanalytic theory does provide a means of thinking about this, but these families challenge these ideas. The families are on the edge of sanity or madness, life or death, uncontrolled violence and sexuality. Continuing to think in the face of these feelings is very hard. But this is a crucial area: children are living through these experiences to become adults, parents. The struggle is to reach them and offer them a useful experience that leaves them aware that thought and understanding are possible and are important. The possibility of hope for the future is what the staff have to convey, the belief that struggling together can bring about change, can make thinking and feeling bearable so that it is possible to hope.

# Chapter 12

# Bringing about change in parent–child relationships

*Maggie Mills and Christine Puckering*

[T]he internal world of the mother, that is, her emotional history and current relationships, forms the external world of the child.

In Britain today, all those working with families of young children where the quality of parenting being provided in the home is causing concern face a therapeutic dilemma. When distressed, depressed, isolated and socially demoralised parents are first encountered they are not, typically, in good enough personal shape themselves, burdened as they are with multiple stressors which preoccupy them, to make use of clinical attempts to facilitate their role as parents and help them form a more positive relationship with their children.

Meanwhile, the preschool years which are such a stressful time for parents are also characterised by the potential for rapid developmental growth and change in their children. Indeed, the message from much recent developmental research is that by the end of the first year of life, behavioural styles of interacting (Murray 1991; Stein *et al.* 1991) and internal representations of the style of early relationships (Main *et al.* 1985) have been established in ways that may already be resistant to modification.

Thus care agencies and clinicians face the dilemma of needing to protect young children while first having to engage 'hard to reach' parents – in itself no mean task when child psychiatric and child guidance services routinely lose a third of families before therapeutic work begins. 'First aid' in the form of extensive support for the parents themselves must be offered before the work of tackling the parental role in all its dimensions can begin. Meanwhile the clock is ticking, and the kind of parent–child interactions we believe to be maladaptive and damaging to the psychological well-being of the child are becoming set in cement, and ever more resistant to change.

So what is to be done? One solution to this dilemma has been the approach adopted by an organisation called Newpin which offers therapeutic and social support for depressed and isolated families where there is serious concern about parenting. Parents are offered the opportunity to engage in the project in a lengthy home discussion in which a project worker describes Newpin and focuses on how the parent sees their life. Attachment to another participating parent follows and there is 24-hour, year-round access to the project network. The project's living room and playroom offer daily support and friendship for both mother and child. Also on offer is a Personal Development Programme, a training lasting nine months and weekly therapeutic group work. There is also the possibility of individual clinical work, an open forum for all users, workshops for supporters and organised in-house and external social events. There are now eleven Newpins around Britain, the majority in London and it is expanding all the time.

In effect the Newpin model offers a real community and a symbolic attachment object similar to – indeed usually safer than – the family of origin, since Newpin's culture is based on respect, support and equality. These essential human qualities are practised by each centre's coordinator who has mothered children herself and frequently was referred into Newpin herself so she has experienced the whole process. Newpin is successful as part of the voluntary sector in its own right (Cox 1993) but its very human and 'user-friendly' approach could be applied to the difficulties statutory services are experiencing in holding and working with problematic families. It offers a genuine 'partnership with parents' as equals, just as the Children Act (HM Government 1989) specifies.

This chapter seeks to abstract aspects of good clinical practice from Newpin and then details an intensive but relatively brief, group intervention with distressed parents called 'Mellow Parenting' (Puckering *et al.* 1994) which is in content and title partly derived from Newpin's pioneering work and shows that this ethos and practice can inform and shape work with difficult families in both NHS and Social Service venues – specifically, community mental health and family centres and a hospital-based child psychiatric day unit.

Long before Clausen and Crittenden (1991) were warning child care practitioners that the severity of actual physical abuse and neglect does not predict the extent of emotional abuse in families, and that grave emotional abuse is frequently found in families where there is no other abuse disclosed, Newpin (Jenkins 1987) assumed that the context for intervention was always going to be emotional abuse, often intergenerational and characterised by basic human obligations not being met in family of origin and creation. Similarly, Billinge (1992), working in the child protection field, observes:

> Among the five categories of 'grave concern' that statutory authorities use, it seems, according to NSPCC figures, that they experience difficulty using the concept of 'emotional abuse' although my own experiences working with families and talking to social workers suggest that many children known to social services are in fact exposed to this adverse family condition.

Young women who were often overwhelmingly preoccupied with the enormous task of mothering were those who had previously experienced unremitting and unresolved childhood emotional turmoil (Jenkins 1987). These unmanageable emotional states would make them resort to inappropriate medication or seek or be referred for psychiatric help within the NHS, which was likely to be of limited duration, on an irregular basis, often never seeing the same psychiatric worker twice, and not necessarily geared to their maternal role. For these reasons psychotherapy became a component of Newpin's work, being both affordable and consistent for mothers in distress.

Today Newpin and other clinicians are seeing parents so beset by current environmental pressures, such as broken parental relationships, the exigencies of lone support, abandonment – often in pregnancy or the first year of a child's life – together with a gross lack of all resources and family support, that they simply have to switch off from their child. They erect a wall, a psychic boundary to limit the pain and preserve some semblance of personal space for themselves. The outcome is not so much the high levels of criticism, hostility and harsh handling which we know leads to disturbed preschoolers with behaviour problems (Radke-Yarrow *et al.* 1985; Stevenson 1982) but an unavailable mother whose physical care-taking is usually adequate but whose style of interacting alternates between pervasive ignoring, which generates uncontained distress in the child (Mills 1994), and maternal resentment in which 'peace' – a brief unbadgered space for the mother – is bought at a price in which the bribed and under-stimulated 2-year-old ticks away like a bomb ready to explode into the tyrannical child more or less out of control by school age.

Possibly the single most negative collective experience for the women Newpin sees is a lack of consistent parental attachment together with emotional deprivation in early childhood. It is through the shared group work and linked therapy (group therapy is accompanied by constant interaction between group members both within and outside the centre which is unusual) that women discover for themselves the importance of secure and positive attachment for their own children. Getting in touch with the distress of an emotionally damaged early childhood in a secure and supportive environment is an important step towards their own emotional maturation. Through this process (Jenkins 1995) they begin to recognise the right of their child to have a loving and secure autonomy of their own.

One could summarise some of the important ways Newpin works with families as follows:

Parents choose to come to the centre of their own accord: it is not prescribed for them. There is no statutory requirement on them to attend or perhaps risk losing their children. After a home visit from a Newpin worker to explain about the centre and meet and talk with the family in a way that can help to attach them, mothers are left to make up their own mind about joining Newpin so that they come well motivated for change to occur. Even then vulnerable women need considerable holding, since the insecurity of many mothers intensifies in the intimate contact a Newpin centre provides. Initial engagement is a delicate dance with defensive rejection never far away and a number of families are lost at this stage, but if the project coordinator can manage to contain women through this stage then the likelihood of continuous successful involvement is greatly increased. No one service, even one as versatile as Newpin, can be appropriate for all families.

Then there is the absence of official bureaucracy or defined links to Social Services. Instead there is a welcome to drop in to the project and hear about it from other mothers like themselves. Typically, Newpin develops a considerable local reputation in the community. All this engenders initial trust rather than suspicion and fear of formal reprisals about any disclosures.

The presence of other mothers like themselves who befriend and share offers the possibility of real friendship and a reciprocity in relationships which are not skewed by professional bias. Most Newpin workers are entirely trained within the project and have made their own personal growth there as new mothers so hope to do – again, a containing model for early anxiety about attachment and difference.

Women are expected to learn by using their own experience in families and sharing it. Newpin's capacity to facilitate change comes from the processes that take effect from being a member of the same group whether for training or personal therapy. Group identity is paramount. The project has hit upon an important phenomenon recently identified by Stern (1994) in which the advent of motherhood permits the emergence of a psychic structure, 'in its own right as important a developmental phase as the Oedipus complex', which essentially allows a reworking of a woman's relationship with her own mother, a process greatly facilitated by membership of a women's group.

Parents are perceived as whole individuals with their 'problem' being only part of their lives, which removes the stigma of being labelled 'child abuser', 'depressive' or an 'inadequate' parent. If parents respond by feeling worthless and scapegoated their capacity for permanent change is nullified and no real dialogue occurs. Professional workers know that they should begin by seeing clients as equal and each one as a person as vital and important as themselves however intractable the problem, although that is often not the manner they use to tackle parenting.

Having an opportunity to internalise the project's ethos which explicitly treats all users with respect and courtesy and expects them to do the same to their children and each other is seen as a necessary step for mothers damaged in their own childhood to be able to meet their child's emotional needs. But personal change cannot be ordained by professionals; offering clinical sessions at a particular time does not mean a parent is ready to use them and as we all know much expensive clinic time can be wasted in this way. The system Newpin adopts allows it to wait, while continuing to give parental support and respite care for the child, and, most importantly, to work with failure as part of the healing process for parents without them dropping out of the project and grave concern and anxiety for the children taking over in consequence.

Newpin has been shown to revolutionise women's psychological well-being. In pilot research (Mills and Pound 1985) and a substantive evaluation with a short-term follow-up (Cox et al. 1991) it has been shown that, almost without exception, women well involved in the project described greatly increased self-confidence and esteem and felt they had better control over their lives. These changes were associated with steady remission of their psychiatric symptoms, particularly depression and anxiety which, for at least half the sample, had been experienced for at least two years previously. Most notable changes occurred in women who had been in the project between six months and a year.

Even where symptoms of mental dysfunction persisted, women described an improved quality of life not usually compatible with mental health problems or the discordant adult relationships (for two-thirds of women) which were reported. Loss and alienation and an inability to sustain intimacy and trust troubled many of the women initially, not surprisingly in a sample where a third had been in care as children themselves and had experienced physical and or sexual abuse and 40 per cent had been separated from parents. In many cases women appeared to have come to terms with their very damaged early lives and to be working through their emotional trauma and coming to an understanding of how it continued to affect their lives.

There was less evidence of a positive 'knock on' effect on the relationship with their children even where women were well involved in the project. Newpin's explicit philosophy is summed up in the training brochure (1993) which states:

> While parents are involved in the Personal Development Programme their children are given an equally fulfilling structure in the playroom with a facilitator who can support each child in developing him/herself through creative play and an acute awareness of each child's emotional needs. Both parent and child have the benefit of an opportunity for self-discovery in a social environment.

It may be that the research's limited six-month follow-up and Newpin's habit of containing mother and child with less emphasis on attention to the actual interactive processes extant in the relationship precluded much change being recorded from the very detailed and subtle observational codes of interaction taken in the home and scored without knowledge of whether the family was involved in Newpin or a control recruited from another deprived, inner-city area.

Significant changes in mothers' ability to anticipate their child's needs and make troublesome caretaking tasks more pleasant and acceptable to their offspring were observed. But overall significant group differences in responding to distress, granting autonomy, coping with conflict, negotiating with the child, responding in a reciprocal and stimulating way and engendering more warmth and less negativity were not observed. Some individual pairs, nevertheless, did change their interactive behaviours on these dimensions in a quite radical and positive fashion. It was not easy to see why some parent–child relationships had improved and others had not, but it was not simply a function of time since some families had been in the project a year or more.

Left untreated, unsatisfactory interaction with very young children could be expected to deteriorate, yet only a few relationships worsened. As the children hit the troublesome second year of life tactful parental handling becomes a much more taxing task, so Newpin's policy of containment does seem to have paid off. Psychological outcome of the children who have received Newpin's care might more appropriately be assessed by observing their adjustment, for example, on starting school, or with a longer follow-up period, since psychoanalytically oriented treatments are characterised by lengthy working through. What may be missing from the programme, which does have excellent lectures on recognising and meeting children's needs and feelings, is direct attention and focus on the mother and child relationship itself and working with 'hands on' experience in the promoting of sharing and enjoyment together. Thus disquiet with the seemingly intractable nature of some relationships characterised by serious emotional abuse, as evidenced by research findings, has led to the development of a more intensive way of working known as Mellow Parenting, which has incorporated from the Newpin experience the good clinical practice detailed earlier in this chapter.

Mellow Parenting works from the theoretical position that the internal world of the mother, that is, her emotional history and current relationships, forms the external world of the child. For many women whose own background includes emotional, physical and sexual abuse and neglect, and whose current relationships with partner and family of origin are conflictual, the additional strain of material hardship and poor housing gives them few resources to bring to a relationship with their child. To teach them parenting skills, while possible, would be ineffective as they would be unable to put these to use in a situation where their own needs and distress completely block their ability to see the child's needs and know they are different from their own.

Just like Newpin, the Mellow Parenting programme therefore explicitly works with mothers to address their own preoccupations with past and current needs and feelings while targeting, with specific parenting workshops using home videotape, the needs and management of the children. What needs addressing is the ongoing relationship to promote sharing and enjoyment between the couple which is usually missing. Looking at themselves on video has a powerful effect but the couple also need practical experience of sharing and joint activities together in the safe environment of the programme with a professional worker alongside to facilitate how they are getting on together without a didactic manner yet ready to contain anxiety and dissipate distress when things go awry.

The programme lasts four months, running for one full day each week. The day consists of three sessions: the mothers' group where discussions of past and present experience are raised while the children are in a creche; the parenting workshop where conceptual dimensions (derived originally from work in Newpin) from an observational coding system (Puckering *et al.* 1994) are illustrated with video and personal examples, and individual homework is set, encouraged and reviewed; and the lunchtime session where children, mothers and staff have lunch together in a structured setting and then have an opportunity to try out an activity together which might be arts and crafts, play, cooking or even an outdoor football game or a visit to the local supermarket.

At all points of the day the links between past or current feelings and functioning are make explicit. For example, it became clear that one mother was quite unable to tolerate any closeness with her daughter. The lunchtime activities (occasionally videotaped to demonstrate how couples are changing) in this case gave unequivocal evidence of this mother's very skilled distancing tactics. When this was raised in the parenting group later the same day, the mother revealed earlier childhood sexual abuse from a stepfather and explained that her daughter's crying acted as the trigger for flashbacks to this painful past which was quite unbearable, hence her avoidance of her daughter. Without the opportunity and support to work on these memories she had been unable to use the considerable previous professional help given and only now did change in her parenting become possible. Thus a vital task in the clinical work is to elucidate and bring into consciousness the links which are blocking mother–child relationships – why a psychic wall has been built up – and then the group can help the parent reflect upon what *has* happened in the 'here and now' of what *is* happening between the mother and child.

The mother's group follows a programme which covers the mother's own family history and current self-esteem and relationships as well as abuse and domestic violence. There is also planning for the future. The group is run on very structured lines initially to facilitate participation by socially unskilled and suspicious parents so they have an opportunity to share ideas. Structure also contains the over-talkative. Sample trigger questions – for example, 'what is the perfect mother like?' (and it is soon agreed that of course she doesn't and shouldn't exist) – are used to promote discussion. Mutual support by the group with its shared experience and identifications is paramount rather than individual or group interpretations of transference material to or by the group leaders. Gratifyingly, anonymous user feedback after the group never mentions the group leaders as a source for change. Women cite giving and receiving advice and support from each other as the most important element in the group process.

The parenting workshops are based around the coding dimensions of autonomy, anticipation, co-operation, warmth and stimulation and the containment of distress and conflict. These are illustrated with video vignettes and discussed in a way which invites the parent to see things from the child's point of view and empathise with his or her feelings. A parenting concept like anticipation, for example, becomes more concrete and will be known in the parenting group as: 'spotting trouble before it spots you'. Group members give each other handy hints such as colouring mashed potato green and making them into ninja turtles as a way of encouraging difficult feeders.

Effective mechanisms involve the mothers' memories of how they remember feeling as children in similar circumstances (how their mother looked or behaved when she was angry, for example, and what it made them feel like), or indeed a woman's reaction now if treated the way we so often treat young children with little respect for them as individuals or for their emotions. As links are made between parent and past, women become able to enter the 'child's world' and manage difficult situations more effectively without losing touch with the child's feelings. One mother who was intrusive and controlling at the beginning of the programme came to reflect, on seeing her videotaped interactions with her little boy: 'I wonder how that feels for him.'

Again, when mother and child are 'practising' a new activity together in the lunchtime session or in the creche, a well-timed reflection from a staff member promotes sensitivity in a similar manner. As a couple were embarking on making chocolate crispi-crackles with mother melting chocolate on the stove and a restive toddler frustrated at her knee, a worker simply said 'I wonder if Johny can see', while nudging forward a stool. Once on equal terms, the couple could share the activity together.

All clinical work is deliberately designed to work with positives. Most women are painfully aware of what is going wrong; they are just helpless to change it. For some women who have been involved with child protection procedures, the group is their first experience of being praised for what they do well – and with many different parenting dimensions it is always possible to find times in the video when things have gone well and point them out; nice interactions which the mothers can never recognise for themselves. Once they start to regain some self-esteem, they are able to take risks and invest energy in trying new ways to tackle problems they define in their own families. Often, they are more critical of themselves than the most discerning professional and know with painful intimacy the nature of the dysfunction in their family.

The Mellow Parenting project was first developed in a local authority family centre. It represents a big commitment in terms of self-examination and time for parents and there are always those who drop out, with some of these coming back to a subsequent programme since they run all the time. But for the majority who complete, towards the end of the programme time in the group is spent working out how to hold on to what has been achieved with a brief refresher course offered every summer. Then there is the planning for what the women want to do next. Some take educa-tional courses, basic literacy to Open University community access courses; some seek personal counselling or therapy to deal with past sexual abuse or trauma; some begin to use mother and toddler groups in the centre or start other groups for themselves. Sub-sequent appropriate use of services is seen as success not failure since many of the families have previously been hard to reach with conventional services and it would be foolish to maintain that all problems could possibly be solved in such a short time.

As for the children, pilot, research findings evaluating the effectiveness of the programme (Puckering *et al.* 1994), which looked at outcome in the first twenty-one families to complete the programme, found that of twelve children on the Child Protection Register ten had had their names removed and the remaining two were out of care and back in their families (area figures show only one third of children being removed annually from the Register).

Change in the interactions between parent and child, comparing pre-post-intervention videotaped codings was also evident. Negative affect, shouting, slapping, hostility, harsh handling, etc., was reduced to about one-fifth of the original level observed before the programme began, while responsiveness – warmth and stimulation and positive examples of autonomy – had doubled in records taken immediately after intervention (a long-term follow-up funded by the DOH is currently in progress). In addition to these frequency measures of observed, sequential interactions, reliable ratings of warmth, sensitivity and effective control showed significant improvement. Most marked were sequences that showed genuine joint activity and sharing characterised by mutual enjoyment, and parental self-report stressed an acquired ability to 'tune in' to the child's interests. Qualitative feedback from the mothers described changes in their perceptions of their children and their own self-confidence in handling difficult behaviour. One parent, for example, commented: 'My children are people with feelings, and their bad behaviours and good are something I can change by my actions. My children are not bad, just wanting something.'

The programme with its three different, but vitally linked components offers a viable context for hard-pressed adults to be receptive to new and often challenging information and a safe space for self-reflection about what makes a relationship. Women tend to be the main carers for children but there is absolutely no reason why this programme should not successfully encompass fathers and partners whose mediating effect on the mother–child relationship and family attitudes clinicians neglect at their peril. The programme incorporates and integrates elements of psychodynamic group psychotherapy, video feedback on parenting interaction which includes behaviour modification principles and a 'hands on' secure environment to reframe, try out and monitor different ways of being with your child. All these equally important elements are represented in the same framework of making links between the mother's childhood and the child's childhood rather than as so often happens, as a piecemeal and separate delivery of disparate services which have no continuity or conceptual linkage.

Clinical emphasis is always on feelings and the nature of relationships in the programme, and how could it be otherwise when the focus of intervention is to break the cycle of emotional abuse? The intervention acknowledges the difficulty and complexity of the task of parenting, which is routinely down-graded in our society, emphasising that there is no one set way to be a good parent and disavowing an 'expert' model where professionals know best and tell the mother what to do. Each parent keeps their own video and makes their own choices about what to share. They feel valued for their advice and participation in the group as a respected member who has shared difficult and painful memories and feelings. Above all, it is the group process exemplified in Newpin and the Mellow Mothering Programme that has brought about these remarkable changes in parenting.

# Chapter 13

# Educational intervention for young children who have experienced fragmented care

*Eva Holmes*

The rise in the number of younger children who present severe behaviour difficulties to their primary school teachers is of growing concern. It is no longer rare for children of 5 or 6 to be excluded from school because of their uncontrollable and often violent behaviour. Their difficulties have usually been associated with complex and disturbing early experiences – of emotional, physical or sexual abuse, of chronic neglect compounded by fragmented care.

In the last ten years several well-intentioned policy changes may have contributed to the rise in these severe behaviour difficulties:

a) Shared care: when children who would in the past have been fostered or adopted are maintained within their own families with frequent 'respite care'.
b) A wide range of flexible day care arrangements which, paradoxically, prevent young children from being in a daily, consistent, alternative setting in which they feel safe.

Both these developments aim to emulate the extended family care of previous generations and non-Western societies, but they differ in one crucial respect: in traditional extended families the other carers are grannies, aunts and elder siblings, committed relatives who are likely to be there throughout a young child's early years. The turnover of staff in family centres or child minders, on the other hand, tends to be very high.

Research into day care (McGurk *et al.* 1993) suggests that high quality care with a high adult–child ratio does not have detrimental long-term effects on children over the age of one. Clinical experience of young children referred to child mental health teams or educational psychologists, however, suggests that many more children are experiencing very inconsistent, fragmented care while still living at home, and that their behaviour is not dissimilar from that of children who are, or were, received into care after several rehabilitation attempts have failed. By the age of 3 these children have often experienced a range of substitute care and of necessity they have learned to be prematurely independent and to expect little support from adults. This pseudo-self reliance can seriously inhibit learning. Children who have spent much of their early childhood in group care find it particularly difficult to adjust to school. They are restless children who cannot settle down or concentrate; their attention span and, in particular, their ability to listen seem very limited. They often behave aggressively or impulsively and their language development is delayed. Others are withdrawn and unresponsive (Holmes 1980).

These observations led to the establishment of a special pre-school unit within a family centre in North London about fifteen years ago; it was a joint project funded by an education department in a social services nursery supported by an educational psychologist working in a child guidance centre. It was set up to reduce the need for special school placement for children who at 3 years were already showing disturbing behaviour and/or delayed development. The unit was based on the nurture group principles developed by Marjorie Boxall for older children with similar backgrounds. She described the difficulties:

Some of the parents were themselves deprived children. Particularly in these cases, the stress of demanding, difficult children may produce in the parent an over-controlling, punitive, or erratic response, more relevant to the feelings and mood of the adult than to that of the child.

(Boxall 1976)

The children spend a great deal of energy trying to please their mothers, to predict their moods but are confused by their inability to find a consistent pattern. The reliability and continuity provided by their teacher in the special class gave them an opportunity to experience a setting in which learning and prediction were possible.

The organisation of the special classroom aimed to provide a stable and consistent setting where trust in adults could be established. Children attended every day for one or one-and-a-half hours in groups of not more than four with a teacher and an assistant. The essential features of the teacher–child interaction were described in the original paper (Holmes 1980):

## 1 THE STABILITY OF THE SETTING

Before looking at what the teacher says and what activities she provides, it is necessary to appreciate the importance for these children of seeing the same person in the same room at the same time every day. This, for many of them, is the first time that they can predict what will happen, with whom, where and when, with certainty. It is essential that the teacher does not allow herself to be distracted by colleagues, visitors, telephone calls or any other interruptions – something no member of the child care staff can guarantee. In the classroom the children are the focus of attention – if they ask a question, it is answered, if they need help it is provided. They quickly learn where things are kept, where their own books and crayons are; their favourite book is always in the same place and the routine is welcomed. For insecure children, who have been moved from pillar to post physically as well as emotionally, the safety of this ordered classroom becomes a haven and a relief. The children's anxious behaviour as soon as any change was introduced is evidence for the importance they attached to the stable setting; in the ordinary nursery setting visitors are often ignored or greeted with curiosity – in the classroom an unfamiliar visitor is an intruder who threatens to disturb a valued routine; the children look anxiously and cling to the teacher, afraid that her attentiveness will lessen, behaving as much younger children do when their mother talks too long to a stranger. The introduction of a new child into the group needs careful preparation and discussion and always brings some reaction from the children already there. Although young children cannot tell the time, they have some sense of the order of the day: changing their classroom time from early in the morning to later, from before lunch to afternoons, also proves disrupting. The children are also very observant: if the teacher moves the furniture, even slightly, they notice and are distracted. In many ways they indicate, again and again, that a predictable structure is essential to them. The classroom, and the teacher of course, because they are not part of the nursery organisation, are able to remain immune from the day to day pressures and crises which impinge on child care staff.

## 2 LEARNING WITH AN ADULT

It is often assumed that, by the age of 3, children can be left to learn through play – by exploration and discovery. The children in the special unit cannot – at first – learn by playing; many of them do not know how to play; they cannot persist in any activity for long enough and they do not know how to use words to give meaning to what they are doing. Only if an adult is with them throughout an activity, putting what they are doing into words for them, helping them, encouraging them, linking the activity with a previous one, can they begin to get any satisfaction from staying with something long enough to see a change – a brick tower built, a puzzle completed. Only then do they seem to gain the impetus to do it again and can begin to learn by repetition and by remembering, and later by predicting: 'Last time the red bit went next to the blue square.'

An essential task for the teacher is to stay with the child till an activity is completed, to see that it is ended with success, not given up in despair, to give it meaning in words, to share pleasure in the achievement, to refer to it the next day. It is almost secondary that the teacher also knows how to extend the skill involved appropriately and does not then introduce a task that is too difficult. Her knowledge of what the child can do and what he did yesterday helps her to know when his 'I can't' is justified or when he needs encouragement to try again. She is also skilled in simplifying a task or a choice: she knows when to say 'Try the red one', or 'Is it the big one or the little one?' or 'Which one fitted in there yesterday?' If her attention had to be shared among a larger group of children this personal knowledge of where a child is at any point would be lost and the child would not have the conviction that what he did mattered and was known to someone else. These children have reached the age of 3 without the conviction that what they do matters to anyone, is consistently of interest to anyone and so their own motivation to achieve anything is very low indeed. This seems related to their observed short attention span.

As the children develop in the special class, they can gradually be left alone to complete something, perhaps calling out to the teacher from time to time. They need a long period (months) of doing things with the teacher there, and only then can they gradually become more independent. If they leave the unit, convinced that they can do things successfully, that persistence is usually rewarded, that a teacher will actually be helpful and is there when needed, they will start off in infant school with the same self-assurance that less disadvantaged children have acquired at home.

## 3 SUSTAINED CONVERSATION

It is characteristic of these children that they have very limited expectations of the adults around them. This became evident when my colleague, Robynne Moore, made systematic observations which indicated that the special class children speak to the teacher about three times as often as they speak to a child care worker and that, when they do speak to an adult, the likelihood of their getting a reply is almost 100 per cent in the classroom and less than 50 per cent in the nursery.

Content apart, one of the essential aspects of the classroom interaction is the intensity of the dialogue between one individual child and an adult. For the first time in his life, the child is exposed to extensive language stimulation directed to him personally – not to a group of children, not from a television set. Gradually language in the classroom is seen as relevant – the child is not allowed to switch off. The content concerns him and he is expected to reply. One little girl expressed her surprise after a few weeks and said to the teacher, 'You listen!' It is essential for the teacher to listen and reply, without being interrupted, if she is to expect a child to listen and reply. These children's initial inability to listen seems to be their most severe handicap. It appears to be a consequence of group living that so much speech around them is irrelevant that they learn to ignore much of the language they hear, and cannot then distinguish relevant from irrelevant speech. In school, where everything the teacher says is likely to be important, not listening is a recipe for failure.

Essentially, what the children learn, especially in their initial individual time with the teacher, and what they will carry over into school is that when the teacher speaks, she is speaking to you, and what she says is important and interesting and demands some response (not always verbal, of course). It is the consistency of the teacher's behaviour that is essential if this is to be learned. Advising child care staff to talk more to children may be helpful, but it is no substitute for the sustained, uninterrupted conversations which the teacher can have every day of the week. She is providing a model of an interested, responsive adult to whom the child is an individual. It is very likely that most infant school children, brought up at home, assume that their teacher, 'my teacher', is personally interested in them and is talking to them personally when she addresses a class; the presence of the other children is probably somehow irrelevant. Children brought up mainly in groups begin with the opposite assumption; what adults are saying is likely not to be personally relevant to them and can therefore often be ignored.

Although the teacher is well aware of the cognitive aspects of language development and consciously extends children's vocabulary, introduces new concepts, etc., the content of much conversation in which this happens may be very personal; the children in this group are constantly exposed to stress, mothers and fathers come and go, housing changes, fostering is planned, familiar staff leave, violence is witnessed or experienced. In the classroom there is the calmness and safety which makes it possible to talk about these experiences, often again and again. The teacher again acts as the child's memory, linking events, recording what happened before: 'Mummy went away and you felt sad, but last week she came back; Mary went to her foster mummy and daddy before Christmas.' Under stress, the children are often very confused; they can become demanding and difficult to manage, because the teacher has them only for a short time, and not in a large group, it is easier for her to be patient and to acknowledge how they feel and to offer some containment. Learning to use language to talk about feelings and to find that helpful is an essential step towards reducing the acting out which is so characteristic of some of these children when they begin school.

This attentiveness to what the children are saying – not always in words, but by their manner, behaviour or by play and drawings – is a special skill demanding more restraint from the usual enthusiastic 'teaching' approach of many teachers.

(Holmes 1980)

Two years later a further paper (Holmes 1982) described the results of following up the twenty-eight children who had attended the unit. Success was measured by their adjustment to ordinary school. A major American study had indicated that at the age of 15 only 19 per cent of children attending a pre-school intervention programme had been placed in special education compared with 39 per cent of a control group (Lazar and Darlington 1982). Of the twenty-eight children followed up at the age of six, twenty-one were coping in mainstream school and seven were in special schools. A smaller group had been assessed before and after attendance; all of them at the age of 3 had been below average in their verbal ability. The children attending the unit made a significant improvement on measures of verbal intelligence, language development and social maturity which was still evident three years later.

The research provides encouraging evidence that an intensive educational intervention which focuses on a reliable adult–child relationship can enable confused, demanding and inattentive children to regain their self-esteem and their capacity to learn.

Subsequent research on early learning (Stern 1985; Dunn 1988; Tizard and Hughes 1988) has confirmed the importance of a sustained, mutually valued adult–child dialogue in a safe pre-dictable setting. As patterns of social intervention and support for young children at risk have changed, and as children are admitted to school soon after they are 4, daily attendance at day nurseries has given way to more fragmented part-time attendance at family centres, with child minders and at playgroups. Teachers based in social services pre-school provision remain the exception rather than the rule.

However, all the principles and practices described above are still valid and are being maintained and developed in a new wave of nurture groups for children in their first two–three years of school (Bennathan and Boxall 1994). The evidence indicates that very deprived young children who arrive in school with very little experience of emotional stability, of adults who have time or energy to think about them or respond to their needs, can make remarkable progress if they spend three or four terms, almost full-time, in a nurture group of ten to twelve children and two adults. The children respond with relief at the attentiveness of the adults, their reliability, the order in the classroom; they begin to initiate conversation, ask questions, play and learn and their behaviour improves.

Marjorie Boxall first established nurture groups in London while working as an educational psychologist in a child guidance centre. She described the children as 'coming from families where severe stress limits and distorts experience and impairs construc-tive interaction between parents and child'. The structure of the nurture group setting with its close teacher–child relationship enables children to retrace early steps of their development, emo-tional and cognitive, in a secure and stable learning environment.

The attention-seeking, over-dependent child can develop greater autonomy and self-esteem by first using the teacher as an attachment figure. In the London Borough of Enfield there are now six nurture groups, based in schools where there is a high incidence of children with special needs. Two hundred and three children have been followed up: 71 per cent have transferred to mainstream classes without difficulty, 17 per cent have transferred with some additional support. For the rest the classes had an assessment function so that the appropriate special education could be identified. Two post-graduate Tavistock trainees in educational psychology have done some valuable research in looking at the quality of the language and behaviour within the groups that contributes to the children's development and some of the characteristics that differentiate the children's and the teachers' behaviour. Jaffey (1990) analysed teacher–child interactions in two nurture groups, having observed 338 conversations in six ten-minute sequences per child, half in the nurture groups and half in the mainstream classroom. The number of exchanges between child and teacher averaged six in the nurture group and three in the main classroom. Furthermore, the children initiated conversation with their teacher three times more often in the nurture group than in the busy classroom.

Henson (1993) compared the development of two groups of children in different schools over one term. The children in the nurture group improved their self-confidence and their social skills and were more able to learn effectively in a group in comparison with a control group. Relationships with their teacher improved so that their experience of school became more positive. The success of these school-based nurture groups is encouraging. The fact that an infant department with a nurture group rarely recommends that a child needs formal assessment demonstrates that this preventive approach – providing sensitive nurturing, so that learning can take place – is successful. Occasionally these deprived children make headline news, more often they drift unsuccessfully through the educational and social system, truanting, being excluded from school, failing. A few children find new families and some are helped by psychotherapy, but for the majority school is their best hope of finding some self-esteem and success. As Henson says: 'Any attempt to modify the way a child approaches tasks and organises his/her learning needs to make use of a relationship between that child and a teacher.'

Ironically, the education system usually provides one to one tuition only when a Statement is issued or when a teenager has been excluded from the system. There is growing evidence that much earlier daily structured support based on developmental principles of attachment can be more successful and cost-effective.

# Chapter 14

# A community group for abused children

*Michael Morice*

This is an account of a psychotherapeutic group for five children, two girls and three boys aged from 8 to 11 years. It ran, as planned, for a period of one year, once weekly during term time. Attention will be given in roughly equal weight to the group process and to the organisation and the thinking that had to go into the weekly running of the group. There is not the scope here to give anywhere near a full description of the group process. I shall confine myself to mention and illustration of two separate though interlinking themes that dominated the sessions and our thinking as the year unfolded.

The first theme is concerned with the very meaning of a 'group'. For most of us this word has connotations of interdependency, mutual concern, learning and growth. For the children in question these were distant goals. We hoped at least to have made a beginning in this direction by the end of our year. The second theme concerns the relationship of the children to the co-therapists, a man and a woman. This, and their perception of the way the adults worked together, became vital to our hopes of forming such a group, in ways I shall describe later on.

Firstly, however, I shall give material from a session which highlights these and related themes that came up over the year. We felt bombarded mentally and physically by such material, and perhaps the reader may, without the benefit of hindsight, have a similar experience.

## CLINICAL EXAMPLE

One of the boys has been reluctant to come this time and the two therapists take up the question of his having been victimised and bitten the previous week. There follows a period of relatively contained play in which two of the boys, including the bitten one, come together to play with marbles. The third boy draws, but defaces or destroys his own capable efforts. The two girls play snakes and ladders, and one of the therapists comments on this being the first time any of them have actually *played* together. Immediately one of the girls makes a loud penetrating noise by shaking the dice violently and drowning out the adult voices. This prompts one of us to wonder if she wants to take everything over with her noise – perhaps this is now the only way she feels she will continue to be noticed. She quietens down but soon takes sellotape and sticks it over her mouth and stands on a chair. She mumbles something to the effect that she is killing herself and goes to bury her face in a plastic bag. One of the two boys playing together goes to hold her face in the bag. He is stopped, but the girl, who has done much to invite this from the boy, pretends to be dead. The boy bitten last week had covered a small monkey figure with plasticine 'skin' in what feels like an attempted act of self-repair. He is now removing the 'skin' from the monkey, but the boy who had bitten him tries to grab it. One of the adults makes a comment that makes him leave the other boy alone, but the latter then offers him the monkey which is to be eaten by an alligator which the other boy holds in his hand.

The girl who had 'suffocated' herself proclaims loudly that her gran, her main carer, is returning from a period away; at this moment there is a note of hope in her voice. The two boys mentioned above are having playful fights with animals and one of them says that the lion had attacked the rhino and now there was a baby coming out of it. The therapists say that mating and fighting seem to be mixed together in their minds, and the girl gives a loud and knowing laugh. The animal fights become more violent, with the third boy joining in. Objects start to be thrown. Then the third boy leads the group in ganging up against the bitten boy. He hurtfully calls his victim a 'poo', then a 'poof' with AIDS.

With ten minutes to go the session deteriorates into a chaotic throwing of missiles, culminating in a visible ganging-up of the whole group against the therapeutic couple. This 'gang' includes the victimised boy and the second silent, but vicariously excited girl.

It is difficult to convey the almost overwhelming immediacy of this group experience. It felt as though the inner and outer worlds of the children had come together to plunge us into a maelstrom of feeling which allowed us at first little space for thought or understanding. Constructive play could not be sustained but instead seemed to be compulsively replaced by destructive or self-destructive activity. Sadistic victimisation and masochistic submission were much in evidence as ways of fending off a sense of helplessness and terror. Apropos the question of terror, membership in a mafia-like gang offered a perverse kind of protectionism, especially towards the ends of sessions when the protection of the therapists was being withdrawn. Noise, disruption and verbal violence went hand in hand with representations of stiflement, suffocation and death. By 'death', in this instance, I mean the death of hope, especially the hope of being noticed, held in mind and eventually rescued.

Procreation and violent assault had become inextricably linked in their minds. They appeared to see themselves as the offspring of this kind of coupling, which is hateful rather than loving. It was therefore difficult for them to see us as anything other than a potentially violent couple. Fear of this was defended against by a heightened sexualised excitement. We were so often seen as a provocative and perversely exciting sexual couple either about to attack them or, towards ends of sessions, to abandon them for the sake of our own violent pleasure. The notion of a benevolent parental partnership could scarcely survive in this highly charged atmosphere.

To complicate matters further, both of us were new to group psychotherapy, although experienced in individual and family work. We had to put aside previously learned ways of working and come together to work out a therapeutic partnership which had to adapt to the needs of this particular group. We had to grow both professionally and personally to meet the challenges.

## GROUP COMPOSITION AND PRE-GROUP THINKING

We had identified certain children in desperate need of help for whom the two main therapies on offer in our clinic – individual and family – had not been suitable. Individual work had been done with some, to no real avail. On assessment, they appeared to lack the organisational and emotional resources necessary to sustain individual once weekly therapy. Likewise, the families did not have the minimum of cohesion necessary to make use of family therapy. In each case, the family were being given, or had received in the past, long-term support by a member of the clinic staff. The idea of therapy in a group was seen to have, for this set of parents and carers, a non-stigmatising and generally far less mysterious quality than individual therapy. Also, we believed they could support the offer of a group because they felt less criticised for their own lack of parenting qualities. A 'group' had an educational and social feel about it which they could more easily accept, without being threatened by questions of mental or psychological disturbance which often come up more starkly in individual therapy. Each child was failing to some extent at school and most were near to exclusion. Their schools had agreed to hold back only because they were being worked with in the group. Even before we started we considered that we were preparing at least three out of the five for smaller groups in a special educational setting or a special school.

Before going further, an explanation of the term 'abused' is necessary. By this term I mean, *not* that the children were particularly known to have suffered from physical or sexual abuse, but rather that they and their families lived in an environment in which abusive experiences of many kinds were widespread. Crime, violence, family breakdown, mental illness and sexual perversity were part of the cultural fabric rather than exceptions to it. These conditions cut across the racial and ethnic differences of the group members. The children and their parents lived in a deprived inner-city area in which emotional deprivation in its various forms far outweighed material poverty.

## THE THERAPISTS: THE THERAPEUTIC COUPLE

Four out of the five children came from broken or single-parent families. Their experience of two adults, most particularly of a man and a woman functioning together on their behalf, was either non-existent or, as we have implied already, was permeated with distrust, fear and sexualised excitement. Their opportunity for normal experience and working through of family rivalries and anxieties in the presence of two parents had been minimal. Therefore, the therapeutic couple had an immediate and intense emotional impact. This is illustrated by the following example.

## CLINICAL EXAMPLE FROM THE TENTH WEEK

At the beginning someone said 'We're going to have a riot' (prison riots were in the news). In the first part of the session there were mutterings about our being 'liars' based on our imposing a necessary but temporary boundary that they had not expected. The older girl became angry. She took a china teapot from the Wendy House and said she was going to break it. She did so violently while the others watched. She proceeded to the cups as the (woman) therapist went to stop her. One of the children saved one of the cups and handed it to the therapist who retrieved the rest. Meanwhile the self-designated 'gang leader' of the group was rummaging in some drawers. He withdrew a book in which he and another boy purported to find our telephone numbers, which they were memorising, and also 'love letters' they claimed we had written to each other. There were insinuations of something 'going on between us'. These insinuations were outwardly of a salacious and sexual nature, but in the light of future material they could be seen to contain darker fears of our plotting together against them for our own sinister purposes.

There followed an attack on the insides of the Wendy House. Dolls were thrown out of the cot. A bag of clothes was emptied and the contents thrown through the windows. Then they tried to smash the house itself and this had to be put outside the room in order to protect it.

While the therapists occupied opposite sides of the room, separated by a table, there was a whispered planning session and then the three boys rushed at the female therapist in a mock-violent way. One of the girls (the heaviest child in the group) launched herself at the man in wanton and violent fashion, ostensibly to pull him away from the door which he was guarding. She succeeded in doing him some actual, but temporary, harm. This appalled the others and prompted two of them to explain that they 'knew they were evil but couldn't help it'. At the end of this session the co-therapists felt split. We felt that each had acted without reference to the other and indeed we had at times been living caricatures of ourselves, having fallen back on safe familiar professional roles: the 'ex-teacher', active, controlling, interventionist; the 'psychotherapist', passive, withdrawn, interpretative.

This session may be seen as a passionate 'over-the-top' expression of oedipal feelings on the part of children who lack the emotional equipment to deal with such problems. From the moment that we *together* imposed a new boundary the session proceeded as an exploration of the nature of our partnership. This exploration, or rather invasion, was clouded with lies, sexual innuendoes and paranoid fears. Whatever 'was going on between us' could not, they felt, possibly be in their interest. The ransacking of the Wendy House, and the throwing out of the dolls could conceivably be seen as a ransacking of the contents of our minds and the conceptual babies they thought we were plotting to produce. This communication quickly degenerates into a vandalising of property and into concrete efforts to possess and control each of the physically separated adults by children of the opposite sex. We came to realise that the idea of the *united* couple held just as many dangers for these children as that of a *split* couple. In the former case, not only could the couple turn its combined aggression on the child, but it seemed that the product of its coming together could be violent thoughts that, far from making them feel held in mind and understood, would be felt to be attacking and rejecting them. In the latter case, that of the split couple, they feared the strength of their omnipotence would have destroyed the protective fabric of the group or family, and left them vulnerable to retaliation without protection. So much of the work of this group, therefore, was aimed at promoting survival of a couple whose benign aspects could eventually be internalised.

Repair of the therapeutic relationship had to take place in earnest between sessions. Our survival as a couple paved the way for future wonder and curiosity about us. Questions evolved about the nature of our partnership. If we were not married (they could see, eventually, that we had different names), and we were not 'sexually related' as one of them put it, then what on earth *were* we doing together, if we weren't harbouring some perverse or otherwise harmful interest in them? They made observations about the matching, different, but complementary, textures of our clothes and their colours. This proceeded to consideration of many more general differences between themselves and between the generations. In these observations, often buried within scenes of chaos and near-anarchy, we saw real gains in their perception and tolerance of reality. Within such a framework a sense of dependency began to be established in which learning and emotional development could take place. Careful scrutiny of the content of each session revealed that this kind of development was usually disguised. We thought that this was to protect the fledgling development from the ever-watchful influence of gang mentality, rather like the growth of an underground movement forming within a totalitarian political regime.

The last clinical example highlights the dangers and the strengths of co-working in groups. We found that the inevitable attempts to split the couple could lead to actual polarisation of our views and attitudes. There was need for constant airing of differences lest our perception of the children's needs, the kinds of boundaries we wished to establish, division of labour, etc., diverged too far without our realising it until it was too late. Much extra time had to be set aside (a minimum of one hour after the group, and fortnightly supervision) to consider the children's material. We needed time to foster a mutual respect of differences with the aim of developing a complementary rather than an oppositional partnership.

For instance, we had to think about our views on sex in relation to children, and how to cope with displays of precocious and perverse pseudo-sexuality. These included obscene representations, both verbal and pictorial, often claimed to have been passed to them by adults in the community. They were testing us critically, and the nature and quality of our combined response was vital to their developing sense of hope in a non-seductive and non-seducible couple. In short, our responses had to be seen as a 'thinking-together' as a prototype of a *group* activity, in contrast to the 'anti-thought' and devotion to lies and confusion of a 'gang'.

## INFRASTRUCTURE

This heading refers to the necessary 'stage management' of the group. I have already referred to the need for discussion between the co-therapists. This included writing up together; a putting together of the pieces of the session directly afterwards, as well as putting ourselves and our minds back together. The children so often made us feel unbearable aspects of their own experiences, which they themselves found impossible to contain. We saw it as our job to feel these for them in the first instance. The latter often had a brutal jarring quality which we found scarcely digestible. We had to remind ourselves that unless we could take these as communications from the children we would never have a gut level understanding of what their lives were really like. One could characterise much of this post-session digestive process as an act of 'turning assaults into communications'. Only *after* this was it some-times possible to relay back to the group, in a more benign way, what we had understood them to be telling us.

Another aspect of general containment was the support of the rest of the clinic staff. We doubt that this is the kind of group that can be seen in a non-professional setting where witnesses and recipients of the sheer noise level, violent language and occa-sional breakages may not understand what is happening.

It may be argued that, for some children, a group held in a school setting offers them a notional (and actual) sense of a latent authority figure, in the shape of a headteacher for instance, which can in itself provide a containing safety factor. However, in our case, this was probably not feasible on two counts: firstly, they were failing badly in school and therefore a non-school setting was felt to be preferable. Secondly, these children were from different schools, and finding the right school with the right space and the right support would have proved difficult to say the least. We believe that sympathetic colleagues and administrative staff, to whom we were able to explain the outlines of what we were doing, contributed greatly to the work and its survival.

Having said this, I must add that we did need the support of the schools, most especially in the matter of releasing the children before the end of the school day (the group met at 3.00 pm). This involved introducing to the schools the various escorts with cars who likewise had to meet the parents or carers of the children to whom the latter were delivered after the group. Paid escorts were necessary because the respective parents were not able, prepared or organised enough to bring the children them-selves, at least not on a regular weekly basis. This fact was in itself one symptom of the children's plight.

Funding of the escorts, as for supervision, was not available from the Social Services, Education or Health Services. Money from a charitable trust fund (Child Psychotherapy Trust) was eventually applied for and granted to cover these costs. The escorts themselves had to be carefully vetted, and even then the most apparently able and dependable of them, who transported three of the children, became the subject of a split.

The disruption that took place at the end of most sessions was enough to persuade her that we let the children get away with bad behaviour. She would have none of this, and in return for their being good she bought the children sweets, drinks and ice creams on the way home. We had established with the children from the start that this was not to be a group that offered food and drink, on the basis that material deprivation was not part of their problem. While this state of affairs went unaddressed, the three children, in the presence of this escort, staged escalating scenes of disruption and unrest in the waiting room at the beginning and the end of every session. This needed careful and diplomatic working out with the escort, and we also had to consider her dismissal, without the prospect of a ready replacement.

While on the subject of cost, it should be said that we did not consider this group as a less expensive alternative to individual therapy. We considered it as a treatment of choice for the children in question and we found that one session lasting one hour a week required several hours of work per week to keep it going. Taking into account the session itself, discussion, administration and fortnightly supervision (including travel time for two of us to and from the supervisor) we worked eight hours per week, or four hours each, during term time, on behalf of the group.

## CONCLUSION

It has not been possible in this paper to give a detailed account of the evolution of the group but we have already highlighted the children's growing ability to tolerate and even appreciate differences between themselves and between the generations.

There were increasingly times when age, gender and emotional vulnerability were not exploited in the services of dominance, scapegoating and the projection of fear into the weakest members of the group. By the end of the year, playing and thinking together in a mutually supportive way were more in evidence. With respect to their increasing tolerance of the differences between the generations, we think that the qualities of a surviving thinking parental couple may have been to some extent experienced and internalised.

The struggle to hold on to our hopes was never-ending. Alongside the gains there were episodes of chaos and destructiveness right up to the end which forced us to the edge of despair. We were reminded constantly that the group did not take place in the context of controlled or stabilised daily existences. During the year, murder, mental illness and suicide occurred within the immediate families of the various group members. We recognise that given such hardships the children may themselves be constantly driven to the edge of despair, just as we were. In such a frame of mind they are more likely to be vulnerable to the spurious protectionism of 'gang' thinking. This, while offering peace of mind, is really dominated by sadism and masochistic submission, and a devotion to propaganda and lies (see Rosenfeld 1971; Meltzer 1968).

It is to be hoped that the group experience equipped some, or most, of the children to cope better with ongoing fear, disaster and hardships in their daily lives by being able to recognise more clearly, and to use, the resources and help that existed in the community around them.

## POSTSCRIPT

The oldest child transferred to secondary school during the life of the group. She was not the subject of a re-referral. Three of them transferred to special school with reasonable success. One of them was re-referred to the clinic when his emotional frailty was recognised by a caring school staff group, and he was seen on an individual basis from time to time. The fifth child settled down during the last two terms of primary school but had a temporary period of severe aggression and disruptiveness during the second term of secondary school, about a year after the death of a member of the family. This was one of the deaths, during the life of the group, that we have already mentioned.

## ACKNOWLEDGEMENTS

My co-worker in this group was Lorraine Tollemache and our supervision was with Sue Reid, to both of whom I would like to express deep gratitude.

Chapter 15

# A community group for depressed mothers and its relation to health visiting

*Zelinda Adam*

## SETTING UP THE GROUP

In 1984 a local female consultant psychiatrist in charge of mothers and babies in the South Bucks area joined forces with a health visitor and special care nurse to launch the first group for mothers suffering from postnatal depression. They were united by the recognition of growing numbers of women in the post-partum period suffering from depression and a need for an opportunity to talk about their problems in some depth. This form of depression, which affects 10–15 per cent of new mothers, is to be distinguished from both the 'baby blues', which can occur a few days after the birth and generally clears up quite quickly, and puerperal psychosis, a psychotic illness which needs immediate hospitalisation, the incidence of which is one or two per 1,000 births, although it has recently been suggested that it may be higher than this (Lucas 1994).

Ten years later that one initial group has grown to five and throughout the South Bucks NHS Trust area there is a comprehensive screening programme for postnatal depression carried out by health visitors on all new mothers. The fact that we find ourselves in such a position today is largely due to the valiant efforts of those who set up the first group. Their insight and commitment has produced immense dividends.

The five groups that are run in the area are led by psychotherapists, health visitors and social workers. Each group has two therapists and a maximum of eight women attending. Attached to each group is a creche, staffed by volunteers and a salaried creche supervisor. They play an important part in the work that is done. The children attending the creche often come full of anxiety and confusion, unable to play or be played with. What our creche workers offer them is patience, understanding and constancy which seems to be able to hold them together in some way while their mothers struggle on.

The groups meet only in term time with mothers tending to stay between six months and two years depending on the character of the group and the particular emotional needs of the mother. Referrals to the groups come from health visitors, general practitioners, psychiatrists and social workers. Before a mother is accepted in a group a therapist will assess her in her own home. Not everyone will be able to cope in a group setting and even if they can the process can be long and difficult. Some evidence of ego strength is needed as is an ability to show some insight into the difficulties they are experiencing. Not an easy task to be achieved in a one-off assessment visit. Sometimes there are mistakes, but sometimes some pleasant surprises.

Over the last few years the groups have started to be seen by the communities they serve as a positive addition to mental health care in the district. This has led to two important consequences. First, the mental health budget has taken over the funding of the groups and has listed the treatment of PND (postnatal depression) as a priority in future funding. Secondly, health visitors have responded positively and have instigated a screening programme to assess all new mothers in the area for PND.

Mothers are now asked to answer a simple psychological questionnaire six weeks after their baby is born. If their score is high they are offered six weeks of weekly visits by the health visitor to talk about their own feelings concerning motherhood: a time for them alone and unlike the usual visit by the health visitor, which is often felt by the mother to be centred around the new baby so that their own feelings about the changes in their lives go unnoticed. The mother is re-assessed when the baby is 3 months old. If the score is still high one of the options is for the mother to be referred to one of the groups.

The questionnaire used by the health visitors is called the EPDS (Edinburgh Post Natal Depression Scale) and is the work of Dr John Cox, Consultant Psychiatrist, who initiated the programme with health visitors in Scotland. He found that after six weeks of intensive 'listening' work with mothers a great deal of improvement was noticed and that more serious forms of depression could be averted. This has been our experience too in Bucks. Our health visitors feel that the EPDS has given a structure to their work and has helped them use their skills more effectively. It has not, however, been an easy ride. Quite understandably the health visitors were initially reluctant to take on what felt like a lot of extra work and the possibility of 'opening up a can of worms'.

I believe that depression in new mothers can be a difficult thing to face for all of us working in this area. The 'pull yourself together' attitude is not just a desperate cry from a despairing husband towards his depressed and seemingly incapable wife, but also perhaps something that can come from deep inside all of us, and, unless we are able to grapple with that and look at PND from a different perspective, we will not be able to offer mothers a place to express their depression and a chance to explore a way out of it.

It was very important, therefore, that the anxieties of the health visitors were met head on, so they too were given a space to express them. A study day was arranged where different speakers from different backgrounds gave their views of PND and how they tackled it. A series of seminars was also offered where the EPDS was looked at in detail and various psychoanalytical aspects of PND were explained. Weekly supervision groups run by a psycho-therapist and psychiatrist were also arranged for health visitors who felt they needed extra support in this type of work. There were inevitably some health visitors who for whatever reasons felt unable to become involved. Their right to do so, although posing problems, was accepted from the start. Everyone reacts differently to this work, a fact we must constantly keep in mind.

Two years into the screening programme health visitors feel the initiative has been very worth while. It has given a focus to their work and has provided the mothers with a very valuable tool with which to express themselves.

## UNDERSTANDING POSTNATAL DEPRESSION

### Unconscious conflicts – unthinkable thoughts

Every woman enters motherhood with a set of experiences from her own history and in particular her own mother–daughter relationship that will determine how she will see herself as a new mother. It becomes very difficult to keep repressed these feelings of turmoil associated with her own experience of being mothered.

Unconscious conflicts can no longer be contained. Joan Raphael-Leff's paper 'Where the wild things are' talks about the effect a baby has on its mother – 'a baby compels his/her mother to re-experience what it is like to be helpless, needy, frustrated, enraged' (Raphael-Leff 1989). To be a sensitive caretaker, to remain 'empathetically receptive' a mother has to keep open the channels of communication between her and her baby, but that means exposure to long forgotten experiences and sensations. How a mother responds to this onslaught is largely determined by her own experience of being parented. If her own feelings of helplessness, neediness as an infant/child were on the whole contained and made sense of then the mother will have been able to internalise an image of a good enough caretaker and she can then draw on these psychic memories to help her through the fraught times with her own baby. If, however, this has not been the case and there is not a good enough memory of mothering to call upon, then the mother feels at the mercy of overwhelming raw emotions. She becomes vulnerable, feels she can't cope with the simplest tasks, blames herself for failing and locks herself into a vicious circle of loneliness and despair.

Winnicott's theory of the 'good enough mother' is worth mentioning here. Winnicott felt that a good enough mother adapts to her infant's needs, allowing the infant some experience of omnipotence and this in turn allows the infant to get started with ego-maturation – real emotional growth. Winnicott sees the infant as someone who 'is all the time on the brink of unthinkable anxiety' (Winnicott 1962: 57). The good enough mother is able to keep this at bay for her infant. The mother who is not good enough repeatedly fails to meet her infant's needs, resulting in the infant not being able 'to get started with ego-maturation, or else ego-development is necessarily distorted in certain vitally important respects' (Winnicott 1962: 57).

We can help mothers break into this cycle by offering them a space to think and express their unthinkable thoughts. It is vital that this is done in an atmosphere that is felt to be understanding, accepting and not judgemental. It often takes some time before mothers can admit to those feelings, not least towards their infants. When they do, their relief is evident not just because they have managed to verbalise such fears, but because they can see from the reactions of others in the group that they are not the only ones to feel that way. Suddenly they no longer feel unique, they are no longer alone.

Gradually the mother begins to experience the group as a possible container for her difficult feelings. Bion's theory of container and contained is very helpful here. Bion believed that an infant projects feelings of anxiety and dread into the mother. If the mother is able to 'contain' these feelings and does not get depressed and unable to respond then she is able to modify the anxieties and send them back to the infant in a digestible form so that he feels understood and comforted. If this does not happen the infant can feel he is too much for his mother and a negative sense of himself starts to develop. With the help of the therapists and the group acting as containers and symbolic mother figures, the new mother can begin to hope that her unbearable fears and fantasies can be survived. In the group, the therapist reflects upon and gives meaning to the tidal wave of unbearable emotion coming from the mother (a projection). It is then offered back to the mother in the form of an interpretation which is felt to be safe and non-threatening. The mother can take it back and own it because she has witnessed someone else as having experienced it and survived it.

In one group session the feeling of anger was very tangible although no member of the group admitted to feeling it. The only person to experience it seemed to be the therapist. The group members had projected their anger into her because they felt it too difficult to bear themselves. When the therapist suggested that there were feelings around that were difficult to express because they were directed at the therapist herself and no-one wanted to be cruel, one by one the mothers were able to admit their anger towards a therapist who was felt to have let them down the previous week by being ill. This led ultimately to discussions about the difficulty of expressing anger and the fear of it being only destructive. Their actual experience, however, in that session had proved different from their fears. The therapist had 'contained' their anger so that they could find a way of expressing it and they and the therapist survive it.

As the process is repeated week after week, the mother's internal view of herself slowly begins to change. Instead of seeing herself as someone who is made up of unthinkable, punishable thoughts, she starts to believe that in her particular circumstances and with her own personal history those thoughts are perhaps quite permissible, that if they are expressed they might not destroy either herself or others. She might not be the bad mother with the bad thoughts that she always thought herself to be.

When mothers are trapped with such negative views of themselves it is easy to see why they turn up to the group with no sense of personal identity – not knowing who they are or what they want from life. As one mother said 'I'm there for everybody else, there's no time for me, there's no time to even think about me.' This lament is used by the depressed mother to suppress any connection with her own emotional needs which are felt to be enormous. It feels easier to deny that she wants anything rather than face the disappointment of not getting it. She feels she spends her day being sucked dry by the constant demands of her infant, that his needs dominate, not hers. This scenario forces the mother to re-experience the conflict that perhaps at some important time in her life she felt her own needs were not met: how unfair, she believes, that now she is expected to meet the demands of her infant without ever feeling that someone was there for her too.

The route out of this depressed state is, in part, along the path of the mother–daughter relationship. In the groups we help mothers to look again at their own relationships with their mothers, where the disappointments lay, the anger, the sadness and, hopefully, the love. We give them a chance to explore those relationships in a more honest way, admitting to feelings which hitherto have been felt to be unspeakable. Once more they and the group have the experience of surviving them. In time they begin to feel they can express their needs, their rights, as human beings. Their needs might not always be able to be met but that no longer prevents them from expressing them. For some women a sign of progress is sitting down and eating when they are hungry rather than thinking only of their infant's needs. For others it might be buying something for themselves without feeling guilty.

## STRIVING FOR THE IDEAL

In their relationship with their infants depressed mothers will often strive mercilessly to create the ideal. The fact that the ideal is not achievable and that they are, therefore, bound to fail serves only to increase their despair. Striving to create an ideal relationship is an important defence in many ways. If one can achieve a perfect mother–infant relationship then one never needs to look at the less than perfect relationship one had with one's own mother. If perfection is achievable then the mother feels she had every right to demand that from her own mother and she can then hold onto the belief that her own mother failed her and she as the child has a right to her grievances and depression. Idealisation is also used as a defence against anxieties which belong to what Melanie Klein described as the paranoid-schizoid position. During this very early period experiences of the mother are split into very good or very bad, which have to be kept apart. If the infant's experiences of mother are not very good in reality, there will be a tendency to cling to an image of an 'ideal' mother, but there remains a constant anxiety of being overwhelmed by a bad persecuting mother.

In the group we try to modify the mothers' need to cling to idealisation by providing an experience of therapists and perhaps other group members who are felt to be receptive and understanding, even if not perfect. Hopefully this provides the members with the opportunity to internalise an object who is helpful and understanding, rather than one who is harsh and critical.

This internalisation of a realistic good mother who is a mixture of good and bad, but nonetheless loved, corresponds to Melanie Klein's description of the processes of the depressive position, something we continue to work on throughout our lives.

It is noticeable how some mothers on leaving the groups can finally allow themselves to say that their own mothers probably did the best they could in the circumstances. They are able in some ways to forgive their mothers for being less than perfect. This releases them at once from the strait-jacket of perfection. Suddenly it is no longer necessary to have a perfectly tidied house, perfectly behaved children, perfectly trained emotions. If they have been able to look at their own less than ideal but nevertheless good-enough mother–daughter relationship and come to terms with that, then they can contemplate the idea that *they* too do not have to be perfect in order for their children to love them. Their internal image of themselves begins to change from a bad/dangerous mother to someone who is loved and is worth loving.

As the mother's view of herself begins to change so too does her view of her infant. Previously her demanding/naughty baby had been evidence that she was a bad mother. Everything the baby did she felt reflected on her in a critical way. Now she is more able to see the baby for what he or she is. He, therefore, becomes less persecuting because she no longer has any need for an external persecutor.

Once a mother starts to pull away from a constant need to idealise and split people into good and bad she can start to see that a mixture of both aspects can be found in others and also herself. As one mother said on finishing her time in the group, 'when I first came I felt you as the therapist had all the answers, now I can see that you don't – the answers are also in me'. Now she feels more able to look at a whole range of feelings which need to be faced in order to get better. These include sadness, guilt and reparation: sadness, at the moments lost and the possibilities missed in her own mother–daughter relationship; guilt, at the recognition that she herself was responsible for her angry feelings towards people whom she also loved. In other words, she now has to deal with mixed feelings. And, finally, reparation which is fundamentally the acceptance of reality. There is a wish to repair the damage that has been felt to have been done to the loved person. The possibility and belief that love can triumph over anger and hate.

## CONCLUSION

The depressed mother needs to exert a huge amount of energy in order to keep her imprisoned fears under control – energy that could be re-directed into enjoying motherhood and the new baby. The work undertaken with PND, whether in groups or individually with health visitors, gives mothers a chance to come to terms with conflicts that have been suppressed, in many cases, for years. The hope is, and our experience shows, that, when they can be faced and worked through, such experiences increase self-esteem, transforming formerly unprocessed feelings into creative potential and true emotional growth can become a reality.

# Chapter 16

# Moving on

## Group work with children from a multicultural primary school

*Bobbie Cooper*

## INTRODUCTION

The emotional upheaval involved in the transition from primary to secondary school is often underestimated. It involves leaving behind many people who have been important in a child's life, as well as the more sheltered environment of early childhood. For children who have suffered physical or emotional upheavals this loss may be particularly painful, and support may be necessary to make a successful transition.

This chapter describes groupwork of a year's duration, with five children in their final year at primary school. The school, multicultural in nature, was located on a deprived inner-city council estate. A considerable number of children from the school were refugees, and had suffered many upheavals and changes in their lives.

Children from this school were frequently referred to the local child guidance unit, where the worker was based. Concerns were expressed about a number of children facing secondary transfer. Following a series of meetings between the worker and the headteacher, groupwork with these children was agreed on.

The children in this group experienced considerable difficulties processing anxiety, particularly in relation to the uncertainty precipitated by change. The purpose of the group was to help them develop a way of managing their anxieties and negotiating change.

## SELECTION OF CHILDREN FOR THE GROUP

The headteacher wrote to parents of children identified for the group (by the head and class teachers) inviting them to a joint meeting, which included the group worker and class teacher. The meetings provided the parents with an opportunity to discuss their child's progress, and to inform them about the proposed group.

Parents who attended these meetings appeared keen for their child to participate in the group, viewing it as a means of aiding a smooth transfer to secondary school. Parents who were unable to attend (two out of five parents) gave their verbal and/or written consent.

The meetings highlighted general family conflicts which possibly contributed to a particular child's school difficulties: for example, bereavement, loss of one parent through separation, domestic violence, fleeing persecution from countries of origin, anxieties centred around refugee status, living in temporary accommodation.

Following these meetings the group worker met with each child individually, seeking to gauge their feelings about being selected and to provide them with an opportunity to ask questions. Generally the children appeared positive, but also initially tentative about being selected. The boys in particular believed they had been identified as a result of their 'bad behaviour', indicating an acute awareness of their school's concern, but also demonstrating concern in their own right. For example, one child (Peter) explained, 'I fight in class but sometimes I can't help it, I tell myself not to.' The group worker met termly with the head and class teacher for a review on all five children.

## THE CHILDREN

I will give a brief description of each child; for the sake of confidentiality the children are not identified by their real names.

### Amy

The eldest of three children, Amy was extremely protective towards her younger sisters. The relationship between her parents had been persistently violent, her father left home shortly after the birth of his third child. Amy was a confident, popular child who frequently bullied others. Her ethnic origins were White English.

### Andrew

The fifth of seven children from a complicated family structure, with five of the children having different fathers. Andrew's parents separated in his third year. He lived with his mother, retaining regular contact with his father. Andrew was a bright child, under-achieving educationally as a result of his difficult behaviour and erratic school attendance. Andrew's ethnic origins were White English.

## Mehmet

The third of five children with considerable responsibility for the care of his younger siblings, as his parents worked long hours. Mehmet was of Kurdish origin with family all over Europe and Asia. Mehmet presented as a sullen, angry child, frequently in aggressive encounters with his peers. His learning difficulties aroused distress and rage in him, further exacerbating his poor self-image. Mehmet was frequently absent from school visiting extended family.

## Peter

The youngest of five, with a large (ten-year) age gap between him and his four older siblings. Peter came to England as a refugee from Zaire at age 8, he has not seen his parents for several years and fears they may be dead. Peter avidly sought acceptance from his peers, frequently playing the clown to gain their approval.

## Sarah

An only child of Afro-Caribbean origin who experienced several changes of home and school as a result of homelessness. Sarah was presented as a sad, withdrawn child, frequently scapegoated by her peers. Sarah's class teacher felt overwhelmed by the constant need to protect Sarah from her peers. This 'protection' exacerbated peer group hostility towards her.

## BEGINNINGS

The group met on a once weekly basis for an hour and a quarter, in a room allocated specifically for this purpose. The room was generally free from interruptions and of a good size. The children arrived following registration with their class teacher. Each session began with a 'group talk' where each child attempted to share with others how they were feeling, they were also encouraged to raise issues from previous sessions. If a child preferred not to participate in the group talk this was respected. The session continued with a 'group activity'. As the group progressed, group members took more responsibility for this part of the group. The session concluded with a second 'group talk' where children discussed the activity and/or their feelings. 'Emergency' group talks arose whenever a crisis or conflict emerged in the group. Examples of group activities included artwork, particularly drawing and painting, for example 'self-portraits' (both in relation to how the children perceived themselves and how they believed they were viewed by others). Other activities included devising 'family trees', detailing biological family plus other significant individuals in the child's life, 'life-maps', illustrating significant events identified by each child in their lives past and current, for example, moves, losses, change.

## FIRST MEETING

The children appeared calm, but also anxious. Peter and Amy talked incessantly, drifting from one subject to another, competing with each other for my attention. Other group members sat silently, looking expectantly at me like hungry baby birds desperate for food. Peter stated, 'I nearly forgot the group started today, I thought it was next week'. Amy replied, 'I knew it was today, I did not want to be late for school.' I acknowledged how anxious, uncertain they might be feeling, as well as looking forward to the group. The children listened attentively, seeming to hang on to my every word. An atmosphere of calm ensued with group members feeling I had acknowledged plus articulated their anxieties.

The session developed with a 'group talk' exploring the children's fantasies about the group. Andrew stated he had come to the group to help him 'be better in class and in my new school'. Mehmet wanted his English 'to be better'. All the children expressed anxieties about their impending transfer to secondary school, hoping the group would help them make sense of this change in their lives.

Providing a space to explore anxieties and fears rendered the children receptive to thinking about the structure of the group, i.e. its boundaries, activities. Group rules represented a particular set of boundaries, seeking to ensure the children would feel safe and contained in the group. Examples of group rules included ensuring disagreements between individuals would be discussed rather than physically fought out, differences of opinion would be respected as much as possible, children would be encouraged to respect each other's belongings, and the room, and not to inflict damage, neither were they to injure each other, themselves or the worker (Reid *et al.* 1977: 34–5).

Formulating group rules was a fascinating process with all the children participating as if this were a means of making an impact on the group. The children's suggested rules were specifically aimed at behaviour and general conduct (for example, 'no kicking, hitting' – 'talking and listening to each other'), indicating these were areas of particular concern to them. The rules were recorded, each child receiving their own copy. The first session ended with the children receiving group folders for their work. These folders were decorated (with names and drawings) and were extremely important to the children. At the end of each session the folders were handed to me for, what Amy called, 'looking after'. Symbolically these folders represented each child, their individual identities.

A group calendar, also indicating group breaks, was explored and constructed in the second session. Mehmet looked anxious, asking 'Why do we need a calendar?' I asked him what his ideas and feelings on this were, he shrugged his shoulders, stating, 'I don't like calendars.' Amy added calmly, 'If we have a calendar then you know what date it is.'

Other group members joined in, exploring their experiences of calendars. Andrew remarked, 'My mum had a calendar once.' I said, 'Perhaps a calendar feels uncomfortable because it makes us think about time, how long things last?' Mehmet looked sad; I added, 'Perhaps it is painful to think about times when the group is not meeting.' Sarah agreed, stating, 'I wish I could come to this group every day.'

The calendar revived fears and anxieties centred around separation. By denying the inevitability of time and change the children hoped these painful feelings would disappear and not have to be faced. Acknowledging these anxieties made it possible for these feelings to be thought about. For example, Mehmet explained holidays made him 'sick and dizzy'; Amy added, 'I only know what time it is when I'm at school, at home I don't even know what day it is.'

Nearly all the children had experienced chaotic family ways of

dealing with and informing others about time and change. However, the children also projected their own panic and chaos into
adults, making it difficult for certain things to be thought about
and processed effectively. Eventually the calendar created a sense
of security for the children, they felt in control, feeling they had (as
Amy defined it) 'known time' to explore their anxieties about endings; it would not merely be sprung on them, neither would they
be encouraged purely to defer responsibility to others, particularly
parental figures.

The first few weeks of the group represented a comparatively
calm period, with all five children participating in their various ways.
Amy and Peter were the most confident of the five, their enthusiasm and strong sense of self encouraged the more withdrawn
children to model more assertive ways of relating. For example,
Sarah and Mehmet in the early sessions often sat silently, but
appeared (in a non-verbal manner) tuned in to the group process.
Andrew at times appeared preoccupied; other group members, in
particular Peter, encouraged him to participate, making him feel his
contributions were valued.

The first half-term break arrived, arousing rage and confusion
in the children. Sarah missed the last session, the other four
children appeared determined to let me experience the full vent of
their feelings. They became confrontational, rejecting, appearing
to sabotage any attempts to think about the situation. I acknowledged their anger, trying to explore with them their feelings about
the break, and about Sarah's absence. In one session Mehmet
shouted contemptuously, 'It's all right for teachers when they say
there's a holiday, there's a holiday, what if we don't want one!'
'Yes', echoed Peter, 'let's go on strike!'

At times their behaviour seemed so unbearable, making me
question whether it was going to be possible to contain it. The children provoked situations with me and each other, precipitating
emergency group talks. I thought about my feelings, stating I
believed the children were actively relaying to me (through their
projections) how overwhelming, frightening separation can be.
Perhaps at these times they feared there would be no respite from
the painful feelings aroused. Gradually they began to process my
words, and comparative calm emerged in the group. The children
seemed keen to ensure I would return after their onslaught, that I
would not retaliate by taking flight from them. For example, Amy
left her 'favourite book' in her folder. I said, 'Perhaps it feels

difficult to believe I will come back, want to come back, when you are all feeling so angry with me.' Mehmet responded, stating sadly, 'Mrs S had a baby and she never came back because we were a naughty class.' Generally, the children feared I would abandon them, replacing them with younger children.

All five children returned from the holiday break in sullen mood, provoking confrontations with me and each other. They became more assertive and competitive with each other for my attention. The periods between group sessions revived feelings about the break, precipitating curiosity about how I had spent it and who I had spent it with. For example, Amy suggested, 'Miss was at home looking after her husband and children.' 'How many children have you got?' demanded Mehmet. 'I bet she's got a baby', added Andrew. Amy in one session angrily demanded to know whether I worked with children in other schools. 'I bet she works with Richard and Germaine in our class', shouted Peter.

The recent break aroused strong feelings of anxiety in relation to their impending transfers to new schools. The children began to denigrate me and their primary school, stating they could not wait to leave us. It seemed the only way they felt able to leave something they valued was by denigrating it, so that it felt easier, necessary to move on. I continued to acknowledge their feelings in spite of their rejecting behaviour. Eventually their rage subsided, leading to group discussions on the various losses experienced by the children. For example, Peter described his feelings at leaving his parents in Zaire, stating, 'It was really horrible, I might never see them again.' Amy described how upset she had become when her parents separated, saying, 'I love them both; it's difficult to choose sides.' Andrew explored his life at primary school: 'I have always been at this school, I was in the nursery, it's weird thinking I won't be here in September.' Sarah described her various moves of home and how difficult it was to believe she would remain in any one place for a substantial period of time. Feeling able to explore painful issues, plus sensing their anxieties had been acknowledged, generated trust between group members, adding to a growing sense of cohesion in the group. The children began to feel they were not alone with their unhappiness, that others existed who could hear their pain, identify with it.

Following the first group break the children began bringing issues for the group to explore. My returning after the break reassured the children, making them feel I did not wish to abandon the group but would try and understand their conflicts with them. The issues brought by the children included how they would be perceived and received by others in their new schools and whether they would retain contact with each other after primary school. A particular anxiety centred around interpersonal relationships which frequently resulted in aggression, violence. The children had fairly direct, abrupt and confrontational ways of relating to each other. This frequently caused conflict and misunderstanding. As a group the children devised 'role plays' exploring various ways of dealing with conflict between individuals.

Interestingly, after the initial teasing, heckling and confrontation, the children became quite skilled and confident in their roles, including Sarah who seemed the quietest member of the group. I was struck by the children's sensitivity and encouragement of each other. These roles encouraged the children to empathise with another's situation, to think, rather than jump to conclusions behaviourally.

The second group break drew near and the children became anxious and irritable. I acknowledged how upset, angry and abandoned they were feeling, trying to encourage them to think about their feelings as opposed to acting them out. The children found thinking about their painful feelings uncomfortable, aggressively expelling these feelings, making it difficult to hang on to coherent thoughts. In spite of their onslaught, and with the aid of skilled supervision, I continued to think about and acknowledge their feelings; gradually they became calmer, their destructive behaviour diminished considerably.

All five children returned from the second holiday break in comparatively calm mood, seeming more receptive to working on their conflicts, a marked difference to their reactions following the first break. The second holiday break aroused feelings and anxieties about individual differences in the group. These differences were, at times, expressed culturally. For example, Sarah, Peter and Mehmet explored life in their countries of origin. Amy confidently joined them determined to be part of these discussions. Initially Andrew became enraged whenever these discussions ensued, attempting to sabotage them with racial taunts, stating 'It's not fair. When they talk about their countries what can I talk about?' Andrew felt abandoned, feeling others had much more to contribute, that I found them interesting and could identify with them more than I could with him.

Andrew also felt this way within his classroom, feeling he was not as interesting to his black teacher as his black peers. In his family of origin, Andrew was a middle child who believed his mother preferred his other siblings, in particular his youngest brother. Andrew displaced his feelings about his family onto other areas of his life, making it difficult for him to relate constructively to his peers. I made a comment about Andrew, as a result of his early history, possibly experiencing me as a maternal figure who had her favourites, would accept particular children and reject others. My comment appeared to clarify Andrew's anxieties and gradually he began to take a more constructive, inclusive role in group discussions.

My comment also addressed similar anxieties in other group members, who began to explore their feelings about their siblings. For example, Peter stated, 'If you are the youngest in my house you get more attention.' Amy retorted, 'I hate my baby sister; she gets away with everything, can't do a thing wrong.' Sarah lamented, 'I wish I had a brother or sister; I have cousins but it's not the same.' Andrew retorted sarcastically, 'You can have all of mine!'

The discussions around cultural differences (and similarities) led to the invention of a game called the 'Map Game'. In this game group members placed counters on a map of the world, in places of particular importance and/or interest to them. When all the counters had been placed, the children took turns to say where they had placed their counters and why. For example, Sarah stated, 'My counters are in Guyana, Gambia and England; my Granny lives in Guyana, I miss her, she looked after me when I was a baby.' Andrew placed his in 'England, Scotland and Africa – my Mum's English, my Dad's Scottish, I want to visit Africa.' The 'Map Game' seemed to energise the children, they became keen to explore, think about other countries and continents. I linked this to them feeling safe to explore their feelings about change, in particular the impending move to secondary school, the group one day ending. I felt it appropriate gradually to explore the children's feelings about change, sensing they were needing to enjoy and feel at ease with their newly gained confidence in exploring.

The focus on the geographical/cultural aspects of the group stimulated curiosity about family structure. Frequently between sessions the children became curious about me and my family structure, wanting to know what my husband was like, how many children I had. Mehmet said, 'I bet you all go shopping together, do lots of nice things!' He explained he rarely saw his father who worked long hours and frequently travelled. Sarah stated, 'I can't remember my dad, he left when I was a baby.' Sarah's words aroused considerable pain in the group as if she had communicated something relevant to them all, i.e. being abandoned by a parent when they were still extremely dependent on them. I commented that perhaps this was how they were experiencing thinking about the end of the group, feeling they would be abandoned by me when they were still extremely dependent. 'Yes,' stated Amy. 'It's not fair.'

The interest in family structure continued to develop. Nearly all the children lived with one parent, remaining curious about their absent parent, frequently their fathers. Often the children idealised their absent parent as if protecting him from feelings of hurt, loss and rage, attempting to keep him alive in their minds. Frequently their rageful feelings towards their fathers were projected onto others, particularly their mothers. In the group (particularly when feelings of vulnerability were revived by a holiday break) I at times represented a denigrated maternal figure who had abandoned her partner and would act to abandon them too.

Loss of their fathers also aroused oedipal anxieties, with the children fearing their hostile wishes towards their father had destroyed, banished them from their lives (Freud 1905). For example, Andrew in one session stated, 'I like my Mum; if I had not been so horrible to my Dad he might still be at home.' As the group developed, I sensed the children were curious, plus feeling safer with the idea of a parental couple, this was often openly expressed through their fantasies about me and my family, following a group break. For example, in one session Amy stated, 'I bet you and your husband talk to each other, don't fight, when I grow up I want a husband I can talk to.'

The impending move to secondary school revived feelings about their fathers. It seemed that the children taking their first steps away from primary school, their maternal base, seeking to venture into the world represented by secondary school, longed to share this major step with both parents. For example, Amy exclaimed, 'I hope I see my Dad before I start my new school'; Andrew added, 'My Dad's not interested in what I do.' Mehmet added, 'My Dad's promised to be at home when I start my new school.'

The final term arrived, with the children feeling anxious, sad but hopeful. They began to deal with group breaks in a comparatively calm, reflective manner, generally taking responsibility for their feelings. The children began openly talking about their new schools, what they looked forward to, what they feared. Alongside the developing interest in their futures, represented by secondary school, the children expressed pain and sadness at the thought of the group coming to an end. Sarah explained: 'I can't think about the group one day not meeting, I want to come forever.' They began to explore ways of keeping in contact with me and each other, trying to resolve the painful possibility of not meeting each other again.

All five children tentatively but openly discussed their feelings, a marked contrast to the early stages of the group where painful feelings could not be thought about, were evacuated and rapidly converted into destructive acting out. As the final session drew near, the children looked back over the year, able to see how far they had moved with their abilities to deal with painful events. In one session Amy explained, 'I nearly know where I am now, I'm not so scared of my new school.' Andrew agreed, 'I will really miss my school, but it's all right.'

The children hung onto their folders, stating their intentions to continue developing, adding to them, indicating a wish to continue the process of self-exploration. The group process had highlighted individual strengths, normalising change and personal reactions to it.

## REVIEW AND CONSULTATION MEETINGS WITH THE CHILDREN'S CLASS TEACHER AND HEADTEACHER

Review meetings were held on a termly basis and involving hearing from the school how they perceived the children were functioning generally and any general concerns about their behaviour. The class teacher noted an improvement in the general behaviour and attendance of all five children. They were perceived to be more cooperative, less destructive and interacted much more constructively with other children. The children appeared more contained, projected less aggressively, thus precipitating more positive interactions between themselves and their class teacher. The class teachers' more favourable impression of the children communicated itself to the headteacher who began to view the class as much more 'independently functioning', obviating the need for constant crisis interventions from senior members of staff.

# Organisations

*Judith Trowell*

Institutions and organisations within the health care and social care or educational domain are highly complex because they have multiple tasks and are in the main dealing with vulnerable individuals. The primary task is to provide the designated service: for example, a school is there to educate the pupils. But education is not just to impart academic knowledge; society also expects schools to play a part in developing the whole person, that is, the child, enabling children to develop into socially acceptable citizens. An additional task is to provide a setting in which future teachers can be trained.

The equivalent is true for other such organisations within health, social services and the voluntary sector. Private sector organisations generally do not have a training remit and more often are more focused on the primary task that is providing the service.

Alongside the aspect of the individual, the body or the mind, that is attended to, the child or young person has an emotional life or emotional world. In the papers in this section organisations and institutions are described which are dealing with a range of children, some of whom have had difficulties while others may not. This means that quite often their emotional development has been impaired or distorted and, alongside their presenting problem, very powerful feelings are likely to be predominant because they have not been ameliorated or reconciled by good enough parenting. These children need 'containment', they need to feel their emotions can be tolerated, can be understood and can be put into words, that their rage will not destroy the organisations and their neediness and longing will not provoke rejection. These children communicate emotionally by non-verbal, unconscious mechanisms, mainly projective identification. Staff need to be able to accept and tolerate these feelings being transferred on to them. The staff need then – perhaps with the help of a consultant – to be able to think about these feelings or allow the child to experience this awareness so that the child can introject this sense of feelings being tolerated and understood – an introjective identification with the staff member.

The papers in this section were written by authors who were functioning as consultants. A consultant is someone on the boundary of an institution who can provide a space for staff to think and reflect so that they can make sense of the projections and the projective identifications. The staff are then able to help the children. Over time the consultant may be able to help the organisation provide a structure within itself so that most of the time an external consultant is not required, a senior staff member from one area perhaps consulting to another division or section within the organisation. When working with emotional, vulnerable or deprived children this way of working is crucial for staff so that they do not burn out or become over-involved with the children and crucial if children are to be provided with the emotional climate in which they can grow and develop.

Chapter 17

# The development of the self in children in institutions

*Isabel Menzies Lyth*

---

*This chapter was first published in 1985 (and republished in Menzies Lyth 1988). Some of the language, such as 'approved schools' and 'matron' is rather outdated. However, the underlying principles remain unchanged and are just as important today.*

The theoretical basis for thinking in this chapter centres on a particular aspect of the development of the self, development that takes place through introjective identification. Healthy development depends greatly on the availability of appropriate models of individuals, relationships and situations for such identification. These models may be found in the adults who care for the children, their relationship with the children and with each other, and the setting for care. Healthy development may also require the management of the child's identification with inappropriate models, for example with other children in institutions for delinquent or maladjusted children.

Institutionalised children are likely to find the most significant models for identification within the institution itself, both in the institution as a whole and its subsystems and in individual staff members and children. This leads to the concept of the institution as a therapeutic milieu whose primary task may be defined as providing conditions for healthy development and/or providing therapy for damaged children. Thus all the child's experiences in the institution contribute positively or negatively to his development, not only those more narrowly defined as education, individual or group therapy or child care. Indeed, it has been the author's experience that the benefits of such provision may well be counteracted by more general features of the institution.

This formulation would then lead one to take a very wide view of the institution in considering its effectiveness in carrying out its primary task. One would include its whole way of functioning; its management structure, including its division into subsystems and how those relate to each other; the nature of authority and how that is operated; the social defence system built into the institution; its culture and traditions. In line with the theme of this chapter, one would consider these in the context of how far they facilitate the provision of healthy models for identification, or alternatively inhibit the provision of such models.

Although one regards the whole institution as the model, in practice, of course, the impact of the institution on its child clients is mediated to a considerable extent through its staff members, who are the individual models for identification. While it is true that they will have their own individual personalities with strengths and weaknesses as models, it is also true that the way they deploy their personalities within the institution will depend on features inherent in the institution, the opportunities it gives staff for mature functioning or the limits it puts on this. The author has discussed elsewhere the severe limits that a traditionally organised nursing service imposes on the mature functioning of both trained and student nurses (Menzies 1970: 43–85).

Thus, in considering the adults as models, one would give attention to maximising the opportunity for them to deploy their capacities effectively and to be seen by the children to do so. Indeed, one may go further: experience has shown that in a well-managed institution for children, the adults as well as the children actually gain in ego-strength and mature in other ways. The adults thus provide better models.

The author's interest in the importance of the whole institution as a therapeutic milieu has developed over many years of working in two institutions for disturbed children where her formal role was that of management consultant and her task was to work with staff in keeping under continuous review the way the institution as a whole was functioning in relation to the primary task. The role involved both a considerable understanding of the way institutions function and a psychoanalytically based understanding of child development. Similarly, in a collaborative study with the Royal National Orthopaedic Hospital designed to improve the care of young children making long stays and to mitigate the long-term effects of hospitalisation, it was found necessary to pay considerable attention to the way the Cot Unit for young children was managed and related itself to the management of the hospital as a factor affecting the quality of child care.

Against this background, it would appear possible that views about the development of children in institutions have been unduly pessimistic. So many of the early investigations were done in institutions whose whole organisation was inappropriate for healthy child development. For example, the bad effects of hospitalisation on young children were demonstrated first in hospitals with inadequate maternal visiting and multiple indiscriminate care-taking by a large number of nurses which effectively prevented attachment between a child and his care-takers. The same has been true, on the whole, for children in day and residential nurseries. In fact, these institutions deviated much more from a good model of care than is realistically necessary, as also from the kind of setting a good ordinary family provides for a child to grow up in. More recent work provides some grounds for a more optimistic view of the developmental potential of children's institutions. They can be operated very differently from, for example, the old-fashioned hospital and can come much closer to the good ordinary family.

The section that follows discusses in some detail ways in which institutions can be organised or reorganised so as to provide improved models for the child's identification and for his development, and gives examples of work in institutions. I will comment on various aspects of this: ego-development, superego-development, the development of a firm sense of identity and of authority and responsibility for the self, attachment possibilities, the growth of a capacity for insight and confrontation with problems.

## THE POTENTIAL OF THE INSTITUTION AS A MODEL FOR IDENTIFICATION

### Delegation and its relation to staff's attitudes and behaviour

It is in general good management practice to delegate tasks and responsibilities to the lowest level at which they can be competently carried and to the point at which decision-making is most effective. This is of particular importance in children's institutions, since such delegation downwards increases the opportunity for staff to behave in an effective and authoritative way, to demonstrate capacity for carrying responsibility for themselves and their tasks and to make realistic decisions, all of which are aspects of a good model.

But this has not traditionally been the practice in many children's institutions; the functions, responsibilities and decision-making are centralised at a high management level, with a consequent diminution of the responsibility, authority and effectiveness of the staff more directly in contact with the children. In my consultancy with an approved school (a residential school for delinquent boys) I became involved in working with staff to change the management structure and functioning in one such area. The setting was traditional, with a matron who dispensed food in kind to the house mothers who provided meals for the staff and boys in the houses where the boys lived. There were all sorts of deficiencies and inefficiencies in the system, both practically in its effects on food provision and psychosocially in its effect on the behaviour of staff providing food and the models they presented to boys. The food allowance was not very generous and there were constant complaints about its inadequacy; indeed, boys were not very well fed. But the effect of the reality of the food allowance was compounded by the fact that, since the responsibility for food provision and decision-making lay with the matron, there was a notable tendency for the house mothers to disclaim their responsibility and authority; for example, to blame the matron if things went wrong, rather than feel an obligation to cope with them themselves.

A small example illustrates this point. Two boys went for a walk one evening and came back hungry. The house mother gave them two of the eggs she had been given for the breakfast next morning, thus leaving herself two short. She was disconcerted and angry when the matron would not – could not – give her more. Matron was blamed instead of the house mother's taking responsibility for her own actions. The model presented to the children was one of irresponsibility and of blaming the other.

The system gradually changed. Ultimately the house mothers were given the money to buy the food themselves. With it they were explicitly given the responsibility and authority for the efficient use of the money. The matron gave up her authority and responsibility for direct food provision and instead became an adviser and supporter of the house mothers if they wished to use her in that way. The former central foodstore became a shop where the house mothers could spend their money if they wished, but they had no obligations to do so if they preferred to shop elsewhere.

In time there were a number of very positive effects of this change. The house mothers visibly grew in authority and stature as they faced and accepted the new challenge and, for the most part, very effectively took over the task of food provision. The task itself was more realistically and effectively performed. One heard less and less about scarcity, and the boys were actually better fed. Most importantly, the confrontation with scarcity and complaints about ineffective provision now became a face-to-face matter between the house mother, her colleagues in the house and the boys. The boys were thus given an important learning experience for life in the world outside: in learning to deal with scarce resources themselves, not just to complain about them. Initiative and ingenuity were freed. The resources of the estate itself, such as fruit, were better used and gardening by staff and boys developed on a considerable scale to augment food supplies. The therapeutic effects of the change in the staff models presented and in the participation of the boys in the new system can hardly be exaggerated.

There was another important consequence in the matter of ego-development and defences. As the author has described elsewhere (Menzies 1970: 43–85), members of an institution must incorporate and operate to a considerable extent the defences developed in the institution's social system. Here a thoroughly paranoid defence system had developed around the provision of food. The matron was regarded as a 'mean bitch'; if only she were more generous, everything would be all right. Responsibility on the part of the house mothers was converted into blame against the matron and the boys were collusively drawn into the system. This defence was primitive and anti-maturational, but gradually disappeared as the new system developed to be replaced by a more adaptive system of acknowledged responsibility and confrontation with reality.

The implications for staff as superego models may also be evident in the carrying of more mature authority for oneself and one's own behaviour and the replacement of blame of the other by more realistic assessment of oneself and one's own performance.

This is but one example of a series of similar changes that gradually changed the provision by staff of ego, superego and defensive models, the importance of which can hardly be over-stressed for children whose personality development is immature or already damaged or both. The ego and superego strength of staff was both fostered by the changes and given more opportunity to be effectively demonstrated to the children. They in turn were also involved more effectively in control over their own circumstances and given less opportunity to regard themselves as helpless and non-responsible victims of uncontrollable circumstances. It was seen as essential to carry out these other changes so as to achieve consistency and avoid presenting the children with conflicting and confusing models.

Effective delegation implies more than taking responsibility and authority for oneself, however; it implies also that the individual can accept and respect the authority of superiors and be effectively accountable to them, and that he can take authority effectively for his subordinates and hold them in turn accountable for their performance. This is again important in the provision of models for children whose relationship with authority is immature and possibly already disturbed. Thus authority channels must be clear; staff must know to whom they are responsible and for what, and for whom they are responsible and for what.

It seems a fault in many children's institutions that they do not handle authority effectively. There may be too much permissiveness, people being allowed or encouraged to follow their own bent with insufficient accountability, guidance or discipline. If this does not work (and it frequently does not, leading to excessive acting out by both staff and children) it may be replaced in time by an excessively rigid and punitive regime. Both are detrimental to child development. The 'superego' of the institution needs to be authoritative and responsible, though not authoritarian; firm and kindly, but not sloppily permissive.

### Institutional boundaries and the development of identity

An aspect of healthy development in the individual is the establishment of a firm boundary for the self and others across which realistic and effective relationships and transactions can take place and within which a sense of one's own identity can be established. Young children and the damaged children in many institutions have not developed effective boundary control or a firm identity within it, and need help from the institution in doing this. How then can the institution provide models of effective boundary control? The institution as a whole must control its external boundaries and regulate transactions across them so as to protect and facilitate the maintenance of the therapeutic milieu. This function will not be considered in detail, since it is less likely to impinge directly on the children than the management of boundaries within the institution. Any institution is divided into subsystems some of which perform different tasks, as with the education and living subsystems in a residential school. Some of them do the same tasks for different clients, for example a number of houses in the living area. The way these subsystems control their boundaries and conduct transactions across them is of great importance for the development of the children's personal boundaries.

A danger in children's institutions seems to be that the boundaries are too laxly controlled and too permeable and that there is too much intrusion into the subsystem from outside and into the individuals within it. There seems to be something about living in an institution that predisposes people to feel that it is all right to have everything open and public and to claim right of entry to almost everywhere at almost any time. Nothing could be more different from the ordinary family home which tends jealously to guard its boundaries, regulating entry and exit and, particularly, protecting its children both from unwarranted intrusions and from excessive freedom to go out across the boundaries. And nothing could be less helpful to the development of children in institutions.

Problems appear particularly in the children's living space, their homes effectively while they are in the institution. It seems important therefore that these present a model of effective boundary control, with realistically regulated entry and exit by permission of the people in the subsystem, notably the staff, not an open front door through which people wander in and out at will. To put it differently, the members of the subsystem need to take authority for movement in and out.

This was an important aspect of the work in the Cot Unit in the Royal National Orthopaedic Hospital where, at first, the boundaries were much too open. The Unit opened directly into the hospital grounds and people walking there seemed to feel free to drop in and visit children *en passant*, often with very kindly intentions of entertaining and encouraging them. Further, the Cot Unit provided the most convenient means of access to the unit for latency children and people *en route* for that often stopped to spend time with the young children. The physical boundary between the Cot Unit and that for latency children was open and there was a good deal of visiting by older children and their families. Altogether the situation seemed highly inappropriate for the healthy development of the children. Individual children were too often 'intruded into' by strange, even if kindly, adults. Relationships between children, mothers and Unit staff could be disrupted by the visitors, as could the ongoing work of the Unit. So the external door was closed to all except members of the Unit. Unit staff and visiting families had the authority and responsibility to control or prevent unauthorised entry. At first an invisible notice saying 'No Admittance Except on Business' was hung in the space between the two units, and again staff and visiting adults helped to control the boundary. Later, a partition was built that effectively separated the two units and made boundary control much easier. The benefits of this boundary control to the ongoing life of the Unit and to the child patients was inestimable.

But there remained the problem of the large number of people from outside the Unit who had legitimate business there: surgeons, the paediatricians, pathology staff, physiotherapists, and so on. Their crossing of the boundary also needed to be monitored to mitigate possible detrimental effects to the children's boundaries. Small children have not developed effective control of such contacts with people who may be strangers and who may do unpleasant, frightening or painful things to them, such as taking blood samples or putting them on traction. The normal way that such contacts are mediated for the child is through a loving and familiar adult who can comfort the child and negotiate on his behalf. It became the rule that such visitors approach the child through his mother if present, or through his assigned nurse, or both. Sometimes the visitor would be asked not to approach the child for the moment if the intervention could be postponed and if the adult care-taker judged the moment inappropriate, for instance if a child was already upset or asleep. The adults both protected the child's boundaries and presented models of boundary control.

Similarly, the transactions across the boundaries outwards which involved children were carefully monitored. Work was done with other hospital wards and departments to ensure consistency in the principles of care between their work and that of the Cot Unit. There was explicit agreement about where mothers or other family adults could accompany children, and so on.

Effective control over boundaries can have another positive effect on the development of identity. It gives a stronger sense of belonging to what is inside, of there being something comprehensible to identify with, of there being 'my place', or 'our place', where 'I' belong and where 'we' belong together. Children cannot get identity from or identify with a whole large institution. They get their identity through secure containment in a small part of it first, and only through that with the whole.

This raises the related issue of the desirable size of what is contained within the boundary if it is to be comprehensible to the child. Too often, it seems, the basic unit is too big. For example, a hospital ward of, say, twenty beds is too big for the small child, both physically and psychosocially. He cannot 'comprehend' it and risks getting lost and confused. The physical space does not contain him securely within its boundaries and the number of staff is such as to risk multiple indiscriminate care-taking, a care system which is inimical to the establishment of a secure identity since it makes it difficult for the child to become familiar with the identity of the other and to have his own identity consistently reflected back to him by the other (Menzies 1975). The Cot Unit was fortunate in being a twelve-bedded unit, usually less than full, which could be staffed by a staff nurse, three nursery nurses and a nursery teacher during school hours. It was physically quite small and secluded once the partition was built.

An effectively bounded small unit is likely to facilitate the development of an easily identifiable and relatively integrated group within the unit, with the staff as its permanent core. This was important in providing support to children and families in the distressing circumstances of long stay in an orthopaedic hospital and in helping to keep anxiety at tolerable levels. This in turn helped prevent the development of inappropriate and anti-maturational defences. In institutions for disturbed children it may also be important in facilitating therapeutic work with the children within the unit through using the dynamics of the group. In a sense it makes escape from appropriate confrontation with realities inside the unit more difficult and facilitates the process of learning from them.

There are boundaries of a more subtle kind that are also significant in providing models for children, notably the boundaries of authority and responsibility. For example, the authority for running the unit needs to be firmly located in its head and his authority should not be undermined by people from outside, such as his superior, directly intervening inside it. The authority and responsibility for managing the Cot Unit was delegated firmly to the staff nurse, and the ward sister did not cross that boundary although she still held ultimate responsibility and kept in close touch with the work there. The ward sister sustained this, although she found it personally depriving and frustrating to be thus distanced from the young children. Similarly, when the head delegates some tasks to his staff the authority needs to be clear and he should not transgress the boundary by direct intervention.

Problems can arise in institutions if the same people work at different times in different subsystems when their authority and the authority under which they operate can become unclear. For example, teachers in an approved school sometimes work in the living area outside school hours. If they continue to think of themselves as 'teachers' under the authority of the headmaster they are confusing an authority boundary, as the headmaster has no management responsibility for the living system. The headmaster in an approved school much concerned for the welfare of his teachers had to learn – painfully – not to think and talk of 'my staff' when they were working in the living area: similarly the heads of the houses had to learn to think of the 'teachers' as 'their staff' and take authority over them effectively. These may again seem strange preoccupations for people concerned with the care of children in institutions, but they do seem appropriate since confusion or inadequate definition of authority boundaries can confuse staff about who or what they are and threaten their own sense of identity and what they identify with. This confusion will subtly convey itself through their attitudes and behaviour to the children, with detrimental effects on their sense of identity and their development.

The final point on this topic concerns the protection of the boundaries of the self and the management of transactions across them, with particular reference to the processes of projection and introjection and their effect on the sense of self. Excessive projection can and does change in a major way the apparent identities of both the projector and the recipient if he cannot control what he takes in. Both can feel unreal and strange to themselves and both can act strangely and inappropriately. Similarly, inappropriate introjections can create a false identity and an unstable sense of self. It seems to be a crucial responsibility of the staff in children's institutions to control their own boundaries so as to manage the effects of both projection and introjection and hold them within realistic and therapeutic limits. In so doing they will help the children to control their projections and introjections and strengthen the development of a true and stable identity. Young children and disturbed children are likely to project massively into care-takers.

Indeed, it is to some extent a normal method of communication, telling the other what the child is feeling or what for the moment he cannot tolerate in himself. For example, the apparent 'conscience-lessness' of a delinquent child can result from the splitting off and projection of a harsh and primitive superego which is unbearable to the child. The deprived, inadequately mothered child may violently project into the care-takers an idealised mother figure with the demand that the care-taker be that mother and compensate for all his deprivations. The danger for the care-taker, and so for the child, is that the projections may be so compelling that the care-taker acts on them instead of taking them as communications. His personal boundaries are breached, his identity temporarily changed and the transaction ineffectively controlled.

The staff of approved schools, for example, may act on the projected primitive superego and treat the children in a rigid and punitive way which is anti-therapeutic. This represents an acting out by staff with children instead of a therapeutic confrontation with the problem. Or staff can respond to the demands for compensation for early deprivation by an overgratifying regime which is equally anti-therapeutic, since it evades confrontation and real work with the problem.

Similarly, staff must be alert to the introjections and false identifications which children use in their desperate search for a self and a sense of identity. These may lead, for example, to false career ambitions in pseudo-identification with idols, identification with delinquent gangs, or apparent and sudden but false improve-ment based on pseudo-identification with the staff or the principles of the institution.

Inappropriate projections and introjections between children and staff are by no means the only problems. One must also take note of projections and introjections between staff and staff, between children and children and between subsystems. For example, it is fairly common to find in institutions a situation where all subsystems but one are said to be in a good state, but one is in a mess. Frequently, this is less a reality than the results in intergroup projections, subsystems projecting their 'bad' into the one and encapsulating the 'good' in themselves. All such phenomena are, of course, anti-developmental and anti-therapeutic and real progress can be made only in so far as people and subsystems can take back what belongs to them, discard what does not and work with the external and internal reality of their situations.

This has always seemed to me one of the most difficult tasks confronting the staff of children's institutions and one for which they need much help and support. This emphasises the need for the staff to be a close and supportive group able to confront together the projection and introjection systems and to help rescue each other when one or more of them are caught. It requires a culture of honesty and mutual confrontation which is by no means easy to achieve. It requires also a certain permanency and long-standing relationship between the staff which is notoriously difficult to sustain in children's institutions, which tend to have a high labour turnover.

A consultant from outside the group who can view the situation with a 'semi-detached' eye may be a great help here in understanding with staff the nature of the projections and introjections and helping to re-establish the basic identity of both the staff group and the individuals with it.

## Institutional provision for the development of the capacity for relationships

The theoretical basis for the discussion here lies in the work of John Bowlby (Bowlby 1969) and many co-workers. Briefly, the capacity to develop lasting and meaningful relationships develops in accordance with the opportunity the child, especially the very young child, has to form secure attachments. The good ordinary family gives an excellent opportunity where the young child is likely to form a focal intense attachment, usually (though not always) with his mother. He forms other important although less intense attachments with others including his father, siblings, other relatives and friends, his attachment circle extending as he grows older. Moreover, the people in his circle of attachment also have attachments to each other which are important to him for identification. He not only loves his mother as he experiences her but identifies with his father loving his mother and extends his 'concept' of the male loving the female. For the most part, although not always, institutions have dismally failed to replicate that pattern. The multiple indiscriminate care-taking system in which all staff indiscriminately care for all children effectively prevents child–adult attachment. This has been traditional in hospitals and can also be seen in day and residential institutions for physically healthy children. The Robertsons' films about John (Robertson and Robertson 1969a,

1969b) show how multiple indiscriminate care-taking effectively defeats John's efforts to attach himself to one nurse. Further, it has been my experience that multiple indiscriminate care-taking also tends to inhibit attachments between staff so that there is a dearth of attachment models for the children. The situation is of course often compounded by staff turnover, hospital wards being staffed largely by transitory student nurses and day and residential nurseries tending to have high labour turnover.

I am indebted to my colleague Alastair Bain (Bain and Barnett 1980) for a dramatic observation of the child's identification with an inadequate model of relationships in a day nursery and its perpetuation in his later relationships. The observation concerns what he calls 'the discontinuity of care provided even by a single care-taker which occurs when a nursery has to care for a number of children'. He writes:

> Their [the children's] intense needs for individual attention tend to mean that they do not allow the nurse to pay attention to any one child for any length of time; other children will pull at her skirt, want to sit on her lap, push the child who is receiving attention away.

One can see this very clearly in *John*. Bain goes on:

> during the periods between moments of attention, the young child experiences his fellows as also receiving moments of attention. . . . He will also experience as the predominant pattern of relationship between adult and child, a series of discontinuities of attention, a nurse momentarily directing her attention from one child to another. . . . He and his moment are just part of a series of disconnected episodes.

The follow-up of these children showed them to have identified with and to be operating on that model, the model of episodic and discontinuous attention, forming in turn a series of episodic and discontinuous relationships with their world shown through fleeting superficial attachments and also in episodic discontinuous play activities and later in difficulty in sustaining continuous attention at school. I have come to call this the 'butterfly phenomenon': the child flitting rather aimlessly from person to person or activity to activity.

Fortunately, institutions do not have to be like that. It is possible to eliminate multiple indiscriminate care-taking and get closer to the family model. Dividing the institution into small units with firm boundaries as described above provides something more like a family setting, even if it is still somewhat larger. Within that setting attachments between staff and children form more easily. Even further, with an institutional setting it is possible to provide something nearer to a focal care-taker by assigning children to a single staff member for special care and attention. What this would include varies according to circumstances and needs. In the hospital the assigned nurse took special care of the child and his family, helping the mother care for the child when she was present, doing most of the general care herself if the mother was absent. She escorted him to theatre or to post-operative care if the mother was not allowed to be present. She comforted him in distress, talking to him if he was verbal and especially talking through problems. For example, a child was overheard having an imaginary conversation with his absent mother on a toy telephone and saying: 'Mummy, I know I've been a naughty boy and that's why you don't come to see me.' The nurse picked that up and worked with the child about it. In residential settings there may be the importance of bedtime for deprived children, of outings like dental or medical visits, playing together, working with distress and problems, having a special relationship with the child and his family together if he is still in contact with his family.

Workers can never equal the mother's almost total availability to the young child since staff have limited working hours, but experience has shown that deep and meaningful attachments can be formed between the child and the assigned care-taker. For example, in the Royal National Orthopaedic Hospital, a small boy came from overseas: his pregnant mother, with a large family of other children, could not accompany him and his father could rarely visit. The assigned nurse developed a closely attached relationship with him (her other assigned children having mothers present). She not only did general care but talked to him about his family, of which the boy had photographs, thus establishing some continuity. She also helped prepare him for going home to find a new baby by talking, by doll play and by relating to babies, of whom there were always some in the Unit. It was very moving to watch them together. Parting when it came was very painful for both, but for both the rewards were enormous. In particular, the child's capacity for attachment was sustained.

The gaps in the availability of the focal care-taker are difficult for the child, but not impossible to handle. In small, firmly bounded units children do form subsidiary attachments to other adults, and indeed to each other, and the care-taking need not become indiscriminate. The Cot Unit had explicit reassignment plans when the assigned nurse was off-duty. Further, with older children in residential settings, adults can and indeed must also relate in an attached way to groups of children engaging in enjoyable activities with the group or handling the group in a state of distress or crisis.

In addition, the small bounded group gives a good setting for the adults to form meaningful relationships with each other. This not only again provides good models of attachment behaviour but also facilitates reassignment when necessary. The child tends to accept the second adult more easily and to use him better if he has seen him in a good relationship with the first. In the hospital, for instance, when a child was admitted and accompanied by his mother, the nurse would frequently have relatively little to do with the child at first, but concentrated on building her relationship with the mother. The good relationship they established undoubtedly helped the child accept the nurse if and when the mother had to leave, and begin to form an attachment to her.

My references to transitory staff and high labour turnover may seem to suggest that attachments are always under threat from adults learning. But, in fact, we found that in units operated as described there would be a dramatic fall in staff turnover. The Royal National Orthopaedic Hospital was fortunate that the Cot Unit was staffed by nursery nurses who were permanent staff and not by transitory student nurses. But in a profession, nursery training, that notoriously has an enormously high labour turnover, there was almost no labour turnover during the study and as the care method developed all three nursery nurses stayed over three years, an inestimable benefit for long-stay and repeat-stay children. The work had in fact become more challenging and rewarding and the attachment to the children increased the nurses' wish and sense of responsibility to stay with the children.

The work is not only more rewarding, however, it is also more stressful. Multiple indiscriminate care-taking can in fact be seen as a defence for staff against making meaningful and deep contact with any one child and his family, a contact which frees the child's expressiveness and makes the care-taker more fully in touch with his distress and problems as well as his joys. It can be quite shattering temporarily for staff to move from multiple indiscriminate care-taking to case-assignment, a move which may include the disruption of concepts about what a child is like. One staff nurse said: 'I have had to unlearn everything I thought I knew about children since you [the author] have been here.' Too often staff think of the healthy normal child as one who is 'settled', calm, accepting of everyone who approaches him, relatively unprotesting about what is done to him. They need to learn that in the abnormal circumstances of the hospital, the 'normal' child is likely to be frightened or miserable quite a lot of the time, to protest at interventions, to object to the presence of strangers and to be apparently more difficult – certainly a more distressing child for adults to work with.

Again the staff may need help with this – help that can come from a strong attached staff group who support and care for each other, from senior staff, or from an outside consultant. In a sense one may say that the staff need to experience the same concern and support for their stresses as they are expected to provide for children and families, a consistency in the method of care.

I will conclude this section by trying to draw together some of the points I have made within a rather different theoretical framework. Bion (1967) has described the importance for the infant's development of his mother's capacity for reverie – that is, how she takes in his communications, contains and ponders over them intuitively but not necessarily consciously, and responds to them in a meaningful way. It is particularly important, in relation to fear and distress, that the mother can take in his projections and return them to the infant in a more realistic and tolerable version. The function of reverie is important also for staff in children's institutions. It can be reverie in the individual staff member or it can be something analogous to reverie in group situations, staff talking things through in an intuitive way together. The communications on which staff must work are often massive and very disturbing and staff in turn need support of the kind I have mentioned. Like the ordinary devoted mother (Winnicott 1958) they need themselves to be contained in a system of meaningful attachments if they are to contain the children effectively. They need firmly bounded situations in which to work and they need the support of being able to talk things through in quieter circumstances away from the core of the children's distress and problems.

## The developmental effect of the institution's social defence system

The author has described elsewhere the development and operation of the social defence system in institutions (Menzies 1970). The institution develops, by collusive interaction among its members, a system of defences which appear in the structure, the mode of functioning and the culture of the institution. Continued membership tends to involve acceptance and operation of the accepted social defence system, at least while present in the institution. However, the social defence system is sustained and operated by individuals, notably staff members, and this plays a part in their effectiveness as models for identification. There appears to be a need for constant vigilance if the defence system operated in the institution is to be sustained at a mature level and indeed to be adaptive rather than defensive, for it will be under constant threat. It will be under threat because the stress and disturbance present in the children will predispose staff to use massive defences against confronting the disturbance in a painful although potentially therapeutic way. I have referred to multiple indiscriminate care-taking as one such defence. It can be associated with massive denial of the meaning of the children's communications, with a manic defence that denies its seriousness, with rigid punitive regimes which try to control disturbance rather than working it through. I also described above a paranoid defence system connected with the evasion of a difficult responsibility.

The children may be a threat in another way in that they in turn tend to operate massive and primitive defences against their distress which are in turn not only individual but also tend to become socialised as they relate to each other in various group situations. This may have a powerful effect on staff, who are usually outnumbered by children as the children try to force staff to enter into collusion with their social defence system. Hard work, courage and suffering are often needed if staff are to resist these pressures and sustain more mature defences as a model and as a facilitation of confronting and working through problems.

In the world of approved schools and institutions for delinquents such phenomena are known as subcultures in which problems such as homosexuality or violence are acted out away from staff or, sadly, sometimes with them, and are recognised to be inimical to the therapeutic culture of the institution.

Work done on a consultancy visit to an approved school may illustrate this. I was told first by professional staff that there was great discontent among the domestic staff in the living units. They felt they could not achieve a high enough standard of work and were not getting job satisfaction. I was at first unclear what I was supposed to do about this, but gradually I felt I was beginning to understand. I heard a lot about violence among boys, of which there had recently been more than usual – some of it very destructive. More than usually violent boys were said to have been admitted recently or were about to be admitted to the school. The professional staff were not only afraid of the boys' violence, but were anxious also about the impulses to counter violence they felt in themselves. Up to that point, they had not felt able to confront the violence adequately as a problem to be worked at. Instead they had developed an anti-therapeutic and subcultural method of trying to prevent it, by gratification and appeasement. They hoped, not necessarily consciously, that if they provided a very high standard of care in living units, they could in effect keep the boys quiet. Professional staff then put subtle pressures on domestic workers to provide a quite unrealistic living standard, a pressure which the domestic workers in turn accepted and tried to put into operation. In reality they could not and consequently suffered painful feelings of inadequacy and failure. We disentangled this in the course of a long day's discussion during which professional staff faced their fears of violence more openly, realised that developing a subculture of dependency to counter a subculture of violence was not likely in fact to deal with the violence or to be therapeutic, and so became more able to work with the violence directly. The domestic workers were relieved of the projections into and pressures on them and could once again apply themselves to a realistically defined task from which they got satisfaction.[1]

Such subcultures are perhaps less likely to appear in institutions which have the features I have suggested as more appropriate for the development of the healthy self in the children – for example, authoritative, responsible staff, well-defined delegation, small, fairly bounded units, effective opportunities for reverie. But no institution is likely to void them fully; hence my comment about the need for constant vigilance, possibly again with the help of a consultant.

# CONCLUSION

I hope I have succeeded in justifying my optimistic view that institutions for children can be developed in such a way as to provide more effectively for the development of a healthy self than has too often been the case in the past and, unfortunately, is still too often the case in the present. Changes in the desired direction can and have been achieved in institutions, although often at the cost of considerable turmoil, doubt and uncertainty among staff while they are being made.

The effect of such developments on children has been encouraging. At the Royal National Orthopaedic Hospital, no children who had been hospitalised under the new care system showed the typical signs of institutionalisation or of any serious damage to their development. There were problems but none serious, nor of a kind that could not be contained in the families and worked with there. Some of the children, indeed, seemed to have gained rather than lost ground. We acknowledge with respect and gratitude the major contribution many mothers made to this result, but it was also evident in unmothered children. I have already mentioned one small boy from overseas who actually developed well, but perhaps the most dramatic example was another small boy with foreign parents who were in this country but who very rarely visited. When the mother did come, she could not really make a relationship with him but only carried out a few simple tasks usually designed to make him look more like a boy from his own country. This was almost meaningless. On admission at nearly 4 years old he had no language, neither his own nor English, and had most violent temper tantrums so that, for example, due notice had to be given of interventions, so that he could be given tranquillisers in advance. Everyone except the author diagnosed him as mentally defective. The author diagnosed him as psychotic, not only on the direct evidence he presented but also from his history.

He had been driven from pillar to post, from foster home to residential nursery, day nursery and round and round again. He had passed much time in inadequate children's institutions with no attachment, no containment, no good models. During his thirteen months in hospital (the longest continuous stay of any child) he was devotedly cared for by his assigned nurse and the nursery teacher especially, but also by other staff in the small, close attachment circle of the Unit. When he left he had an age-appropriate

English vocabulary, had completely lost his temper tantrums, and had begun to use toys and other methods to work over in a constructive way his hospital experience. A fortunate coincidence for him was that the staff nurse had to resign her post for family reasons and decided to foster children as a means of working at home. She took the boy home with her, thus sustaining an important attachment. He then continued to develop well and settled well into a normal school.

The results in the desperately damaged boys in the approved school do not usually match up to that level, but it is notable that there is in general much less acting out in the school, fewer abscondings, less violence and much more constructive activity than one usually finds in such institutions. The results are also above average in terms of life performance in general and, in particular, in fewer of the repeated delinquencies that take so many such boys later into other institutions like Borstals, prisons or mental hospitals.

Much remains to be done, however, to convert other children's institutions into places more suitable for children to grow up in a healthy way. Since powerful pressures are now evident in our society to put children into institutions, there appears to be an urgent and serious need to improve these institutions if children are to be given the best opportunities for development and the 'vicious circle' effect of early institutionalisation prevented, such as delinquency, mental illness, or repeated institutionalisation.

## NOTE

1   What I have described as subcultures of violence and dependency are closely linked with Bion's formulation of basic assumptions of fight/flight and dependency as observed in small groups (Bion 1961). The point Bion makes about the basic assumptions is that they are characterised by psychotic phenomena, are evasive of reality instead of confronting it, and do not evidence a belief in work as a means of carrying out tasks or in the time and suffering needed to do so. So they are anti-therapeutic.

# Chapter 18

# Issues in residential work

*Christine Bradley*

Those who work in the field of residential care of children and young people often feel that the commitment and concern they offer to the children they are responsible for goes unrecognised by those engaged in other professions. At times it seems as though they are used merely as a dumping ground for children whose emotional lives are in such a state of anxiety, panic and rage that they are unable to be contained in any other setting. All too often there are not the resources available to support and train care staff effectively. It is, therefore, of little wonder that staff, who are not sufficiently equipped to understand and meet the needs of such children, become overwhelmed by the primitive forces of their behaviour and fall into misinformed and unprofessional practice. When the outside world is aware of what is happening there is a public outcry, with the staff being accused of either being too permissive or too punishing towards the children. In some circumstances such an outcry is valid, although at times not enough thought is given to the difficulties involved in creating an environment where staff and children can co-exist satisfactorily. It is no simple task to establish a structure which will enable both staff and management to assess the emotional needs of the children and develop effective treatment programmes geared to meeting these needs.

To understand the dynamics involved in developing such a process we must examine what must be the experience of the child who is in need of residential care.

> Children are especially vulnerable to disturbance, their emotional immaturity makes it difficult for them to discriminate between fantasy and reality. Events in childhood or within their

families can either strengthen their capacity for healthy development or lead to self destructive relationships, or a damaged capacity to make healthy relationships.

(Passey 1994: 172)

For the majority of children in residential care, sadly this has often been the case in an extreme form, and physical, sexual and emotional abuse has been a central part of their life experience. Many of them have grown up believing that the psychic pain they have endured is a part of childhood. When they discover that many other children have not experienced such abuse but have known a childhood which contains predominantly happy memories, it makes them even more aware of their unhappiness and emotional vulnerability. They begin to believe that the primitive and self-destructive feelings which have overwhelmed them in their life will always be there and that they have no choice but to act out, against others and towards themselves.

Robin Balbernie, in his paper 'Looking at what professional carers do: the therapeutic context and conditions of change' (1993), writes, 'A child's relationship to his or her parents determines his or her inner world and the earlier this is disturbed or traumatized then the greater will be the consequent pathology. Here we are considering such fundamental areas as the establishment of the attachment and basic trust, and the growth of ego-integration.' If we apply this statement to children in residential care, we realise that for the majority of them their inner world has been disrupted at a very early stage of development. Often, vulnerable parents have been unable to provide them with the emotional containment, consistency and reliability necessary to enable the child to develop sufficient strength of ego identity. If this is compounded by a series of rejecting and abusive situations, it is not surprising that, by the time they arrive in residential care, they are suspicious and hostile towards those caring for them.

Let us think about the child who has been removed from such a family setting and the response he may have to this action. Possibly there is relief at being taken from the situation which was fraught with anxiety and fear, whilst at the same time anger at those who have removed him and placed him somewhere they consider more suitable. If the child has experienced the parent or carer as rejecting and abusive then in residential care she/he may well 'idealise that person' for fear of recognising the true hostility and rage they feel towards them. The residential worker will receive the negativity which belongs to the actual parent. If the worker does not understand that the child needs to split these feelings, it will be difficult for them to cope with the anger and they may find themselves reacting inappropriately to that child. Alternatively, there may well have been a genuine love between the parent and child but because of the extreme vulnerability of the adult the child has had to assume the parenting role, and has become the care-taker. The pressure and the responsibility become unbearable for them. In this case the child experiences excessive anxiety and guilt at leaving that person and needs constant reassurance that they are still intact. At the same time the child needs to be helped within the residential setting to relinquish the adult role and to be able to become a child with needs of their own to be met.

Whatever is the context of their separation they bring with them their inner set of personal experiences and feelings which need to be listened to and accepted by those caring for them in the residential setting if there is to be any possibility of recovery from the original trauma.

I have been thinking about the position of children and staff in residential care and it seems to me nothing short of a miracle that there are not many more crises which occur in these settings. Indeed, there are a great many community centres and children's homes which provide children with extremely satisfying nurturing experiences and where considerable appropriate emotional involvement is achieved. It is only with this kind of involvement that effective communication becomes established and the child really feels that their helplessness is being heard and listened to. Through this experience the possibility of hope becomes a bearable thought but without this kind of involvement the child remains convinced of the impossibility of change and is stuck in an anti-social, often subcultural, way of living. In the present climate of allegations and child protection issues such involvement can come up against much criticism. However, as Mrs Dockar Drysdale said in her book *The Provision of Primary Experience*, 'I do not believe that therapeutic management can be achieved without considerable involvement – something stronger and perhaps more primitive than empathy' (Dockar Drysdale 1990).

Good child care practice is crucial. Increasingly, however, children in need of residential care are emotionally disturbed at a very deep level and without effective therapeutic management it is

not possible to help them recover from this disturbance. By therapeutic management I mean a plan which is established for the child
that is geared to his/her individual needs within the context of a
relationship with a grown-up who is able to be sufficiently preoccupied in such a way that the child comes to depend upon the
provision offered. The reliability of this provision makes them feel
that they really do exist in relationship to that person, a feeling
they have rarely experienced before. It is only then that the child
is able to communicate fully about his inner hurts.

Communication rarely comes easily for the child in residential
care, and those working with such children have to be particularly
sensitive to some of the precarious ways in which they do let their
feelings be known, which is often not through words. In many
cases their emotional pain and conflict happened at a time when
they did not have the words with which to express themselves.
Often they have experienced words as attacking and annihilating.
Unless the worker is able to achieve effective communication with
the child at this very primitive level, the child will continue to feel
that the depth of his inner turmoil is such that he is in complete
isolation with it, and that nobody could survive the level of his
pain. If this continues to be the case and the workers are not able
to reach this part of the child's world then it is inevitable that
the child will 'act out' their turmoil in an unacceptable and often
delinquent way.

How would we define the therapeutic quality of communication
needed to perform this task? The group of students I was teaching
on a therapeutic child care course recently defined therapeutic
communication as follows:

> It must be based on an understanding through a relationship
> – the worker must be aware of what the child is saying, verbally,
> and non-verbally, and must be open to questions from the child.
> Such communication heals, offers comfort and unconditional
> acceptance and promotes change.

The following case example from Samantha Morgan, a Residential
Social Worker at the Caldecott Community, illustrates the precarious state children find themselves in once they become attached to
workers, and highlights the importance of the worker allowing
themselves to be open and responsive to the child's communication
once it emerges.

Brian had some good experience as a baby, but there was a

failure of maternal preoccupation. He was seen by his mother in retrospect as 'a demanding baby'. From six months Brian could not tolerate being separated from his mother. She had to tie him to her side throughout the day because he screamed uncontrollably if she put him down, eventually this became unbearable for her and she ceased to keep him with her. Now Brian is demanding because his primary needs have never been successfully addressed and satisfied. Brian also has a very strong disruptive and attacking force and one has the sense that as an infant Brian demanded a great degree of containment on the part of his mother. Brian to this day continues to be an uncontained child. His feelings can be very powerful, and are thus experienced by him and others as overwhelming. He is unable to contain his anger and destructive feelings, and projects them outwards onto another. The recipient of Brian's negativity is then ferociously attacked by Brian. He can be very violent. His violence tends to erupt after hearing what he wants has been refused. He cannot tolerate the difference between his inner reality and outer reality. Reality does not accord with Brian's inner reality particularly if it involves a need Brian cannot tolerate.

His real self is at the developmental stage of a baby, but he has created his own 'caretaker' self to take care of the baby whom nobody else is allowed to reach. He attacks and rejects help and experiences it as threatening and even intrusive. It *is* threatening because he risks undergoing a deep and needed dependency which is terrifying as the person he becomes dependent upon may abandon him. This was his experience when he was very small. As a 'caretaker' self Brian has often referred to himself as a 'middle-aged child'. The caretaker, not surprisingly, often fails to take care of the real self.

Samantha Morgan writes:

Brian is a very needy child and he talks of gobbling-up those he is attached to. On a number of occasions he has told me that I am the food he loves, and has said, for instance, 'you are my low fat custard, Sam'. In recent months he has begun to hand over his caretaker part to me. I have consistently been the adult carer of Brian's bunny rabbit, Tom, from the day it came into his care four months ago. Tom, is a symbol of Brian's little self, through which we communicate. I have cared unconditionally for Tom's primary needs whilst Brian watches. He has said whilst watching,

'I wish I was Tom'. The initial stage of the transference of Brian's caretaker self to me produced three weeks of constant violence directed at me. Having moved through that phase, he has been tactile, affectionate and very possessive not wanting to share me with the other children or adults. Brian has since been faced with my absence for a two-week holiday. Two days before I left Brian became very violent and distressed. He spoke of suicide, and repeatedly threw himself on the back of an armchair, while being caught by a member of staff. Brian significantly said there was no one else who could care for Tom, and I was not to tell anyone how one cares for him. Brian alternated in saying, on the one hand, 'I will have to tell someone how to care for Tom' and on the other, that he was not going to tell anyone and Tom was going to die. On the one hand he was angrily taking back, in my absence, the responsibilities of his caretaker self and on the other hand his rage at being 'abandoned' was so intense that he was preferring to murder his little self. Pain was uncontainable and unbearable so it was better if Tom – the baby Brian – was denied the real emotions of existing. Assurances of constant contact from me and leaving something of mine to look after seemed to help a little.

(Morgan 1994)

The responsibility Samantha experienced with Brian once he became dependent on her highlights the awesome and responsible task of the residential worker. It is all too rarely recognised by those to whom they are professionally accountable.

To be in a position where they can offer the child the quality of involvement and emotional provision necessary, the worker is placed in an extremely vulnerable position. 'They are working in an involved and undefended way, only thus can they provide the primary experiences needed' (Dockar Drysdale 1990: 3).

As soon as the child begins to feel emotionally located with a worker they will transfer many of their unresolved feelings of hostility and conflict from previous relationships, which for sensitive and intuitive workers can feel unbearable. The worker is being asked to meet the emotional needs of these very damaged children, to provide some of the missed primary nurturing experiences they should have had in early life, to offer the child cultural opportunities and to help them to develop a value system which mothers and fathers would provide; yet at the same time the workers have to remember that they are none of these! To allow themselves or the child to create an illusion that they could become the *actual* parent is dangerous and misleading and can often result in the child developing fantasies about them which both would find extremely difficult to deal with.

In this profoundly demanding relationship child care workers are enormously vulnerable and this may well open up emotional wounds for them. In fact, it is not possible to have true empathy and understanding for the child without this happening and, without adequate support, supervision and training, the workers could become confused and overwhelmed. They will be in danger of either over-reacting to the children or becoming depressed and then leaving the work. If workers are to meet the needs of the children in their care with reliability, consistency and responsibility then it is important that they experience their own supervision with the same quality.

> We have often seen very competent workers reduced to severe doubts about themselves and their abilities to function in the work through absorbing disturbances from clients. The supervisor's role is not just to reassure the worker, but to allow the emotional disturbance to be felt within the safer setting of the supervisory relationship, where it can be survived, reflected upon and learnt from.
>
> (Hawkins and Shohet [1989] 1993: 4)

It is all too easy, given some of the stressful situations residential workers find themselves in, to neglect the basic requirements necessary to enable them to survive, of which good supervision is the most urgent. One of the most difficult feelings for workers to live with is that of the destruction of their self-esteem. The projection of the child's lack of self-worth and dreadful feelings can without adequate supervision lock the worker into feelings of negativity towards the child and they begin to feel that the task in hand is an impossible one. Good supervision can enable the worker to feel better about themselves and, as with good training, can help to objectify feelings and ideas which have become subjective.

For workers to undertake therapeutic work there has to be a way in which they can assess the impact of deprivation in order that they can determine the child's level of ego integration. This makes it possible for them to develop a treatment plan for the child appropriately and ensures that the therapeutic relationship between a worker and a child is safely contained within a structured conceptual framework.

At the Caldecott Community the use of a need assessment developed by Dockar Drysdale in 1970, has proved a valuable tool for this purpose. On the assessment form basic questions are asked.

1  Does this child panic? (a state of unthinkable anxiety)
2  Does he disrupt?

If the answer to both these questions is yes then it is quite likely that the child is in an 'unintegrated state', and his level of ego identity is at its best fragile. His level of unintegration is then measured upon levels of personal guilt, dependence on a person, potential for merger, ability to feel empathy, ability to cope with stress, levels of communication, identification, depression and aggression, and also the capacity to play. If these questions are answered by a group of workers it is possible to formulate a treatment programme for the child, which enables the group to meet both his individual and group needs. The following example from Julian Brooks, a worker at the Caldecott Community, will illustrate the use of such a programme.

John had an emotionally deprived first two and a half years of life. He was taken into foster care and looked after by an elderly woman who appears to have sexually abused him. At 6 he was taken into a children's home. An adoptive family was found for him when he was 8 and this broke down quickly, fuelled by the jealousy of another adopted son. When he arrived at the Caldecott Community he was extremely chaotic and appeared to be fixed at an early developmental stage. A need assessment was completed on him.

The answer to the question 'Does he panic?' was 'Yes – he can often feel very unsafe and become aggressive and chaotic'; to 'Does he disrupt?' was 'Yes – both consciously and unconsciously'.

Answering the rest of the questions it emerged that, although John showed signs of guilt and had become dependent, he merged with others and under stress became aggressive and sexualised. He could often communicate symbolically through play, but could not reach depression. He appeared to be blocked and denied feelings. He had a rich vein of play and appeared more comfortable communicating in this way than verbally. Through his assessment it was determined that John had large pockets of his personality which were emotionally frozen and difficult to reach. Having completed an assessment on him it was now possible to develop ways of adapting to his emotional needs, which hopefully will help him move on from his angry and sad state.

Julian Brooks writes:

When I first became his key worker he was in a fragile state, destroying his room and acting out delinquently. I first concentrated on his basic child care which included the continual tidying of his room. I moved his bed away from the window as he explained about having graphic nightmares of people coming through the window to get him. He was also picking up sound from other areas of the unit which carried round to his room through the vacant loft spaces, adding further to his distressing fantasy that people were out on the roof.

I formed a very close working partnership with my co-keyworker, and we made two fundamental adaptations to his particular needs. The first was my consistent reading of a book about rabbits called *Watership Down*, which became a special book which I only read to him at his special settling time for fifteen minutes at bedtime. This, in due course helped to stir his interest in stories and facilitated immense progress at school. The second piece of therapeutic management that brought him a dividend was special food. First, tomatoes, which helped to stave off stress and anxiety. Secondly, he has a passion for Marmite which he is allowed to take directly from the pot in his room, rather than having it spread on toast. Soon he was collecting Marmite pots of varying sizes on his shelf. A little later I noticed he was arranging them into family constellations and this was a valuable means of symbolic communication which helped me to communicate with him about his family.

During these months John appeared to feel more safe and contained. He curtailed much of his delinquency and running away and made rapid progress in school. He retained an outlet for his negative feelings, aggression and sexualization by dumping it on one female member of staff. This went awry when she left the group and there was a feeling I had at the time that John might have fantasized about having killed her off. He began to internalize his anxiety and became extremely manic in his behaviour, more delinquent and unmanageable through the summer. Then his female key-worker announced she was pregnant and would be leaving by Christmas. This threw up issues of jealousy of the pregnancy and anxiety at the forthcoming separation from and loss of the staff member to whom he was most attached. I too was promoted to assistant manager and had been moving out of a key-working role with him.

With all this happening at once, he regressed back to the kind of uncontained, less integrated state he was in when I first came. He had also initiated some sexualized contact with a girl in the unit which was stopped before it could get very far and he has become sexualized around female members of staff.

From all this information and observation we now need to come up with a treatment programme for John and here the use of a twenty-four hour management programme sheet is helpful. The programme has been devised with participation of the entire staff team, after the discussion upon John's needs and the therapeutic management required.

**Management plan**

*Waking/getting up*

To be woken at eight, staff to check whether the bed is wet and to remove sheets for washing if necessary. Space given before breakfast to talk about dreams and nightmares. Help with brushing hair and teeth, doing tie, buttons etc. Marmite and warm water as a morning drink.

*Meal times*

Needs to sit with an adult and be encouraged to use knife and fork properly and to try different foods. Adult to keep John at the table and to concentrate on eating. Needs reminding to use toilet and wash hands before meals. Adults to be aware of possible mergers.

*In-between times*

High level of pre-occupation with adults. Encourage play and monitor television programmes. Anticipate mergers and panics and confront with firm boundaries. Look for opportunities for nurturing experiences.

*Behaviour in groups*

Adult support through group discussions and playing with peers. Adult supervision and anticipation of mergers.

*Communication*

Communication encouraged using playroom, life story work and special time. Localized regression only with key-workers. Other adults to encourage age appropriate speech and actions.

*To and from school*

John to walk to and from school with an adult holding his hand. Clear hand-over between school and group.

Work closely with teachers to keep John in class until an adult arrives. Very careful management of these transitions required.

*Bedtimes*

Bath on boys' bath nights or in the morning if he has wet the bed. Supper of his choice but no drink. 'Time' given rather than staying up to watch television. Time spent encouraging him to read or read together. Time allowed after 'time' for play, then return to say good-night. Use night light. Always shut window and pull curtains.

*Special needs and adaptations*

Special foods – tomatoes and Marmite – to be given only by key-workers. Save Marmite jars for John to collect.

(Brooks 1994)

This case example shows how progress can be achieved with disturbed children, given an appropriate and adequate structure. However, it is crucial that residential workers have the opportunity for adequate training which equips them with the skills to understand the external influences affecting the children in their care, and also the internal dynamics which have influenced the way in which they view the world. Without a theoretical structure to identify with, I do not think it is possible to engage with the world of the child in a creative and helpful way without becoming over-whelmed and engulfed by their anxieties and fears. Residential work should be seen as a highly specialised task for which workers need a specialist training which offers the possibility of developing the skills essential to perform that task effectively. After several years of no such training being available it is reassuring to see it beginning to appear in the form of a Diploma/MA in Therapeutic Child Care at Reading University and a new Certificate and Diploma in Therapeutic Child Care at Caldecott College in Ashford, Kent. One hopes that in time there will be more of these around the country.

Whatever the task the residential unit decides to take on, there has to be a theoretical conceptual framework within which workers can exercise their skills. Otherwise it is not possible to formulate healing strategies which can effectively meet the emotional needs of children. What is most difficult for residential workers to recognise is that they cannot take away the original damage and cure the child completely. All they can do is to be able to bear the child's pain, listen to them, and offer them the possibility of a more creative way of living. In my experience that is the most difficult and painful realisation for residential workers to absorb. Here one has to remember the words of Winnicott:

> One-has to allow the possibility that there cannot be a complete destruction of a human individual's capacity for creative living and that, even in the most extreme case of compliance and the establishment of a false personality, hidden away somewhere there exists a secret life that is satisfactory because of its being creative and original to that human being. Its unsatisfactoriness must be measured in terms of it being hidden, its lack of enrich-ment through living experience.
>
> (Winnicott 1969)

In this chapter I have examined and illustrated some of the psychodynamic influences and approaches which, in my view, demonstrably contribute to the development of the residential task as an effective, healing service, part of the community's care for children in desperate need. Winnicott's conviction of an individual's capacity for creative living is supported by the progress made by children who experience the commitment and insightful practice of trained residential child care workers. Such experience is the right of every troubled child.

# Chapter 19

# What is good day care?

*Lynn Barnett*

Summarising some of the major studies that have taken place in non-parental day care recently, McGuire and Earls state: 'These studies suggest that, rather than [children] becoming socialised in day care, the opposite may be taking place' (1991). This chapter summarises the findings of two research projects, and a rare example of putting research findings into practice. Unfortunately the major recommendations, made twenty years ago, are still not implemented in most local authority nurseries.

## 1 THE DESIGN OF A DAY CARE SYSTEM IN A NURSERY SETTING FOR CHILDREN UNDER 5 YEARS (BAIN AND BARNETT 1976, 1980)

### Summary

Action research was carried out at the Tavistock Institute of Human Relations with a grant from the DHSS in 1975–9. The project director was Alistair Bain, the senior social scientist and child psychotherapist was the author and the consultant to the project was Isabel Menzies Lyth, training psychoanalyst and social scientist. There is a dual commitment in action research to study a system (in this case child care) and concurrently to collaborate with members of the system in using the observations and analysis to help to change it in what is regarded as a desirable direction. The research team looked in detail at the social system within which the day nursery operated (social services department, visiting doctors, social workers, etc.); nursery staff (their backgrounds, ways of working and turnover); the children and families (a sample of twelve children (and their families) was followed in the nursery and later at school over the three-year period and assessments were made by an educational psychologist, child psychotherapist and independent observers). The causes of stress to both children and staff were investigated and also the defences employed by staff to avoid stress and experiencing intimacy with the children.

A major conclusion of the study was that exposure to the day nursery was a cause of increased aggression and retarded language development in children and, in some cases, damaged or severely hindered their personality development and their learning potential. On the other hand, the research also indicated that it is possible for a day nursery to function more therapeutically and with an educational role, but that, for this to take place and be sustained, changes in practice and policies are required in staff/children ratios, recruitment, training and role of nursery nurses and matron, structure and organisation of care in the nursery and increased coordination with other professionals. It was found that, as the nursery culture changed from an emphasis on domestic care (cleaning and minding the children), to child care (understanding the behaviour of children and case assignment), the staff turnover was reduced, parental involvement increased and the roles of nurses, matron, teacher and social services department changed.

## Setting

The research was based at what was considered to be one of the best local authority day nurseries in a London borough. Such nurseries are second to child minding in terms of the numbers of children cared for on an all-day basis. They are generally managed by the social services department, within guidelines laid down by the Department of Health and Social Services. Thus there is no statutory regulation, only recommendations, about conditions and levels of staffing so this varies from one local authority to another.

In the nursery we studied, there were forty-seven children from 3 months to 5 years and ten staff (including the matron). Nine were permanent staff and one was temporary from an agency. Most of the staff were young and all (except the Deputy Matron) had been in post for less than a year. Staff turnover was 438 per cent when we arrived. Twenty-five staff had arrived and left the nursery during the previous six months. Also, each member of the permanent staff was, on average, losing fifty-three working days per year. Both sickness rate and staff turnover can be an indication of, among other things, stress and dissatisfaction at work. Both figures decreased considerably during the project.

Children are admitted to some nurseries soon after birth and cared for within the nursery for up to 10½ hours a day. In the study nursery, children were admitted at 3 months old. The opening times were 7.30am to 6.30pm. Children once admitted to a day nursery are likely to be there until they start school at 5 years. Some children in their most formative years therefore spend more of their waking hours in the nursery than in their family. As well as general observations made in the nursery a sample of twelve children and their families was studied, assessed and followed up in great detail.

## Aggression

### i) Individual dynamics

We found that there was a high level of aggression in the nursery children; most had difficulties in this area, for example:

In an observation made of Ricky in the nursery, when aged 3.8 years, he was in turn aggressive with the other children and then seductive. The observer noted at the beginning of the observation that 'Mother didn't say goodbye to the children but said goodbye to the staff and the children showed no reaction when she left'. The observation continues: 'Ricky thumps the head of K and takes K's hand to bump his head with it again'. Five minutes later 'Ricky is now sitting down and takes K's milk'. One minute later 'Ricky pretends to smack K's face, he sings a song and then holds K's hand and claps it up and down'. He says 'Daddy pushed me in the water,' turns to K and says 'and he'll put you in the water'. Then follows a touching scene of affection between himself and a little girl. A few minutes later, he says 'I'll be your friend if you get the car', trying to persuade her to play with him. Three minutes later, he again uses his buying technique, seeing and wanting a child's bike. 'I'll buy you some bubble gum if you let me have it'. He showed protection of his sister and concern about her and another girl's cough, saying that he would get some cough sweets for them, but some minutes later kicks another boy in the spine and makes him cry badly when he suspects, wrongly, that he's made his sister cry. He then takes the car of another child by sheer dominant behaviour.

(Bain and Barnett 1980: Appendix, 4)

For related work see McCartney *et al.* (1985); Melhuish *et al.* (1990); Belsky (1988); Haskins (1985). This is a controversial issue (see Melhuish and Moss 1991; McGurk *et al.* 1993), as findings on aggression in nurseries depend on the quality of the day care and research methodology.

In the nursery we studied, the nurses, because of their youth, inadequate training, own past experiences, the emphasis on physical care, the large numbers of disturbed children, the stress involved in their work and other factors, were not able to be sensitively in touch with the children and deal adequately with their aggression. Nor were they easily able to resist being manipulated into placating behaviour or into giving reassurance, neither of which helps diminish the omnipotence of children's fantasised and real aggressive attacks and their consequent fears of retaliation.

Further, the children, most of whom had come from deprived and traumatic backgrounds, appeared to experience the repeated broken relationships with their nurses not just as further deprivation but also as persecution and punishment. As the project continued the nurses were able to improve their capacity to understand and handle the children's aggression more effectively.

Another factor associated with the aggressive behaviour of the children was their language difficulties. Verbalisation of feelings leads to an increase in control. They had great difficulties in the use of language, particularly expressive language. In comprehensive language only three of the eight sample children were below average, but in expressive language six of the eight sample children were below average. This meant that angry feelings tended to be expressed as indiscriminate aggressive outbursts or attacks on other children or equipment. Language difficulties also affected reading and formal school work. Emotionally and intellectually no children were achieving their potential and some were failing badly at school despite average and above average IQs in all cases (Barnett 1983). Other researchers have found that children receiving day care from more responsive, sensitive and contingent care givers have higher language and cognitive skills (Carew 1980; McCartney 1984; Rubenstein and Howes 1983).

## ii) Institutional factors

We were also interested to discover what institutional factors might lead to increased aggression and stress in the children. We created a measure called 'exposure to the nursery' which consisted of the average number of hours spent daily in the nursery combined with the number of months or years the child had attended. We tested the hypothesis that aggressive behaviour in individual children was related to 'exposure to the nursery' by carrying out a series of paired observations of children in the same room over a period of time: one observation was of a child with a high score on 'exposure to the nursery', the other was of a child with a low score. The behaviour recorded was of aggressive incidents performed by each child either to children, adults, toys or objects. (It was not known by the observer how the child was ranked on 'exposure'.) Firstly, we observed that children with high exposure to the day nursery were more actively involved in aggressive incidents than those with a low exposure. Secondly, when the nursery nurses in the 2–5-year groups rated *all* the children in their particular rooms in terms of their aggression (also their maturity, passivity and disturbance) those rated most aggressive by their nurses had had more 'exposure' to the nursery. What was it then about the structure and culture of the nursery which led to such findings? We found there were several complex factors.

## Pathology of the nursery structure

### i) Discontinuity between nursery and home

At the time we entered the nursery there was little real contact between staff and parents. Thus the children were often subjected to very different routines, ways of communicating and values at home and at the nursery.

At the beginning of the project we observed how children were taken to the nursery by busy mothers on their way to work or left later by non-working mothers. In both cases the mothers' attitude seemed to be that the nursery staff, as experts, were taking over their children. However, dealing with parents was seen as the matron's job; nurses were not trained in this area despite the fact that they were the ones with the intimate day-to-day knowledge of the children they looked after. Nurses could deny their responsibility for a child's behaviour by saying it was the fault of the parents who in turn blamed the staff. This projective system decreased as the project developed and contact between parents and nurses increased through the establishment of parents' meetings and weekly staff and room meetings.

### ii) Multiple indiscriminate care

When the project began, there were two rooms for eight babies (often joined into one room and cared for by only two nurses) and there were three rooms for so-called 'family groups' of children, mainly from 2 to 5 years but sometimes also including children as young as 18 months. This organisation was causing problems for children and staff: toddlers coming into family groups from the babies' room were often upset and disturbed, frequently trampled on and pushed about by other children and they themselves interfered in the more structured activities of the older children. One of the nurses, commenting on the difficulties of being a child in a nursery, said, 'It's we, we, we all the time, not you. It must be very difficult for a child to fit in being an "I" and not a "we"' (Bain and Barnett 1980: 56).

In all the rooms, because any nurse attended to any child at any time, children were prevented from forming an attachment to one nurse and nurses were able to minimise their emotional involvement and communication with the children, all of whom were seen as having more or less the same demands and needs which could be met by any of the nurses. The drawings we asked staff to do were instructive in this respect. We asked the nurses in each room to 'do a drawing of how you, in your room, see the nursery'. The following comments are from Nurse M, who worked in the babies room at the time when there were six babies being cared for indiscriminately by two nurses. She drew only one *named* child in her lap, child O, who, unless he was on her lap, cried constantly. He had thus created for himself a way of becoming 'a person', which the other crawling, faceless children had not.

> Nurse P who worked with Nurse M said, looking at Nurse M's drawing:
> 'That's O – crying'.
> Nurse M: 'He practically lives on my lap so he isn't crying'.
> Nurse M, as she continued the drawing, said at different times:

'I always feel encumbered with the children all around me. This one's a crawling thing'.
'I don't imagine individual children, except for O; the others are just round and about'.

Nurse M drew some feeding bottles on the window sills saying:

'I imagine all these demands for bottles all over the place'.
'I see myself as encumbered all about with crying ones who are pushing the others away'.
'I thought of a mass of children around me'.

(Bain and Barnett 1980: 72)

The resistances to changing this structure of care to a form of case assignment were considerable. Where one nurse becomes responsible for a small number of children in her room, and is 'their' nurse in terms of caring for them through most of the day, the possibilities of forming a stronger attachment are immediately enhanced. However, this directly threatens a nurse's defences against the experience of intimacy with a child and awakening to his normal developmental needs. Thus objections were raised: the present system was all right, the children didn't need it; a child would suffer more when 'his' nurse was away and particularly if 'his' nurse left; to form a strong attachment between nurse and child would weaken the child's attachment to his mother; mothers would resent it and it wasn't practical and wouldn't work because of the shift system, staff leaving and staff absence. However, change did occur despite these objections, and by the end of the project a case assignment system of varying degrees was being used in all five rooms, separate age groups were given separate rooms and a teacher was provided for the 3–5-year-olds. The changes occurred at different times in different rooms and with different intensities, depending on the individual nurses' changing perceptions as to their roles and capacities and the needs of the children and their parents. Change occurred through regular discussions – pairs of 'room nurses' were seen by each member of the project team (the same each week) and there were also regular staff meetings (which included the project team).

What is meant by 'a case assignment system' is that particular nurses were responsible for particular children (lunched with them, put them to bed, washed them, etc.). With this increasingly personalised work, there was a reduction in staff sickness and turnover and less disturbance in new entrants who were given a new attachment figure from the moment they arrived and were helped to separate from their mothers or previous nursery nurses in a planned way.

### iii) Defences against stress and experiencing intimacy with the children

Nursery nurses have to work under intense stress, due to large numbers of small children with similar needs, inadequate staff ratios, highly disturbed children and parents, inadequate staff training with a too narrowly conceived role of nursery nurse leading to under-functioning and a cutting off from feelings. There were also difficulties in local authority organisation and management practices which contributed to the high stress rate. We found, however, that, with changes in working methods, not only were occasional staff absences less, but staff also carefully prepared children when they went on leave or left for other employment.

### iv) Absence of thought and curiosity in nurses

It is literally difficult for nurses to think in such a dependency culture, partly because of all the discontinuity, partly because it is felt that a child will behave in a certain way because of its innate characteristics, not as a result of particular social and emotional situations involving oneself as a nurse. Not surprisingly, child development was measured by physical accomplishments: what could be seen rather than thought about. There was also a belief that others would do the thinking for you. We were seen at first as 'the Experts' who would tell the staff what to do; at first idealised and then resented and rejected as critical interferers. However, these two stages were worked through with the staff and led on to another stage in which they withdrew their projected criticism, expertise and capacity for thought and developed these attributes themselves, together with a greater capacity to be in touch with and deal with, rather than deny, the pain of their work. This was often a difficult and painful experience as it meant facing change in oneself and taking more personal responsibility. The Matron described this when she said she thought the other nursery matrons would probably be expecting a list of instructions to be written down at the end of the project about changes they should make in their nurseries. 'But', she said, 'I can't even explain . . . to my husband so how can I explain . . . to them. It seems to be it's a change in *me* that's taking place, it's very hard to put into words' (touching her heart) (Bain and Barnett 1980: 81).

### v) Fleeting and discontinuous attention in the nursery

With a large number of young children to look after a nurse cannot pay attention to an individual child for more than a second without other children pulling at her skirt, having 'an accident' or behaving in some other attention-seeking way. Thus children experience as a predominant pattern of relationship a series of discontinuities of attention. They internalise no model of continuity of care with sensible beginnings and endings to actions and longish periods of attention to the same thing, but episodic and discontinuous moments. A typical reaction to this is frustration and aggression and an inability to sustain any but a fleeting attachment or interest. The Robertsons (1969a, 1969b, 1989) and Isabel Menzies Lyth (1988) have highlighted the damage caused to children in institutions by exposing them to multiple indiscriminate caretakers and we showed that added damage is caused by discontinuity of care and attention from a single caretaker. It was striking that, when the nursery children were followed up at school, it was, in every case, their lack of capacity to concentrate which was consistently remarked upon by their teachers, e.g. the teacher of a 5-year-old boy who had been in the nursery since he was 2.4 years old said of him: 'He just couldn't sit still . . . for a long time he couldn't do anything and was not interested in work.' One year later his school report reads: 'His behaviour is very variable and he cannot sustain quiet working for periods longer than about ten minutes.'

A girl, aged 6.11, ex-nursery, highly intelligent, was in the lowest reading group in school and was described by her teachers as follows: 'Does the opposite to what is asked for – is the worst child in the class, chats a lot in school . . . not in a defiant way . . . disengages.' During 10 minutes observation of this girl she had written only one word (Bain and Barnett 1980).

## 2 THE MEDIATION OF PSYCHOLOGICAL DISTRESS AND ANXIETY IN A DAY NURSERY (IDEMA 1990; IDEMA AND BARNETT 1990)

In 1990 Mathilde Idema carried out some research in a small seaside town where there was a private non-profit-making nursery for thirty-five children aged from 6 weeks to school age. It had only been open for fifteen months so had no legacy of old day care procedures to overcome. Nevertheless it too operated on the same defensive model of care as had the old Exeter day nursery (see p. 23 below) and the nurseries Bain, Barnett and Menzies Lyth had investigated twenty years earlier. It was open for long hours, there was no case assignment as the nursery practised multiple indiscriminate care- a child might be fed by four different nurses, and comforted by as many in the space of fifteen minutes. The supervisor, a keen advocate of strict nursing routines, periodically devised schedules for each nurse, specifying a particular duty for every fifteen minutes of the day, which often left a nurse at a loss what to do when no specified duty was 'required' of her. No assessments of the children were made on entry and parents were discouraged from staying after the first 'settling-in' morning.

The focus of Idema's work was on observing the communication and behaviour of children and nurses using a mixture of an event-sequential approach and time sampling. She particularly observed separations, distress, aggressive behaviours and attention seeking from nurses.

Because the nursery was under threat of closure for financial reasons, any consistency and continuity of care which did exist was disrupted as parents who could no longer afford the fees withdrew their children and staff were laid off at short notice (usually without preparing the children or even saying goodbye as they found this too painful). With the lack of government money for under-5s provision and encouragement being given instead to the · private sector to make provision, this dire situation will not be uncommon in the future.

Idema's findings may be summarised as follows. Very few *distress events* (distress events included children's overt and covert behaviour, e.g. crying, expressions and body movements) were terminated by nurses comforting the distressed children. *Aggressive behaviour* occurred most frequently in the 1-year-olds while the 3-year-olds showed aggression to objects rather than people. (One wonders whether by this age they had found adults are 'absent' or non-containing.) Aggression, like distress, was dealt with by a 'telling off' or was ignored, rather than being managed and talked about. Where aggression was the result of jealousy or possessiveness of a nurse (i.e. attachment behaviour), shouting and reprimanding by nurses merely increased the aggressive behaviour and did not lead to a good involvement with a nurse.

Idema showed that when there were fewer children in the nursery non-verbal communication between nurses and children improved, but with fewer children nurses spent more time on domestic tasks rather than being with the children. Most parent–child *separations* took less than two minutes in duration from the entry of a parent and child to the nursery to the departure of the parent. Adults thus avoided dealing responsively with children's inevitable anxiety associated with these separations and, of course, it was a way parents defensively tried to deal with their own painful feelings. However, as Bain and Barnett (1980, 1986) and Hopkins (1988) discovered, once parents and nurses are encouraged to be more in touch with their own feelings, they can improve their way of handling both their own and their children's feelings about separations.

Idema's work not only showed that young children's needs, particularly for attachment and comforting, are not met in day care settings where multiple indiscriminate care is practised, but also that the expression of these needs may even be punished and is often ignored. As a result, children learn either to withdraw and become passive (more common in girls) or to escalate their demands into aggression and destructiveness (more common in boys). It was against all expectations and of great concern to Idema that the children under 2 were treated less well than the older ones in that they earned more reprimands and had fewer individual contacts.

## 3 APPLICATION OF THE LONDON RESEARCH IN DEVON (BAIN AND BARNETT 1986 PART 2)

Together with a colleague, the author was invited to join a joint steering committee of the Departments of Health, Social Services and Education, aiming to transform a nursery established pre-war in Exeter into a modern family centre. In the existing nursery physical care was the main focus, staff did much domestic work, multiple indiscriminate care was practised and parents were discouraged from spending time with their children. There were no staff meetings and no records were kept.

With some urban aid money and an additional building, a new principal (no longer called matron) and three members of the Exeter Child Guidance Clinic attending weekly staff and room meetings, many important changes were made. (For a more detailed discussion of the process, see Bain and Barnett 1986 Part 2; also two videos: Barnett 1987, 1989). The major change was in the philosophy of care. The whole family was now seen as needing to be involved in care rather than just individual children, and nurses' roles were reframed to include psychological and educational care, with supervision from the principal who also conducted staff meetings and training events.

*Continuity of care* for children was implemented. This involved individual assessment at entry and home visits by the child's future key worker beforehand; staff were attached to small groups of children on a permanent basis; the centre opened for shorter hours (and there was no longer a shift system for staff); parents' meetings were begun and a parents' newsletter; staff worked regularly with parents together with their children (for example, where attachment problems existed); parent and toddler groups were set up and many of the children attending them continued attending the family centre when older; links were made between staff in the other units of the centre, local playgroups and schools so that transitions both within the centre and outside it could be carefully planned; holiday play schemes for older children, particularly the siblings of those attending the centre, were organised and record keeping was established to record each child's (and parent's) progress. A 'float' member of staff was employed so that strange temporary staff did not need to be brought in to replace staff on sick leave or holidays.

*Educational opportunities* were provided for the older children (the principal was a teacher as were some of the new staff).

*Staff ratios reflected the changing attachment needs of children as they develop.* Thus, there was a higher staff ratio in the units for younger children where there was more work with parents.

*Joint work with other professionals and individual case assignments* were undertaken and there were regular review meetings to which parents and relevant professionals were invited.

All these changes, as in the London nursery, led to a dramatic reduction in sick leave and staff turnover as staff took more responsibility for 'their' children and families and their work, as a consequence, became more rewarding.

The changes came about largely through the staff being given time and space (and the support of a skilled outside 'consultant') to think about their work and its implications – not only for the children, but also for themselves. Through this process came the change in the philosophy of child care from impersonal 'minding' to more intimate 'caring'.

In the London situation the researchers acted as catalysts, or agents of change, while in the Devon Family Centre the child guidance team supported and encouraged the newly appointed principal in implementing shared ideas, as well as regularly consulting with the staff of each room.

Thus, the vehicle of change was through discussion: some, more general, which took place at the newly introduced staff meetings and some, more specific and personal, at the new weekly room meetings. It was in the latter that staff built up enough trust to begin to explore with their 'consultant' their personal feelings and anxieties about their difficult work.

Such discussion took a different form at weekly meetings with staff from seven different infant care nurseries which took place at the Tavistock Clinic over six months. They were conducted by child psychotherapists Juliet Hopkins and Dilys Daws.

> The changes achieved through the group discussions were reached through combining the nurses' knowledge and experience with the group leaders' psychoanalytic understanding of group processes and child development. The group leaders made it clear that they were there to help the group to learn from each other and find their own solutions to problems, rather than to tell them what to do. ... In particular, the leaders' individual interest in them and their work probably contributed to their own growing interest in the individuality of the children in their care, while the leaders' toleration of their feelings helped them to feel more tolerant of the infants, and, to some extent, of the infants' parents.
>
> (Hopkins 1988: 108–9)

In this setting change occurred in the nurses' outlook but, understandably, it did not lead to structural change in their workplaces as this would have needed more intensive consultation.

This brings us full circle from the initial quotation. We know why and how young children learn to become antisocial and unhappy in day care. We also know that changes can be made, both in the ethos and structure of day care to prevent such damage. Who will take on the responsibility for making sure such changes are made?

# Link section

# Social issues

*Marion Bower*

In this section we have focused on some issues which are part of wider social and political concerns. The theme which runs through the chapters in this section is that of human destructiveness, violence and cruelty, its effects on children and its enactment in the wider political sphere. This is an issue worthy of a book in itself, and many of course have been written on this subject. What we have tried to illustrate is the value of psychoanalytic ideas in understanding these processes and some of their practical implications.

In our introductory chapter we referred to the murder of James Bulger. This is by no means the only murder which has been committed by children, but what were particularly disturbing were the sadistic and sexual elements, which emerged only during the trial, and the youth of the murderers. Felicity de Zulueta's chapter reminds us that children are more often the victims of murder. However, her chapter makes it clear that the *roots* of this violence lie in disturbances of the normal attachment processes in childhood.

The family backgrounds of James Bulger's murderers are examples of the type of experiences of rejection and emotional deprivation described by de Zulueta. It is also true that these experiences are common for many children in large cities, and it is hardly surprising that there is concern about the levels of violence in young people; perhaps it is more surprising that it is very rare for children to commit murder.

This raises the question of how human beings come to murder. Freud believed in the existence of a death instinct which operates in all human beings in conflict with the life instinct. The idea of a death instinct was unpopular at the time and has remained so; however, the implications of this theory have been explored by

Paula Heimann. Following Freud, Heimann believed that the force of the death instinct is largely neutralised by a fusion of the two instincts. Heimann suggests that under certain circumstances an 'instinctual disaster' can take place (Heimann 1952: 329), and the two instincts become defused leaving the forces of the death instinct stirring without mitigation by the life instinct. The only way the person can defend themselves is by deflecting this instinct outwards, which takes the form of a murderous act of excessive and merciless cruelty.

This model of the human mind in constant conflict between the impulses of love and constructiveness and those of hate and destructiveness has implications for understanding social relationships. At the time of writing this book the perilous balance existing between the forces for peace and war in Ireland are a vivid illustration of this.

Our remaining two chapters illustrate the interaction between social manifestations of hate and destructiveness and individual experience. Sheila Melzak describes how families are affected by living in political regimes where murder, torture and intimidation are a part of life. She draws attention to the complex interaction which takes place between these externally imposed sufferings and the unconscious inner world.

Savi Mackenzie Smith's chapter describes how racial identity can be used for good or ill as a way of dealing with and organising our emotional needs and experiences. In one case she describes a little girl who needs to be aware of her mixed race identity to understand the meaning her father has in her life and to be able to mourn his death. The other case is a boy who has made black people the carrier of angry feelings about a black stepfather as well as his own more vulnerable feelings. Had this not been dealt with in therapy he might have turned to politically organised racism as an outlet for this feeling. Psychotherapy or psychoanalysis cannot deal with organised racism, but it can give us insight into some of the forces behind it.

In a sense, these chapters strike a positive note, as they draw attention to the human capacity to survive physically and emotionally in the face of terrible adversity, and the capacity that many people have to face psychic pain in the service of personal growth and development.

# Chapter 20

# Cross-cultural issues and racism in a multi-cultural society

*Savi Mackenzie Smith*

## INTRODUCTION

The purpose of this chapter is to convey and consider cultural, cross-cultural and racial issues as experienced in my work as a child psychotherapist. Most inner cities, and especially London, have now become multi-racial. Britain saw an influx of an Afro-Caribbean population who were encouraged to come here in the 1950s to assist with the manual labour shortage. The migrant groups at first settled in ghettos to be with their own people, whilst finding a space in a new environment. They became more and more established and a second generation was born and grew up here. The younger people were accommodated in their local schools. They expected to be treated with the same equality and to enjoy similar advantages as their English counterparts. They did not particularly want to be classed as the future labourers of Britain. Some expected to move into the professional arena.

The 1970s saw another influx of British ex-colonials coming to the country. The Asians from Uganda, India and Pakistan came for protection due to the political unrest in their countries. Most of them looked upon Britain as their only hope and security. Some of these people already had enjoyed being a privileged class in their country and expected to be treated likewise here. Unexpectedly, they experienced being treated as second-class citizens mainly through the racial and cultural background.

Racial identity is classified in an amorphous way into two main categories of black and white. Within these two parameters there are obviously a range of differences in several respects: physically, culturally, religiously and semantically. One could meet a very pale-skinned, green-eyed Asian who spoke fluent English and was a Moslem or Hindu. In contrast, one could meet a fairly dark, sallow-skinned person from the south of France who would be classed as white. Customs, traditions, language and eating habits also vary dramatically. The younger generation are continually caught up in different cross-cultural issues and dynamics. For example, the traditional custom and tendency for most Asian parents to arrange marriages for their daughters and sons is becoming a painful dilemma for the present generation, who are caught up in cross-cultural emotionality. The younger generation often attend school and mix socially with their local peers, enjoying the western life style to some extent.

Present-day Britain also has a population of children from mixed parentage who have difficulties in identifying with any one racial category. As Wilson conveys, 'As children develop in social awareness they come to realise that who or what they are to some extent depends on how society defines them' (1987: 21). She goes on to add, 'The dictates of society become an intrinsic though distinct part of each child's identity.'

## EXTERNAL REALITY

On a superficial level one can easily identify a child or adult from their physical traits. In the external world or visually, identity is recognised by the colour of the skin, colour and texture of the hair and broadly by the language spoken and general mannerisms.

Many years ago my experience of what during present times would possibly be considered as a racial remark was made by a 4-year-old. I stepped on to a bus and sat next to a young English mother and her son, both blonde and blue-eyed. The little boy looked at me intently. I smiled at him and he responded with a tentative one and buried his face into his mother. Intermittently he peeped from that position. His mother smiled at me and encouraged him to say 'Hello'. He promptly said, 'She is chocolate colour!' The mother blushed, looked embarrassed and confused. She quickly explained that they came from a little village where there were no foreigners. A few days ago when he became curious, her father had jokingly associated dark-skinned people with having eaten too many chocolates. She added that she had reprimanded her father for telling him lies and tried to explain to Tom as best as she could. But he has obviously stayed with her father's explanation. She looked concerned and I assured her that I understood.

I jokingly said to Tom that, although I might look like chocolate, he was not going to be able to eat me. The mother laughed and the boy joined in. We chatted pleasantly until they got off. The mother prompted the boy to wave and I reciprocated as the bus moved on.

As our society becomes more alert to such experiences of prejudice it can make it harder to allow such views to emerge and understand what they mean to the individual.

## INTERNAL REALITY

Child psychotherapists focus on the emotionality of the children concerned. This could be conveyed through play, conversationally or by acting out their unconscious phantasies. Very young children cannot always verbalise their feelings distinctly, especially if they are too painful. Sometimes they are not consciously aware of what it is that is making them feel so vulnerable, unhappy, sad, angry, disruptive or aggressive and unsociable, either at school or at home.

Klein explains projection: 'The processes of splitting off parts of the self and projecting them into objects are thus of vital importance for normal development as well as for abnormal object-relations' (Klein 1946: 8–9).

Klein makes it clear that the individual projects bad feelings as well as good, which helps with psychic growth and integration of a good internal object, whereas with projective identification 'these bad parts of the self are meant not only to injure but also to control and to take possession of the object'. The (m)other 'is not felt to be a separate individual but is felt to be the bad self.' Sometimes it is evident that there is often a process of 'projective identification' where much of the bad self is attributed to others because of the unbearable mental pain involved. This pain is then 'acted out' and can be used to externalise an internal conflict.

This is true for both adults and children, although in this chapter I will examine its manifestation in children. These are two clinical vignettes.

## CASE STUDY A

Mark was nearly 11, a red-haired, freckled-faced, tall boy who looked more like a 14-year-old. He was referred to the clinic because he had been expelled from three schools. The question of a suitable school for secondary transfer created obvious problems. His mother in desperation asked for an appointment, saying that Mark needed to sort out his problems. As there were emotional difficulties involved, I was asked to see him. I decided to meet with him and his mother for the initial appointment before arranging anything for Mark individually.

I was surprised to see Mark dressed in a dark suit, looking like a grown up. I was informed by mother that the family unit consisted of just herself and Mark and then as an afterthought she added that there was a lodger who had been with them for about two years. It transpired that he was black and mother's partner. During the interview mother related that Mark had often been in fights with boys at school and more and more it was with black boys. At his last school he had pulled out a knife to attack a black boy, who snatched the knife from him. When it was discovered that it was Mark who had perpetrated the incident he was expelled. Mother also informed me that he had been going to marches with the National Front movement. She accused Mark of being a racist and said that she felt disgusted with his interests and attitude.

Whilst listening and responding to mother's outbursts, I observed that Mark had not so far contributed to the session. He sat with his arms crossed, in a manly fashion and looked very angry and tense. A few times when I tried to engage Mark, mother cut across incessantly or answered for him. When I managed to get a word in, I said, 'I, as you can see, am a black therapist! How do you feel about me trying to help you?' There was complete silence with mother being more shocked than Mark.

For the first time he looked directly at me and then at his mother. Quite vehemently he replied, 'I don't care one way or another. I only came because she pushed me into coming.' He looked exceedingly angry and explosive. I felt slightly uncomfortable and said that I had probably been very directive and placed him in a spot. By now mother had regained her composure and started to apologise profusely.

Surprisingly, Mark turned up for his first assessment session twenty minutes early. Once in the room we discussed a few peripheral matters. I found Mark to be very different to the boy I had met with his mother previously. When I brought up the issue of his fights at school, he shrugged his shoulders and explained that peers constantly 'cussed' him and he retaliated by at first asking them to 'shut up' and if that did not stop them, he hit out. Tentatively I tried to explore the last fight entailing the knife episode. He started to recall the incident fairly calmly, but suddenly became very emotional and screwing up his face shouted, 'I hate myself! I hate her! She is a liar.' Surprised at the response, I gave him a few minutes and said that he was conveying some very strong feelings. Perhaps he would like to explain.

This brought on a deluge of very vibrant feelings and he related the following:

> My mother is a liar. For years she made me believe that Joe, whom she had met soon after coming to London, was my real father. He used to beat me when he came home drunk for no reason. I used to think, 'Why does my father want to hurt me?' I used to ask my mother and she used to say it was because Joe did not know what he was doing when he had too many drinks. I told my cousin one day and she said that Joe was not my real father. My mother only met him when she came from Ireland when I was a year old.

Mark's mother had run away from his father because he was an alcoholic and physically abused her, but she cohabited with Joe who also drank heavily. He looked quite distraught and I could see his eyes go moist, but he did not cry.

It was later that he learnt that his father also had an alcohol problem which was the reason for his mother deserting him. Mark clenched his fists down on the arms of the chair and said disbelievingly, 'She lied. She lied for nearly nine years.' I tried to share with him the pain of experiencing Joe's abuse and the struggle to forgive him, all the while, because he thought he was his father and then came the shattering discovery.

He divulged how on one occasion when Joe physically abused him he kicked him really hard on the groin and Joe doubled over in pain. He thought he had killed Joe and ran out. He was surprised when he later came in to find Joe snoring. He felt both relief and guilt. He tried to make it up with Joe the next day, but Joe could not remember what exactly had happened. Sneeringly he said, 'Too p— to remember anything!' Mark came several times after that and we worked through some very painful experiences. I had almost forgotten that he was supposed to be a racist.

Looking at Mark's behaviour from a psychoanalytical viewpoint I would associate his 'acting out' at school as mainly due to his immense murderous anger, which could be related to the concept of 'projective identification', identification with his father as the aggressor. Later on the 'acting out' of oedipal rivalry aggression towards mother's black partner became evident. The feelings of being physically abused by Joe from a very young age made him feel that he was bad. The pain of being physically abused by a father, who should have loved him and not beaten him, also became psychically unbearable. He split off this part of the ego and perceived it in his peer group in the outer world. He happened to be in an environment where there were more black people than white, resulting in a higher proportion of black children in the schools. The splitting could also be associated with bad as being black and therefore targeting black pupils. The fights at school also started at about the time when his mother did not want to know about Joe's beating of him or made excuses for Joe. Klein (1927) found 'the mechanism of projection important in the externalization of internal conflicts in play with external objects'. She added, 'This form of projection in delinquent acts confirmed Freud's view of criminals who act out of an unconscious sense of guilt.' Mark was a very confused angry boy due to the circumstances he was reared in.

## CASE STUDY B

Liza was a 6-year-old of mixed parentage. Her mother was white English and father Afro-Caribbean. She was referred to the clinic by her mother, saying that she had been a happy child until not long after she had started attending infant school. Her father had died recently but her school refusal problem had started before the sad event. She had settled in well for the first term but almost overnight she became anti-school. She constantly complained of aches and pains. Once it was established that she was going to be at home, she relaxed and was better. The GP could not find any physical reasons for her complaints. He suggested that she contacted us but about that time her husband who had gone into hospital for a routine check up, was told that he should stay for some tests. He was soon afterwards operated on, and died suddenly, after surgery, from a damaged liver in an advanced state of sclerosis.

The mother informed me that she, as well as other members of the family, was puzzled by Liza not shedding a tear or showing any feelings of sadness. 'Liza had been very fond of her father and it might sound odd but, I think she looked relieved when she was told that he had died' was what mother conveyed. She also told me that when the family went to see her husband, Liza had, after a fleeting glance, stepped back and ignored him. The family had thought that she found the sight of her father in hospital too painful to bear. Liza also had nightmares, saying that there was a ghost in the house and that she heard voices. Something she had never done before was to expect her mother to stay with her until she fell off to sleep, which could take hours. In desperation mother had kept her on the sofa downstairs until she herself was ready for bed. Mother's worry was also about how Liza was going to react to returning to school after the holidays.

Liza, who had been quietly drawing a picture of a colourful summer garden, spontaneously called out, 'I'll go to school. I want to see my friends again. I'm not worried about going to school any more.' Mother looked astonished and puzzled. I was trying to think about what might have brought about the sudden change in Liza's attitude regarding school. I tried to explore this by asking her about her friends, hoping that she might enlighten us about what had happened at school, but could not derive anything definite.

The next few sessions were taken up with issues of bereavement and Liza spent much of her time painting or drawing colourful pictures of trees profusely bearing fruit. She remained silent when any reference to her father was made either by me or her mother. I often noticed that Liza smiled at these times but it was a false kind of smile and far from a genuine, happy, childlike smile. It made me feel uneasy, and mother related that the nightmares continued but she did not talk about hearing voices as much. She could not explain what the voices said but that they sounded angry.

On the first day, Liza had gone back to school without presenting any difficulty. She had waved cheerfully to her mother and showed no signs of concern or worry. This continued all week and they came to see me on the Friday. We talked a little about her first week back and she drew me a picture with two figures. She casually mentioned that it was herself and her friend Jade, who was now her best friend. I tentatively tried to explore Liza's experiences at school before the holidays, when the school phobia had started. This developed into my expressing that her father was not around any longer to take or fetch her from school. Liza gave me a strange screwed-up look which prompted me to ask her exploratively if she preferred her Mum taking her to school. She nodded and her mother asked her if she could tell us why. Liza looked a little tearful and then burst out, 'Donna said that Daddy was black. It's disgusting.' I could see mother jerk back as if she had been struck. Liza burst out crying. After a pause and having been comforted by her mother, she was able to respond with more details.

It transpired that when Donna said this about her father she had said to her teacher that Donna had been very rude to her, but could at that time not repeat what Donna had actually said. The teacher, probably thinking that it was some trivial thing, ignored her plea. Liza had not mentioned it at home but her mother recalled that there was something about her attitude towards her father at about that time. She once or twice caught Liza staring at her father in an intense manner. She further informed me that she had met her husband over twenty years ago and that she had never distinguished people by their colour. To her 'people were people for whom they were and not what colour they were'. Her husband, being an intellectual, came to Britain to study. Ever since they had been together, she had thought of him as her husband and partner. The issue of being mixed parents had never created any problems in their household. Interestingly, she did inform me that her two older children were in relationships with white partners. Liza had absolutely adored her father and they had been really close together.

In Liza's conscious world she had never associated black ethnicity as part of herself. There had been no room for such thoughts in her home. She had a pale coloured skin with gingerish, curly, but not tightly knotted hair and identified with her English mother culturally and in all other respects. Donna's reference to her father's colour had an immense impact on her psychically. She found the association unbearable and unconsciously wanted to disown and split it off. From a conscious level she could stay away from school, as that was her only means of dealing with the problem. She therefore somatised the psychic pain and developed all kinds of physical complaints. Her teacher, obviously not realising the seriousness of what Liza was trying to tell her, was unable at the time to deal with her problem. She could not verbalise her feelings and thoughts at home.

In Liza's unconscious phantasy she might have wished her

father to disappear or perhaps even more seriously wished him dead. Perhaps she felt that this might eradicate her blackness altogether as she could not cope with the evidence that she was partly black. In reality and most unfortunately her father died. His death made her think that her phantasies had come true and this terrified her. She strongly felt that she had caused his death, because there came a point in her therapy when she revealed that she had wished that he would go away.

Liza's nightmares fairly soon came to an end and not long afterwards she informed me that she did not hear frightening voices any longer. After almost a year of once weekly psychotherapy, Liza fully accepted that she was not the cause of her father's death. She was a very intelligent girl and settled well in school, producing some excellent work. Her mother said that she socialised more and had both white and black friends. She was able to remember anecdotes involving her father and herself and spoke very fondly of him. She could also talk to me about her feelings about black friends.

Her mother realised that their protected but open-minded lifestyle had made her overlook some of the problems. She could see that she should have taken into account that her children were of mixed parentage and that it would have some repercussions. She often conveyed that things might have been different if she had made her children aware of their mixed ethnicity and arranged for them to be aware of that cultural part of themselves. Her husband, she informed me was a 'true colonial' and British to the core.

As Wilson says 'Mixed race children not only have the dilemma of identification of the two ethnically different parents, but also adjusting to peer groups' (Wilson 1987: 44). She goes on: 'What seems to have happened in the sixties and seventies is that black children's tendency to identify themselves as white has decreased rapidly, whereas their preference for the white race has been more slow to change. "The Black Consciousness Movement" seems to have heightened children's awareness of their blackness and to have eliminated all shame in declaring who they are.'

Unfortunately, this has not been so for Liza. She had not been encouraged to recognise her Afro-Caribbean identity. One white parent does not give her a complete white identity even though she might not show physically any obvious traits of a black parent. Liza had to start to learn about herself from a very different viewpoint.

## CONCLUSION

> All a child's activities and those of adults too, even those most geared to external reality, also express and contain their phantasies. External reality affects our phantasies and our phantasies influence our perceptions of external reality.
>
> (Daniel 1992: 21)

As Daniel conveys, both Mark and Liza displayed their inner phantasies in their respective ways. In Mark's case he was overtly aggressive, to countermand the excessive physical pain and mental pain he had to endure from someone he had hoped would love him. He also experienced immense anger due to his mother's lying. Liza invested her anxieties and the shock of her friend's remark in psychosomatic illnesses. Both children were 'acting out' their feelings and the outer behaviour could be seen by parents and other adults.

Both Mark and Liza experienced racial and cross-cultural anxieties and conflicts. If Mark had not had the opportunity to discuss his feelings he might have developed strong racist feelings and developed an allegiance with organised racial organisations. He had chosen the most vulnerable target to project his anger into.

In Liza's case issues of race and identity had not been addressed. Children's behaviour needs to be thought about not only as conscious behaviour and activities, but also as to what its unconscious significance is. Issues of race and racial identity need to be addressed not only at their social or political level but also at the level of their unconscious use and significance.

# Chapter 21

# Working to support refugee children in schools

*Maureen Fox*

## INTRODUCTION

In recent years, many people from a range of countries, including Lebanon, Somalia, Eritrea, Ethiopia, Tibet, Afghanistan, former Yugoslavia and Khurdish homelands in Iran, Iraq and Turkey, have applied for asylum in the United Kingdom. In 1993 alone, some 22,000 applications were received by the Home Office (Home Office Statistics 1994). The anonymous distress and suffering of refugees which the media brings into our lives on a daily basis is barely manageable, but we find our defences more substantially challenged when these upheavals are embodied in the account of one particular individual, or form part of the life history of the child sitting in front of us. Thinking about the experiences and needs of refugee children can be daunting and disturbing. In these moments, it is often the voice of our own fears, conscious and unconscious, that speaks loudest, as in our imagination the sufferings of these young people come to represent our own worst phantasies of atrocities and terror. Through our identification with these survivors we ourselves feel traumatised, and, as a consequence, our capacity for rational thought gets interfered with. We may experience an impulse to turn away, unable to identify what we can offer that would be of any use, whilst simultaneously hankering to respond to the need that has been evoked in us. Confronted by the recent arrival of so many refugee youngsters, schools have been turning to psychological services and other specialist agencies for help in identifying ways in which they can meet the needs of these young people and the staff working with them.

In this chapter I would like to discuss some of the ways in which schools have responded to the arrival of these children. In particular, I will focus on work with teachers and with schools as a whole. However, I will begin by saying something about the legal status of refugee children.

## LEGAL STATUS

The description of these children as 'refugees' in the strict sense of the word is a misnomer. The majority of them are more likely to be asylum seekers awaiting the outcome of their application for asylum, which in this country takes up to two years to be processed. They may have come to the UK with some members of their family, but more frequently they will have been accompanied by an older sibling, relative or family friend who acts as their guardian. A substantial minority of them will have arrived as unaccompanied minors, that is children who have made the journey by themselves or in the company of a sibling or siblings under the age of 17. Very young unaccompanied children will be received into care by the local authority, but for a youngster of 15 or 16 reception into care is less likely, particularly if he or she has come with an older sibling who will be regarded as the legal guardian.

An application for asylum results in:

- *Refusal of asylum*, in which case steps will be taken to deport them although they are entitled to appeal against this decision.
- *Exceptional leave to remain*, in which case they will most likely be allowed to remain in this country for one year with the right to apply for an extension at the end of this period. They may then be granted further leave to remain for a specified one-, two- or three-year period.
- *Refugee status*, in which case permanent residency is granted (Applying for Asylum: Refugee Council Leaflet 1994).

It is notable that in recent years the number of people being granted refugee status has been reduced substantially.

Asylum seekers are entitled to housing benefit and to receive 90 per cent of the basic rate of income support. They are entitled to care under the NHS and their children have the right to education. Refugees are required to have been resident in this country for a minimum of three years before they may enter university. After six months in the UK they may apply for a work permit, which can take up to a year to be allocated. It is difficult for refugee children and their families to find their way round our bureaucracy, and they often seek help from teachers in understanding the many letters and forms they receive from the Home Office relating to their legal status and conditions of residence.

Recent changes in legislation (Asylum and Immigration Appeals Act 1993) have resulted in the introduction of finger-printing for asylum seekers at the port of entry, the limiting of housing to temporary accommodation (which usually means bed and breakfast) and the reduction to ten days of the period during which an appeal against deportation can be lodged.

A government-funded scheme has been set up recently under the auspices of the Refugee Council to offer advice and guidance to unaccompanied minors (Panel of Advisers: Refugee Council Leaflet 1993). Two hundred and fifty such young people arrived in the UK in 1993. This pilot programme, which was introduced in April 1994, will run for twelve months.

## WORK WITH TEACHERS

For refugee children, teachers and school assume enormous importance, becoming their substitute family and home. Indeed, these phantasies on occasion become reality, as happened recently when a teacher was asked by a hospital consultant to authorise an operation on a 15-year-old Somali boy, as there was no other adult from whom permission could be obtained. As we would anticipate, in the absence of a mother or father, these youngsters transfer their trust and expectation of parenting onto those adults around them most likely to fit the bill. This transference (Saltzberger-Wittenberg 1975) places an enormous stress on teachers who may find themselves overwhelmed by the need of their pupils and their wide-ranging problems: these problems may relate to housing when they have nowhere to live or have just been allocated a dirty, empty flat which they have no means of furnishing; or to finances when they have no money for food or their bus fare to school; or to offering guidance when they do not know how to complete an application for asylum (a form which is available only in English); or to nurturing when they have raging toothache and want some-one to comfort them. For these children, weekends and school holidays are anticipated with dread.

Some teachers protect themselves against these intrusions by becoming rigid and irritable or acting out angrily with colleagues and management. Others internalise the pain and trauma of their pupils and become traumatised themselves, losing confidence in their teaching skills and doubting their own competence. Consider the example of the conscientious teacher who wonders how to teach war poetry to a child from Lebanon or the arithmetic of a family budgeting to a youngster who has walked across a desert and watched her family die of hunger. Others give themselves until they near burn-out becoming mother, father, aunt and uncle, social worker, lawyer, financial adviser, doctor, furniture remover and even, at times, interior decorator.

Under these circumstances the task of the teacher is a complicated one. Whilst managing the pressures of recent changes in education legislation, the national curriculum and new assessment schemes, together with the demands of their own specialist subjects, they find themselves offering pastoral care to emotionally vulnerable refugee children, having received little or no support, guidance or training for this task. Increasingly schools are becoming aware that, in order to provide adequately for these youngsters, they must first provide adequately for their staff. Some local authorities have responded by appointing a peripatetic specialist teacher with responsibility for the needs of refugee pupils, whilst a few schools have established a post of responsibility for a Refugee Co-ordinator from within their staffing resources.

Creating a supportive setting in school, either within departments or in small groups, where teachers can talk about their experiences of working with refugee youngsters elicits much sensitive and painful discussion. In this context hitherto unexpressed debilitating anxieties can be shared. With the help of a facilitator, staff can allow themselves to contemplate how they themselves might have coped under similar circumstances, express outrage at what is and is not being done by the international community, other governments, our government, the local authority, school management and themselves. Guilt and shame and ignorance of other cultures can be owned and paralysing fears contained. Once staff have been supported in managing their own anxieties and frustrations, they are in a stronger position to support their pupils with theirs. It then becomes possible for the teachers to consider their refugee pupils, not as projections of their own worst fears, but as individuals, each with a unique history of family, school and community which has been traumatically disrupted; to perceive them as children who have suffered emotional and perhaps physical abuse, having lost parents, family and friends; to understand that they are people who have had to abandon their homes at short notice leaving all that is familiar behind them. By withdrawing their projections, teachers relinquish their disabling identification with these youngsters, and re-establish contact with their own considerable competence and experience in understanding and working with children whose lives have been disrupted.

## WORK DISCUSSION GROUP

Most schools have an identified teacher, or group of teachers, who carry particular responsibility for working with bilingual pupils, including refugee children. Whatever the structure, it is often this group of staff who find themselves most intimately involved in the lives of these youngsters. In response to a request to the Tavistock clinic from an English as a Second Language Department of a large comprehensive school, we decided to set up a work discussion group. The group, which consisted of the staff of the department, arranged to meet in school on a monthly basis to discuss individual children. The teachers took it in turns at the start of each session to present a short account of the child's situation and staff concerns. This presentation formed the basis of the ensuing discussion: I would like to describe one such session to you.

### Case study

Tesfa is a 14-year-old Ethiopian boy who had come to the UK seeking asylum. All that was known about him was that he had arrived in Britain six months earlier to join his mother who had travelled ahead. He has four siblings and his father is not with them.

His teacher was concerned because Tesfa was always alone, seemed very sad and rarely spoke. In the large group she would often feel him looking at her. When this happened she would approach him but he avoided eye contact. She would then look at his work or ask him a question. She felt this put him at his ease even though he rarely answered. She noted that he had a beautiful smile.

Tesfa's English was excellent and it was felt that his comprehension and oral skills were greater than he let be known. In an essay entitled 'My Likes and Dislikes', he had written that he did not like loud noises or screaming; he liked to be happy and cared a lot about people; he did not like people being cruel to each other.

His teacher believed that he felt secure in the year room or when he was being taught by one of the English as a Second Language staff. However, she was aware that he needed something more but she had no idea what that might be.

During the discussion that followed, the group wondered how they could make contact with Tesfa: how could they get him to talk? One of the teachers suggested that he seemed to be talking with his eyes, projecting a sense of sadness and loneliness. Everyone acknowledged how moved they had felt by his teacher's sensitive observation of his non-verbal communication. In fact, it was felt that the poignancy of his communication was almost too painful to think about and it had made everyone feel uncomfortable.

Then his teacher remembered an occasion when he had talked spontaneously. On this particular wet and miserable November day, she had been supporting him in a maths class. At the end of the lesson she had found herself commenting aloud on how cold it was in this country and how much she missed Africa. Tesfa's face had lit up with pleasure to discover that she too was from Africa, and together, for a few minutes, they shared memories of the warmth of the African sun. The teacher now remembered how touched she had been by this exchange at the time, and she could not understand why she had forgotten it until now.

She went on to recall an English lesson when Tesfa had written a letter to a friend in Ethiopia recounting his painful journey through a number of countries, in the company of strangers, to reach his family in London. The letter was confused and poorly structured, and, as it formed part of his GCSE course work, she had encouraged him to improve upon it, helping him reorganise it into a more acceptable format.

In this discussion, Tesfa was perceived as communicating his sadness and loneliness by projection, a projection which served the dual purpose of letting others know how he was feeling as well as involving them in sharing the burden of some of the painful feelings he was carrying (Saltzberger-Wittenberg et al. 1983). Through his eye contact, Tesfa drew attention to the fact that he did need something more, as his teacher had understood. He needed her receptivity and capacity to bear his memories of screaming, noise and cruelty. He needed her to know about his mourning for his homeland, which she had sensitively articulated in her apparently spontaneous remark about the weather. However, Tesfa's sadness was enormous and difficult to listen to, and she had defended herself by 'forgetting' their conversation, and later by responding to his account of his journey to London merely as a grammatical exercise. It was only after the combined resources of the group had been able to bear and articulate the poignancy and discomfort of Tesfa's communications that the teacher could allow herself to remember what had passed between them. Fortunately, Tesfa was also a child who wanted to be happy, who cared for people, and who sought contact by using his eyes and beautiful smile to engage and enlist the help he needed.

This case study contains many of the elements that need to be borne in mind when working with refugee children. Rarely do they have difficulty in communicating in the presence of a receptive adult, although their communications may not always be verbal. It is the painfulness of what is being communicated that makes it difficult for them to be heard.

## WORK WITH THE SCHOOL

I would like now to describe a school's response to requests from staff for some training in working with refugee children. The school management decided to devote two days at the start of the following terms to INSET (in-service training) on this topic. In order to provide the maximum opportunity for participation, it was arranged that the same event would run on both days with half the staff attending on each. Ancillary workers, technicians, teachers, management, governors and visiting professionals were all invited to participate, and the event was chaired by the headteacher. The day began with three short talks given by invited speakers from a refugee community, the Refugee Council and the local authority Specialist Teacher for Refugee Children. During the small group exercises which followed, staff were divided into groups, each of which was allocated one of the following topics for discussion:

The Induction of Refugee Children into the School
Refugee Children and the Curriculum
The Management of Refugee Children in Class
Staff Communication with reference to Refugee Children
The Impact on Teachers of Working with Refugee Children
The Pastoral Care of Refugee Children

These topics were selected from the range of concerns identified by staff in a series of discussions held the previous year.

The groups met for an hour and a half and were co-ordinated by an outside facilitator. Group members were invited to discuss their allocated topics and to come up with three recommendations for improved practice. During the last half hour they were asked to identify three ways in which their recommendations could be implemented, without incurring any increase in resources. At the final plenary session each group presented its suggestions for discussion.

The two-day event proved to be a stimulating and satisfactory experience, providing a helpful balance of information and application. Many creative and innovative ideas emerged, including the setting up of an induction programme for refugee pupils on arrival; recommendations to exam boards with a view to establishing an equality of opportunity for refugee children; the preparation of cassette tapes, welcoming the pupils in their mother tongue and providing information about the school, which could be prepared by pupils themselves; cross-cultural, cross-curricular projects which would provide the opportunity for pupils and staff to learn about other cultures and religions; and the appointment of a Refugee Co-ordinator from within current staffing resources. It was recognised that many of the recommendations put forward would also serve the needs of a range of non-refugee pupils in the school.

Shortly after this event, a group of sixth form students sought help in exploring ways in which they could most appropriately support their refugee classmates. In discussion with the newly appointed Refugee Co-ordinator, it was agreed that they would set up an after-school club which would meet for two hours once a week. Refugee youngsters were invited to come along and share games, music and songs from their own country over coffee and hot chocolate. The students also made themselves available to help out with homework. Very quickly the popularity of the club grew, and some eighty youngsters began attending regularly once the membership was opened to include anyone who wanted to come along.

## SUMMARY

In this chapter I have discussed some of the difficulties experienced by refugee youngsters prior to their arrival in the UK, and described how their suffering and loss continue even though they have reached physical safety. I have highlighted some of the key aspects of legislation which have a bearing on their daily lives. The important role of teachers and schools has been emphasised and the profound impact of working with these children explored. A number of accounts have been given of ways in which schools, teachers and fellow pupils have attempted to support asylum-seeking youngsters in coming to terms with what they have been through and in the task of building a new life in this country, whilst uncertain of the duration of their stay.

# Chapter 22

# Refugee children in exile in Europe

## Sheila Melzak

I work as a community child and adolescent psychotherapist for a charity that works with refugees who have survived organised violence and war, and who came to Britain seeking a safe place to live and to make a home (asylum). My work requires me to develop, carry out and support direct therapeutic work with refugee children. These children will all have had direct or indirect experience of violence. We work with the assumption that it is therapeutic for children who have experienced extreme and unusual events that may have been quite overwhelming to communicate their concerns verbally or non-verbally to adults who care for them, and with whom they are able to develop a relationship.

Often parents and members of their extended family can listen to them and thus help them to contain their feelings and integrate their difficult and often extreme experiences. Some refugee children have no adult care-givers to parent them, or have parents who are preoccupied and disturbed by their own exposure to repression and violence. Our work is carried out at the Medical Foundation for the Care of the Tortured, in schools, within the refugee communities, in family consultation centres and in any situation where children and adults meet together, to work, to play and to live.

I will try to sketch out here a philosophy of assessment and therapeutic work with refugee children, which essentially acknowledges the context in which refugee children lived in the past and in which they live now. Their community, their home, their school and the spaces in between these can provide an environment which is sensitive to the needs of refugee children. However, their needs can be invisible.

Most refugee children live in exile in the 'Third World'

(Summerfield 1993) as a result of organised violence, war and repression in their home country. It is a relatively small proportion of refugees that reach Europe. These will, as Maureen Fox describes, be victims of the increasingly punitive European asylum laws that separate families from their communities. These laws underline Europe's unwillingness to support refugees and give them a real home in exile. While political repression and war divide families, they are further divided by asylum laws that increasingly keep parents and children separated.

For me, as a child and adolescent psychotherapist, there is, at the centre of every refugee's internal experience, a conflict between being entitled to life and being an expendable individual, part of an expendable culture, social or religious group. All refugees become refugees because the established powerful authority in their country is challenged by their presence (directly or indirectly) and cannot tolerate their difference and therefore their continued existence.

These are the powerful dynamics that refugee children carry with them. They remind us, as workers, of the capacity for violence and destructiveness within all human beings. They also may generate in us extreme emotions such as terror and rage and extreme help-lessness. The dynamics of perpetrators, victims, bystanders and rescuers are repeated in every situation where refugee children find themselves. It is as a result of these dynamics that workers attempting direct work with refugee children may become easily overwhelmed, feeling in their work as if they are perpetrators or victims of organised violence and war.

In this situation it is helpful to consider the context of the experience of each refugee child, in order to be clearer about which feelings belong to the child and which are our own. This thinking will include consideration of the family, the political, the social and the historical context of each refugee child's experience, both in their own country and in exile. It is perhaps also helpful to consider each child's experience in the light of the following framework of eight concepts. This is useful both for assessment and understanding and for supportive direct work with children and adolescents. This framework was developed to help adults working with refugee children to conceptualise and understand their concerns, their muddles and their worries.

This framework includes eight concepts which connect to a series of questions.

(a) Developmental issues
(b) Repression
(c) Violence
(d) Secrecy
(e) Scapegoating
(f) Loss (problems in mourning and acknowledging loss)
(g) Trauma (problems with remembering, thinking and forgetting)
(h) Change (problems with adaptability and coping strategies).

Refugee children will have had a variety of experiences of violence. These range from direct experience of fighting and torture, to observations of physical brutality towards close family members and community, to having to deal with changes in their parents resulting from the complicated consequences of torture, exile, change and loss, which are often emotionally violent.

In our thinking about the effects of organised violence on communities, there is often a confusion between events, context and meaning, and the effects of the event or context (Richman 1993). An event may be *potentially* traumatic, but may not in fact be traumatising, as individuals and families may be able to use various personal, social and community factors to mediate against the effects of extreme events. The combined effects of these 'coping mechanisms' at an individual, family and community level will be towards resilience. These 'coping mechanisms' protect individuals against potential threats to increase their vulnerability.

Refugee children may live in a wide variety of situations. Some may live with parents who are able to understand and meet their children's developmental needs; some arrive in Britain with one parent, having lost the other parent through death or disappearance or unexplained absence; some have two parents who are unable to consistently give care to their children, as they are preoccupied with past and present traumata, and some arrive in Britain alone and unaccompanied by adult care-givers, having been sent to Britain for their safety. Many refugee children live with adults who are not their parents and who are unable to act as parents, e.g. elder siblings, cousins, etc.

It is undoubtedly true that having functioning parents, the capacity to be active rather than helpless and the capacity for self reflection, all three help children to be resilient in the face of adversity (Rutter and Garmezy 1987; Fonegy *et al.* 1992; Anna Freud 1939–45). These act as mediating factors between potentially traumatic events and their effects.

## THE FRAMEWORK

### a). Developmental issues

In any work with refugee children it is important to establish whether or not the child or young person has a good enough care-giver, and, if not, how ways might be found within the community to complement, supplement or step up the existing care.

Refugee parents often worry that their children will identify with perpetrators, victims or bystanders or organised violence (these identifications can be swift, sudden and powerful when, for example, soldiers enter children's homes and parents are seen to be helpless). Psychotherapists call this 'identification with the aggressor'. Psychotherapeutic work within the black South African community (Straker 1992) and the Palestinian community (Punamaki 1992) shows that these swift identifications can be transformed within 'good' relationships with caring, thoughtful adults.

The second important developmental question is about the link between chronological and developmental age. Refugee children often show uneven development, having both strengths character-istic of older children and vulnerabilities characteristic of younger children. Refugee children may develop a variety of strategies to care for adults around them at some cost to their own development towards integrated and mature adulthood. Refugee children have often good reasons not to trust authority and may be disconnected from adult authority. They may be unable to play or may play out their experiences of killing and fighting (something which could be alarming in a European school). These behaviours will have different meaning from children showing the same behaviour with a different history.

It is helpful to ask these four developmental questions about each refugee child:

1 Does the child have a functioning parent or parent substitute?
2 Is the child's emotional and intellectual development in accord with their chronological age?
3 Can the child play, and does he or she have other ways to express their feelings and a situation in which to do this?
4 At what level of emotional development does the child function?

## b). Repression

A repressive society is one where a powerful minority governs the majority in an autocratic way, often using divisive strategies such as organised violence, torture and the creation of refugees to divide the population and to prevent dissent (Chomsky 1991).

Refugee children come from many different societies and have very different histories. It is helpful for workers to inform themselves about the history of each child, the social, political and family history. Parents will have had different relationships with the repressive government and may be proud, ashamed or bewildered. They may be victims, perpetrators of violence or bystanders. They may be rescuers.

Question: What techniques of repression were used in the country the child you are concerned about came from, and what was their relationship to this system of organised violence?

## c). Violence

Refugee children are exposed both to physical and to emotional violence. In addition to physical violence there is the violence of loss and change. Often the worst kind of violence is the violence of losing the idealised perfect parent who protects the child from pain and from too much discomfort.

Violent acts have different meanings for powerful and for powerless groups to which refugees usually belong. Experience of violent events can thus not be separated from meaning.

Questions: What kind of violence has the child experienced? What did this mean for each child?

## d). Secrecy

Secrecy is the central element by which repressive societies function and divide the population (Martin-Baros 1990). Refugee children may have to keep various secrets, some conscious, some unconscious. These include secrets about the whereabouts of adults, about adults' political activities and about their own identity and history. There are also secret worries and anxieties about the cause of various events. Young children (and older children and adults under stress) will think in an egocentric and magical way, assuming that they have caused certain events, e.g. a child angry with a parent who is later imprisoned and arrested may assume that their thoughts have caused the arrest.

We know that the central pathogenic factor in childhood abuse is secrecy (writers such as Bentovim, Finklehor, Shengold and Glazer all writing that childhood abuse that is not acknowledged and worked through is likely to cause disturbance in adult life). It is important that the conscious and unconscious secrets in the lives of refugee children are unravelled, both in order to reconnect these children to the past and their own history, and to help them to integrate their experiences. Central to the internal experience of secrecy is the inhibition and restriction of thinking and feeling, making learning and developing relationships difficult.

Questions: What secrets is the child having to keep? Are these conscious or unconscious?

### e). Scapegoating

Scapegoating means that individuals and groups are persecuted because of their own difference and often as a result of what they represent for the persecutor (which may be an unacknowledged part of themselves).

Refugees have always experienced scapegoating in their own country. This is one aspect of organised violence. Refugees may also be scapegoated in their country of exile. Refugee children may experience not only racist asylum laws, but also racism, bullying and discrimination in schools and inequality of opportunities to learn.

Questions: What discrimination has the child experienced? What could you do to challenge present discrimination?

### f). Loss

Refugee children always experience many losses of people and of culture. Some find difficulty in acknowledging losses as they do not know whether a loss is permanent or temporary. Refugees do not know, usually, whether they will be able to return to their homes or not. They do not know the extent to which their home will be transformed. They may feel they have lost who they are.

Refugee children are thus often stuck in the mourning process and unable to mourn members who have disappeared, or with whom contact is broken. Refugee children need opportunities to work through concrete and abstract losses.

Questions: What losses has the child experienced? Has the child been able to begin the mourning process?

## g). Trauma

As I wrote earlier, not all refugee children are traumatised. For some the same event may be overwhelming, while others will have coping strategies which make them more resilient to this event. Violence, loss and change can all be potentially traumatic for refugee children.

I define a traumatic event as one where even briefly the child becomes shocked and loses contact with familiar faculties such as being able to think, to concentrate, to sleep without intrusive thoughts, to control bladder and bowels. A traumatic event is one where the effects of the event repeat themselves at irregular intervals for a long time after the event. This is especially frightening and humiliating for children and young people who are growing up and enjoying newly acquired developmental skills. Trauma can interfere with learning and with making friends. Trauma is an isolating experience. Children may feel that no one else has had the same difficult psychological consequences as a result of exile and organised violence.

The central character of trauma is that of disconnection. This includes disconnection of past from present, of external events from their internal consequences and of feelings from memories. Children may remember the past and not connect to the present, for example.

Any therapeutic work with refugee children must not assume that the child has been traumatised. The aim of any therapeutic listening work is the reconnection of memories and feelings.

Questions: Has the child been traumatised? What events were traumatic and what were the consequences?

## h). Change

Refugee children must all make a transition from one culture to another (Blackwell 1989). Some children are adaptable and resilient and quickly learn the new language and new cultural rules. For others, the task of transition is prolonged and difficult, especially when children have not accepted exile and deny the losses involved. This internal problem for the child will not be worked through if the child's experience and needs are not acknowledged by the host community and in schools.

Many young refugees, as a result of war and political repression, have missed years of schooling and arrive in exile in adolescence bright and keen to learn, but without the basic skills to begin this task. This is often deeply humiliating, especially when their one hope for a good life in exile is an education. Schools may also be unfriendly and racist.

Questions: What changes has the child had to negotiate? What could schools do to meet the special learning needs of children who have missed years of schooling – in a way that is not humiliating for the child?

## CONCLUSION

These eight concepts are helpful in thinking about the special needs and special experiences of refugee children in exile in Europe. The central concern of my work is always with children and parents, and institutions in the community that work with children. This has the aim of maintaining, if at all possible, the bonds of attachment between children and their parents and finding a comfortable place in a school where a refugee child can meet their entitlement to learn.

This applies whether children are with their own parents or not. We all need to be aware that the natural bonds of attachment between children, parents and their community are threatened, loosened and can be distorted by organised violence and its concommitants. Refugee children in exile in Europe provide us with the challenge of reconnection at many different levels, internal and external, emotional and practical.

# Chapter 23

# Children and violence

*Felicity de Zulueta*

The origins of human violence have been a subject of considerable speculation over the last few centuries. Are children born 'evil' or do they become 'bad' as a result of their upbringing? The argument could carry on for ever, as it is essentially a philosophical debate about human nature (Zulueta 1993: 11–24). Meanwhile, whilst the debate continues, some of our infants grow up into cruel, self-destructive, abusive and even murderous children. Those who attempt to give these boys and girls the loving care they seem to need often become desperate in their apparently futile struggle to communicate with them. To others, these children are seen as evil monsters whose misdemeanours can only be dealt with through punishment and increasing control. This polarisation of opinions was made manifest in the aftermath of the murder of James Bulger in November 1993. It reflects a failure to understand the root cause of childhood violence, a failure which in its turn stems from our difficulty in acknowledging how much human beings need one another and how vulnerable they are to failures in their attachment relationships.

## VIOLENCE AS ATTACHMENT GONE WRONG

Bowlby and his followers made us aware of the attachment and behavioural system we share with other primates. It is because of this innate behavioural system that the human infant selects a primary attachment figure (which need not be the mother) whose whereabouts will require constant monitoring. The developing child will remain in fairly close proximity to this caregiver, otherwise described as the 'secure base', even under non-stressful conditions. As the infant develops, secondary attachment figures play an increasingly important role.

The attachment system is activated by both internal stimuli, such as illness, or external threats which drive the infant to seek close proximity and contact with the caregiver(s). If separated from these parental figures, infants protest strongly before manifesting despair and, finally, detachment. At this point, these infants will no longer respond to the return of their caregivers; they might even snub them (Robertson and Bowlby 1952). As we will see, this 'avoidant' response will be crucial to our understanding of destructive human behaviour.

Bowlby originally suggested that the attachment behavioural system's main function was to provide the infant with protection from predators, but we now know that it also protects the young both from other members of the species and from extreme environmental conditions. Recent studies also highlight its role in enabling the psychobiological process of mother–infant attunement to take place (Field 1985).

It is important to realise that the attachment behavioural system is continually active, even if, at times, the infant's monitoring of the caregiver is unconscious. As development takes place, the infant gradually learns to be alert to the physical and psychological accessibility of the caregiver; through repeated interactions, the child may come to experience his or her caregiver as either rejecting or unpredictable, in which case different strategies for gaining and/or maintaining access will be developed. These different behavioural responses to the caregiver have become the focus of much of the American research in the field of attachment behaviour.

Ainsworth and her team (1978) carried out a series of studies on 1-year-old infants using the Strange Situation Test in which they demonstrated that those babies who had been emotionally deprived or rejected showed an 'avoidant' response towards their mother after a very brief separation of only a few minutes. In other words, they showed no distress when separated and ignored their mother on her return though their rapid heartbeat belied their apparent indifference.

This insecure-avoidant (Group-A) behaviour was found in 20–25 per cent of infants in the USA, whilst 63 per cent were found to be securely attached (Group-B). The remaining 12 per cent of infants were described as insecure–ambivalent: they became very distressed when separated from mother but were unable to obtain comfort on her return (Group-C).

In later studies, Main found a group of children who did not fit into Ainsworth's categories. These infants were given 'disorganised'/ 'disorientated' D-attachment status. Some of these infants displayed behaviours typical of both the 'avoidant' and 'ambivalent' resistant infant in addition to other strange, undirected movements and postures. One such infant would approach her mother by moving backwards or sit for a while staring into space. This particular attachment status has been linked to frightening parental behaviour, such as is observed in maltreating families, and/or, more specifically, to their parents' traumatised, frightened and often dissociated state of mind (Main and Hesse 1992). What these infants appear to suffer from is a collapse of their attachment behavioural strategies.

Whilst the possible links between D-attachment status and human violence are still unknown, there is considerable evidence linking the A-attachment behaviour with human destructiveness. If we bear in mind that we are looking at research carried out on a quarter of the American or European infant population, we cannot be too surprised to discover that human violence is a widespread social phenomenon both in children and adults. These findings may go some way to explaining why apparently 'normal' people are involved in family violence, bullying, racist attacks and other more sinister mass forms of violence such as took place in Nazi Germany. So, whilst the more severe and perverse manifestations of human cruelty might well be ascribed one day to the D-group of infants, what we can learn from the Group-A infants is significant in terms of our everyday understanding of human violence in our society.

What the study of the 'avoidant' infants provides is an understanding of the importance of dissociation as a defence against the trauma of loss. Their particular attachment behaviour can be explained by the fact that these children are placed in an intolerable conflictual situation by their parent: we know that, if threatened in any way, all infants will be driven by their attachment behavioural system to seek comfort from their main caregiver; however, if that caregiver becomes both threatening and/or forbids physical contact, as many rejecting parents do (Main *et al*. 1979), their infants learn to displace their attention elsewhere, to 'cut themselves off' from their feeling of anger and fear in relation to mother or caregiver, so as to remain as close as possible to those on whom they totally depend. In this way, these children have learnt to 'dissociate' so as to maintain a close relationship with their caregiver. The price they pay in terms of their internal world is that, in order to preserve their 'good internal objects', these children have to see themselves as 'bad': this requires 'splitting' and identification with the bad rejecting objects, an identification that the child will cling to in order to preserve some sense of control and some hope of redemption. For Fairburn the resulting 'guilt must be regarded . . . as partaking of the nature of a defence'. As he put it on behalf of his patients: 'It is better to be a sinner in a world ruled by God than to live in a world ruled by the Devil' (Fairburn 1952: 66). A similar phenomenon can also be observed in adult victims of abuse or trauma.

Studies on 'avoidant' children have shown that they express frequent hostility, unprovoked aggression to both adults and children and that their peer interactions are generally negative. These findings were confirmend by Troy and Sroufe (1987) who carried out a study of nineteen pairs of children, aged 4 to 5. They found that victimisation took place in all the pairs where one or both the children had been found to display an 'avoidant' attachment response; in other words, one partner continually abused his or her partner both physically and verbally. In all these couples, the abuser had a history of an 'avoidant' attachment and the partner was also insecurely attached (type A or type C). Children with secure attachment patterns (type B) were not observed to be either abusers or victims. This study is very important in our understanding of human violence. It is also of particular interest in understanding the development of internal object relations because the fact that a group A child can be both a victimiser and a victim suggests that it is indeed the relationship, the 'self' in relation to the 'other', which is internalised. These same children whose parents have shown little empathy also develop a poor sense of self-esteem, and show little empathy themselves: they are essentially egocentric and this predisposes them to maladaptive behaviour towards others. For example, avoidant toddlers respond negatively or even violently to signs of distress in their peers: they will hit a crying child whilst their more secure counterparts are able to show interest and sadness (Main and George 1985). The violent behaviour of these children to those in pain could arise because they find their peer's distress intolerable, a reminder of their own pain and, possibly, of the way their parent dealt with their tears.

A battered wife who was in my group reported how when she cried her father would beat her up and then say: 'Now you have something to cry about.' This example and countless others in both children and adults have led to the realisation that children whose attachments have been damaged through deprivation, loss or other forms of rejection have a similar way of dealing with their painful experience as those who have suffered psychological trauma. This is not surprising, since for both what is involved is the disruption of the attachment system with all that this means in terms of psychological defences, biological manifestations and violence. Whilst this resulting violence can be ascribed to both the narcissistic rage that arises following damage to the individual's sense of self and to the more physiological underpinnings of the attachment system itself (Zulueta 1993: 64–7), how do we explain the re-enactment of childhood traumas?

## VIOLENCE AND TRAUMATIC RE-ENACTMENT

Faced with terror and pain of what cannot be endured and feeling utterly helpless, the child, like the adult, will literally dissociate himself from feelings and thoughts which are too disturbing to acknowledge. This is how abused and traumatised children cope with the unspeakable pain in their past. It is only when these split-off feelings are triggered back into consciousness by an external or internal stimulus that the dissociated rage and its accompanying perceptions are brought back into action (though not necessarily into consciousness), often to recreate the very experience that the child was originally exposed to, either in himself or in the 'other'. This leads to a repetition of the traumatic experience, a repetition that has correctly been described as having a compulsive quality to it. The latter is due to the fact that children whose early attunement experiences were less than satisfactory cannot modulate emotional or physiological arousal either symbolically or physiologically. It appears that they can become literally addicted to the trauma whose re-enactment leads to the release of endogenous opiates. In Van der Kolk's view (1989), the victim's compulsion lies at the heart of the traumatic origins of violence.

Mr Brown illustrates very clearly the links between childhood physical abuse and violence in adulthood. He was referred to me after several years in custody for killing his small daughter. He now felt depressed and wanted to know if therapy could help him.

When I met Mr Brown, he was in his fifties but his white hair and pale looks made him look much older. He seemed anxious to help me with the interview, though he knew it would be difficult for him. The subject of his 2½-year-old daughter's death soon emerged. He sketched out her life prior to the 'incident' as he put it. She had been looked after by her grandparents abroad before being brought to this country to live with Mr and Mrs Brown. It was not long before she was being abused by both him and his wife who had apparently always hated her child.

As an infant and toddler his daughter was systematically starved and beaten. He described a pitiful scene of this pale little girl tottering barefoot in the freezing cold. She was so cold her feet stuck to the ice. In his attempt to warm them up her father burnt them with lighted cigarettes and hot coals. She ended up in casualty, her feet covered with blisters.

On the day of the fatal 'incident', this little 'waif', as he called her, had been locked up in her room without having been changed or fed. On arriving home Mr Brown was told by his wife to clean the 'thing'. He found her in a mess of faeces and urine. After cleaning her, he brought her to the living room and then attempted to get her to talk to him but she only stood in silence, pale and distressed. He became desperate and bullied her to speak so as to feel better himself. He recalls going up to her and shaking her . . . nothing else. That night, he must have been worried because he told his wife to keep an eye on her. The next day his daughter was found dead in her bed. In recounting these events Mr Brown was quiet and subdued. He seemed to have split himself off from the violent feelings that drove him to kill his child. He did not recall beating her but he knows she died from chest injuries.

Sensing that I could not get any closer to what actually happened between this child and her parents, I asked Mr Brown to tell me about his early life. He began by talking about his mother and as he did so his face lit up. She had been a devoted mother who fell ill with tuberculosis when he was still small. She often had to go to hospital for treatment and when she left he missed her so much he would walk several miles in order to be with her. It was during the war and food was scarce. Mr Brown recalled how this frail woman would give her children the food she had in hospital so that they had enough to eat. 'She was like an angel', he said. His mother died when he was only 8 and he remembers feeling distraught at her funeral. From then on Mr Brown was in the hands of his father, a man whose violence he feared though he tried not to be too critical of him as if he needed to keep his real feelings at bay. He described how, one day, on his mother's return from hospital, he had found her being beaten up by his father. Though only a lad of 7, he had grabbed an axe and threatened his father with it.

Later on in his childhood, his father injured his arm and asked his son to take over the cobbler's business. Though Mr Brown proved to be good at the job, one day his knife slipped and pierced a leather boot he was making. His father saw this and in a fury he picked up a large stick and began to beat his son on the back of his head. The boy tore down the village street with blood pouring from his head and his father at his heels. A kindly neighbour came to his rescue: for once in his life someone had actually stood up for him.

At this point I attempted to explore whether Mr Brown could begin to acknowledge how much he had missed as a result of his mother's illness. Bearing in mind his need to idealise his 'angel' mother and the fact that she could not be blamed for her illness (though he might have felt to blame), I wondered if there had been a little boy who may have felt that he had so little of her, he had suffered consistently as a result. He could acknowledge such feelings and this led him to link his experience of the little 'waif of a daughter' with the picture he had of his pale sick mother in hospital. It seemed likely that his unconscious rage against his mother, who failed to care for him, was finally discharged on his daughter. Like his mother, she had appeared helpless and in pain, evoking in him his own desperate needs and his old pain. He had not been able to find in himself the love she needed from him. Instead, he appears to have coped with his own pain by identifying with his violent father and, in his destructive rage, he found the power to inflict the pain he had once been made to suffer. It is likely that on the night of his daughter's death, Mr Brown did not 'see' his child before him. What he probably experienced were his old memories and feelings being brought back to life, those unbearable moments of pain and helplessness which had been 'split off' in his mind, just as they were again on the day of our interview. Splitting is a dissociative process that enables us to cope with the overwhelming fear of feeling utterly helpless in the face of abandonment and abuse. Mr Brown could not recall what happened on that fatal night nor will we ever really know what took place between this man, his wife and their child. However, it seems that in some strange way she was to become the little 'waif' who reminded Mr Brown of his dead mother whose helplessness and ill health was to be her undoing; this same helplessness was to be his child's undoing (Zulueta 1993: 5–8).

Childhood violence cannot be understood without first acknowledging the importance of attachment in child development. Such a conclusion does not deny the importance of genetic predisposition and personality, factors which may make it more difficult for a satisfactory attunement and attachment to take place between infants and their parents. What it does show is that affiliative and destructive behaviour are the reciprocal manifestations of the same underlying attachment system and its psychological representation at the level of the self. The violent child does to his objects what was once done unto him. The implications of these findings are important both for the way we judge and treat destructive children.

# Endpiece

*Marion Bower*

Throughout this book we have tried to keep in mind the political, social and legal framework in which we all operate. At this point we would like to return briefly to the organising theme of this book which is the value of psychoanalytic understanding in helping us work with families and children and institutions.

There are many ways of helping people, but we would like to end by stating what we feel is uniquely valuable about this approach. First the psychoanalytic approach assumes we are all driven by unconscious emotions, conflicts and patterns of behaviour which were established early on in our lives (hence the great value of working with *young* families). Problems arise when we become stuck with unhelpful patterns which may have a compulsive or repetitive quality.

Such patterns are easy to see in adults and children but difficult to change, because they involve an emotional shift which may involve facing a good deal of psychic pain. Second, a psychodynamic approach enables this type of change to take place by creating a space for the difficulties to emerge, and offering a new way of responding to them. The great value of this type of change is that it provides an element of *choice* and *control*, as we become free of some of the forces that drive us. This offers freedom to make the best of our own potential and the social situation in which we find ourselves.

For those who do not use psychodynamic ideas in a therapeutic context, we believe that the concept of 'a space for thinking' where information can be gathered and reflected on and its significance considered *before* taking action is a valuable one. This is particularly well illustrated by the chapter on infant observation, but we hope that the book as a whole will be a convincing illustration of the value of these ideas.

# Appendix 1
## Topic reference list

For further details of books, see bibliography.

### Dictionary/reference texts

Laplanche, J. and Pontalis, J.-B. *The Language of Psychoanalysis* (PB)
Hinshelwood, R. *A Dictionary of Kleinian Thought* (PB)
Rycroft, C. *A Critical Dictionary of Psychoanalysis* (PB)

### Freud

The Penguin Freud series (PB), especially:
*The New Introductory Lectures* (Vol. 2), *Case Histories* Vols 8 and 9,
   'Three essays on sexuality', in *On Sexuality* (Vol. 7)

### Freud, A.

*The Harvard Lectures* (PB)
*The Ego and the Mechanisms of Defence* (PB)

### Klein, M.

Segal, H. *Introduction to the Work of Melanie Klein* (PB)
Klein, M. *Envy and Gratitude and Other Works* (PB)

### Winnicott, D.W.

*The Maturational Processes and the Facilitating Environment* (PB)
*Through Paediatrics to Psychoanalysis* (PB)

### Bion W.R.

*Second Thoughts* (PB)

## Child abuse

Goldstein, J. *et al. Beyond the Best Interest of the Child* and *In the Best Interest of the Child* (PBs)

## Adult psychotherapy

Anderson, R. (ed.) *Clinical Lectures on Klein and Bion* (PB)
McDougall, J. *Theatres of the Body: A Psychoanalytic Approach to Psychosomatic Illness* (PB)
Klauber, J. *Difficulties in the Analytic Encounter* (PB)

## Child psychotherapy

Szur, R. and Miller, S. (eds) *Extending Horizons* (PB)
Boston, M. and Szur, R. (eds) *Psychotherapy with Severely Deprived Children* (PB)

## Family therapy

Box, S. (ed.) *Crisis at Adolescence: Object Relations Therapy with the Family*
Sharff, D.E. and Sharff, J.S. *Object Relations Family Therapy* (PB)

## Group therapy

Bion, W.R. *Experiences in Groups and Other Papers* (PB)
Foulkes, S.H. and Anthony, E.J *Group Psychotherapy: The Psychoanalytic Approach* (PB)

## Institutions

Obholtzer, A. and Roberts, V.G. *The Unconscious at Work* (PB)
Dockar Drysdale, B. *Therapy and Consultation in Child Care* (PB)

## Social work

Saltzberger-Wittenberg, I. *Psychoanalytic Insights and Relationships: A Kleinian Approach* (PB)
Yelloly, M. and Henkel, M. (eds) *Learning and Teaching in Social Work* (PB)

## Schools

Saltzberger-Wittenberg, I., Henry, G. and Osborne, E. *The Emotional Experience of Teaching and Learning* (PB)

## Medical

Balint, M. *The Doctors, the Patient and the Illness: Balint Revisited* (PB)
Holmes, J. *A Textbook of Psychotherapy in Psychiatric Practice*

## Attachment

Bowlby, J. *A Secure Base* and *The Making and Breaking of Affectional Bonds* (PBs)

## Bookshops

Most of these books can be obtained from **KARNAC BOOKS**
58, Gloucester Road, London SW7 4QY Tel: 0171 594 3303 and 118, Finchley Road, London NW3 5HJ Tel: 0171 431 1075.

# Appendix 2
## Useful organisations

### Young Minds

The National Association for Child and Family Mental Health, 22a Boston Place, London NW1 6EN. Tel: 0171 724 7262

### Gaps

Group for the Advancement of Psychodynamics and Psychotherapy in Social Work, *Secretary*, Peter Pearson, 120 Church Road, Hanwell, London W7 3BE

### APP

Association for Psychoanalytic Psychotherapy in the NHS (and Related Services), *Secretary*, Linda Kaufman, Tavistock Clinic, 120 Belsize Lane, London NW3 5BA

### British Confederation of Psychotherapists

Psychoanalytic psychotherapists, 37, Mapesbury Road, London NW6

### TMSI

Tavistock Marital Studies Institute, Tavistock Centre, 120 Belsize Lane, London NW3 5BA

### Tavistock Institute

Consultation to organisations, etc., The Tavistock Institute of Human Relations, 30 Tabernacle Street, London EC2A 4DE

## FAETT

Forum for the Advancement of Educational Therapy and Therapeutic Teaching, *Secretary*, Gerda Hanko, 3 Templewood, Ealing, London W13 8B

## Balint Society

*Contact*, Sue Littlechild, Adult Department, Tavistock Clinic, 120 Belsize Lane, London NW3 5BA, Tel: 0171 435 7111 Ext 2411

## Charterhouse Group

An association of therapeutic communities, The Peper Harrow Foundation, 14 Charterhouse Square, London EC1M 6AX

## The Squiggle Foundation

To study and cultivate the tradition of D.W. Winnicott, *Director*, Nina Farhi, 11 North Square, London NW11 7AB

# REFUGEES

## Children of the Storm

Hampstead School, Westbere Road, London NW6, 0171 435 4880

## Medact

601 Holloway Road, London N19 4DJ, 0171 272 2020

## Medical Foundation for the Care of the Tortured

96 Grafton Road, London NW5 3CJ, 0171 784 4321

## Minority Rights Group

379 Brixton Road, London SW9 7DE, 0171 978 9498

## Red Cross

9 Grosvenor Crescent, London SW1X 7UJ, 0171 235 5454

## Refugee Council

3 Bondway, London SW8 1SJ, 0171 582 6922

## Refugee Support Centre

King Georges House, Stockwell Road, London SW9 9ES, 0171 733 1482

## Refugee Workshop

Child and Family Department, Tavistock Clinic, 120 Belsize Lane, London NW3 5BA, 0171 435 7111

# Bibliography

Abraham, K. (1924) 'A short study of the development of the libido', in *Selected Papers on Psycho-Analysis*, London: Hogarth, pp. 418–501.

Ainsworth, M.D.S., Bleher, M.C., Waters, E. and Wall, S. (1978) *Patterns of Attachment: Assessed in the Strange Situation and at Home*, Hillsdale, NJ: Erlbaum.

Anderson, R. (ed.) (1992) *Clinical Lectures on Klein and Bion*, London: Routledge.

*Applying for Asylum* (1994) Refugee Council leaflet. *Asylum and Immigration Appeals Act* (1993) London: HMSO.

Bain, A. (1982) 'The Baric experiment: the design of jobs and organization for the expression and growth of human capacity', *Tavistock Institute of Human Relations Occasional Paper No. 4*.

Bain, A. and Barnett, L. (1976) 'The design of a day care system in a nursery setting for children under five', unpublished report to the Department of Health and Social Security.

Bain, A. and Barnett, L. (1980) *The Design of a Day Care System in a Nursery Setting for Children Under Five*, London: Tavistock Institute of Human Relations (TIHR) Document No. 2T347.

Bain, A. and Barnett, L. (1986) *The Design of a Day Care System in a Nursery Setting for Children Under Five* (Part I Abridged version of Bain and Barnett 1980; Part II Application of Principles in Devon), London: TIHR Occasional Paper No. 8.

Balbernie, R. (1993) 'Looking at what professional carers do: the therapeutic context and conditions of change', *Maladjustment and Therapeutic Education* 1(1).

Balint, M. (1964) *The Doctors, the Patient and the Illness*, London: Pitman Medical.

Bamford, T. (1990) *Myths of Welfare: Political, Professional and Personal Implications*, paper to BASW conference.

Baritz, L. (1965) *The Servants of Power: A History of the Use of Social Science in American Industry*, New York: Wiley.

Barnett, L. (1983) 'Language and intimacy: some comments arising from action research in a local authority day nursery', *J. Ch. Psychother.* 19(1).

Barnett, L. (1987) Video *Buddle Lane: A Day Nursery Becomes a FamilyCentre.* VHS: 40 mins. Obtainable from Lynn Barnett, Iddesleigh House Clinic, 97 Heavitree Road, Exeter, Devon.

Barnett, L. (1989) Video *Enriching Day Care.* VHS: 38 mins. Available from Lynn Barnett, Iddesleigh House Clinic, 97 Heavitree Road, Exeter, Devon.

Belsky, J. (1988) 'Infant day care and socioemotional development: the United States', annotation in *J. Ch. Psychol. Psychiat.* 29: 397–406.

Bender, H. (1981) 'Experiences in running a staff group', in *Colloquium: Hospital Care of the Newborn: Some Aspects of Personal Stress, J. Ch. Psychother.* 7(2): 152–60.

Bennathan, M. and Boxall, M. (1994) *Nurture Groups: Successful Early Intervention in Mainstream Primary Schools*, East Sutton, Kent: AWCEBD.

Berelowitz, M. and Horne, A. (1992) 'Child mental health and the legacy of child guidance, some issues for the 1990's', *ACPP Newsletter* 14(4): 161–7.

Bergman, T. (1965) *Children in the Hospital*, New York: International Universities Press.

Bick, E. (1964) 'Notes on infant observation in psychoanalytic training', *Int. J. Psycho-Anal.* 45: 558–66.

Billinge, M. (1992) 'Assessing families where there is "grave concern"' *Child Abuse Review* 5(3).

Bion, W.R. (1955) 'Group dynamics: a re-view', in Klein, M., Heimann, P. and Money-Kyrle, R.E. (eds) *New Directions in Psycho-Analysis*, London: Tavistock, pp. 440–77.

Bion, W.R. (1961) *Experiences in Groups*, London: Tavistock, New York: Basic.

Bion, W.R. (1962) *Learning from Experience*, London: Heinemann.

Bion, W.R. (1962) 'A theory of thinking,' *Int. J. Psycho-Anal.* 43: 306–10; also in Bion (1967).

Bion, W.R. (1963) *Elements of Psychoanalysis*, London: Heinemann.

Bion, W.R. (1967) *Second Thoughts: Selected Papers on Psychoanalysis*, London: Karnac, 1984.

Blackwell, R.D. (1989) 'The disruption and reconstitution of family network and community systems following torture, organised violence and exile', available from the Medical Foundation for the Care of the Tortured.

Blom Cooper, L., London Borough of Brent (1985) *A Child in Trust: Report of an Inquiry into the case of Jasmine Beckford*, London: HMSO.

Boston, M. and Szur, R. (eds) (1990) *Psychotherapy with Severely Deprived Children*, London: Karnac.

Bott, E. (1957) *Family and Social Network*, London: Tavistock, 1971.

Bowlby, J. (1951) *Maternal Care and Mental Health*, Geneva: World Health Organization Monograph Series No. 2, Columbia University Press.

Bowlby, J. (1958) 'The nature of the child's tie to his mother', *Int. J. Psycho-Anal.* 39: 350–73.

Bowlby, J. (1969) *Attachment and Loss*, Vol. 1, *Attachment*, London: Hogarth.

Bowlby, J. (1979) *The Making and Breaking of Affectional Bonds*, London: Tavistock.

Bowlby, J. (1988) *A Secure Base: Clinical Applications of Attachment Theory*, London, Routledge, 1993.

Boc, S. (ed.) (1994) *Crisis at Adolescence*, New Jersey and London: Jason Aronson.

Boxall, M. (1976) 'The nurture group in the primary school', *Therapeutic Education* 4(2): 13–18.

Brafman, A. (1988) 'Infant observation', *Int. Rev. Psycho-Anal.* 55: 45–61.

Brazelton, T. B. (1992) *Touchpoints*, London: Penguin.

Breen, D. (1989) *Talking with Mothers*, London: Free Association Books.

Bridge, G. and Miles, G. (eds) (1995) *From the Outside Looking in: observation essays*, in press CCETSW.

Briggs, S. (1992) 'Child observation and social work training', *Journal of Social Work Practice*, 6(1).

Brooks, J. (1994) 'Assessing the needs of children', Unpublished, Caldecott College.

Butler-Sloss, Lord Justice, DBE (1988) *Report of the Inquiry into Child Abuse in Cleveland (1987)*, Cm.412, London: HMSO.

Carew, J. (1980) 'Experience and the development of intelligence in young children', *Monographs of the Society for Research in Child Development* 45: 6–7, serial no. 187.

The Children Act (1989) *Guidance and Regulations* V1, 2 and 3, London: HMSO.

Chomsky, N. (1991) *Deterring Democracy*, London: Random Century.

Clausen, A. and Crittenden, P. (1991) 'Physical and psychological maltreatment: relations among types of maltreatment', *Child Abuse and Neglect* 15: 5–18.

Cockett, M. and Tripp, J. (1994) *The Exeter Family Study: Family Breakdown, its Impact on Children*, Exeter: Exeter University Press.

Cox, A. (1993) 'Befriending young mothers', *Brit. J. Psychiat.* 163: 6–18.

Cox, A., Mills, M. and Pound A. (1991) 'Evaluation of a home-visiting and befriending scheme for young mothers', *J. Royal Soc. Medicine* 84.

Cox, J. and Holden, J. (1994) *Perinatal Psychiatry: Use and Misuse of the EPDS*, Gaskell Press.

Daniel, P. (1992) 'Child analysis and the concept of unconscious phantasy', in Anderson, R. (ed.) *Clinical Lectures on Klein and Bion*, London: Routledge.

Daws, D. (1985) 'Standing next to the weighing scales', *J. Ch. Psychother.* 11(2): 77–85.

Daws, D. (1989) *Through the Night: Helping Parents and Sleepless Infants*, London: Free Association Books.

Daws, D. (1993) 'Feeding problems and relationship difficulties – therapeutic work with parents and infants', *J. Ch. Psychother.* 19(2): 69–83.

*Defence against anxiety*, Tavistock Papers No.3

DES (1988) *Five Post-Qualification Social Work Courses: A Research Study*, London: HMSO.

DHSS (1984) *Guide for Guardians ad Litem in the Juvenile Court*, London: HMSO.

DHSS (1985) *Social Work Decisions in Child Care: Recent Research Findings and their Implications*, London: HMSO.

Dockar Drysdale, B. (1970) *Consultation in Child Care*, London: Longman.

Dockar Drysdale, B. (1990) *The Provision of Primary Experience*, London: Free Association Books.

Dockar Drysdale, B. (1993) *Therapy and Consultation in Child Care*, London: Free Association Books.

DOH (1989) *The Care of Children, Principles and Practice in Regulations and Guidance*, London: HMSO.

DOH (1991) *The Health of the Nation: Consultative Document for Health in England*, London: HMSO.

DOH (1992) *Manual of Practice Guidance for Guardians ad Litem and Reporting Officers*, London: HMSO.

Dunn, J. (1988) *The Beginnings of Social Understanding*, Oxford: Blackwell.

Elkan, J. (1981) 'Talking about the birth', *J. Ch. Psychother.* 7(2): 144–8.

Fairbairn, W.R. (1952) *Psychoanalytic Studies of the Personality*, London: Tavistock/Routledge & Kegan Paul.

Field, T. (1985) 'Attachment as psychological attunement: being on the same wavelength', in Field, T. (ed.) *The Psychology of Attachment and Separation*, London: Academic Press, pp. 415–54.

Fletcher, A. (1983) 'Working in a neonatal intensive care unit', *J. Ch. Psychother.* 9(1): 47–56.

Foulkes, S.H. and Anthony, E.J. (1957) *Group Psychotherapy: The Psychoanalytic Approach*, Harmondsworth: Penguin, 1965.

Freud, A. (1936) *The Ego and the Mechanisms of Defence*, London: Hogarth Press.

Freud, A. (1992) *The Harvard Lectures*, ed. J. Sandler, London: Institute of Psycho-Analysis/Karnac.

Freud, S. (1895) 'Paranoia', *Standard Edition of the Complete Psychological Works of Sigmund Freud*, Vol. 1, London: Institute of Psycho-Analysis/Hogarth Press.

Freud, S. (1905) 'Three essays on the theory of sexuality', *S. E.* 7: 226.

Frodi, A.M. (1981) 'Contribution of infant characteristics to child abuse', *Am. J. Men. Def.* 85(4): 341–9.

Gay, P. (1988) *Freud: A Life for our Time*, London: Dent.

Goffman, I. (1958) 'The characteristics of total institutions', in *Symposium on Preventive Psychiatry*; also in *Asylums*, New York: Doubleday, 1961.

Goldstein, J. et al. (1973) *Beyond the Best Interest of the Child*, New York: Free Press; London: Macmillan.

Greenwich, London Borough of (1987) *A Child in Mind: Protection of Children in a Responsible Society*, report of the inquiry into the circumstances surrounding the death of Kimberley Carlile.

Haskins, R. (1985) 'Public school aggression among children in varying day care experience', *J. Ch. Dev*, 56: 689–703.

Hawkins, P. and Shohet, R. (1989) *Supervision in the Helping Professions*, Milton Keynes: Open University Press, 1993.

Heimann, P. (1952) 'Notes on the theory of the Life and Death instincts', in Riviere, J. (ed.) *Developments in Psycho-Analysis*, London: Hogarth Press.

Henson, S. (1993) 'Nurture groups as a resource for children with special needs', unpublished MSc thesis.

Hinshelwood, R.D. (1989) *A Dictionary of Kleinian Thought*, London: Free Association Books.

Holmes, E. (1980) 'Educational intervention for pre-school children in day or residential care', *Therapeutic Education*, 8(2): 3–10.

Holmes, E. (1982) 'The effectiveness of educational intervention for pre-school children in day or residential care', *New Growth* 2(1): 17–30.

Holmes, J. (1991) *A Textbook of Psychotherapy in Psychiatric Practice*, Edinburgh: Churchill Livingstone.

Home Office Statistics (1994) Research and Statistics Department, Home Office, Lunar House, Wellesley Road, Croydon CR0 9YD.

Hopkins, J. (1988) 'Facilitating the development of intimacy between nurses and infants in day nurseries', *Early Ch. Dev. Care* 33: 99–111.

Idema, M. (1990) 'The mediation of psychological distress and anxiety in a day nursery for the under fives', unpublished paper.

Idema, M. and Barnett, L. (1990) 'The mediation of psychological distress and anxiety in a day care nursery for the under fives', research dissertation for MSc in clinical and community psychology, Exeter University, unpublished.

Jaffey, (1990) 'An evaluation of nurture groups', unpublished MSc thesis.

Jenkins, A. (1987) 'Recognising and treating the hurt child within parents', in Whitfield, R. and Baldwin, D. (eds) *Families Matter*, London: Collins.

Jenkins, A. (1995) *Opening the Door to Change*, book in preparation.

Jones, A. and Bilton, K. (1994) *The Future Shape of Children's Services*, NCB.

Jordan, B. (1984) *Invitation to Social Work*, Oxford and New York: Blackwell.

Joseph, B. (1989) *Psychic Equilibrium and Psychic Change: Selected Papers*, ed. M. Feldman and E. Bott Spillius, London: Routledge.

Kerbekian, R. (1987) Video: *Caring for Premature Babies*, Ipswich: Concord Films.

Kerr, A., Gregory, E., Howard, S. and Hudson, F. (1990) *On Behalf of the Child: The Work of the Guardian ad Litem*, London: Venture Press.

Kiernan, K. (1991) 'Changing marriage patterns', *J. Social Work Practice* 5(2): 123–31.

Klauber, J. (1986) *Difficulties in the Analytic Encounter*, London: Free Association Books and the Maresfield Library.

Klaus, M.H. and Kennell, J.H. (1979) 'Early mother–infant contact', *Bull. Nenn. Clin.* 43: 69–78.

Klein, M. (1927) 'Criminal tendencies in normal children', in *Love, Guilt and Reparation*, London: Hogarth Press; reprinted Virago, 1988, pp. 170–85.

Klein, M. (1935) 'A contribution to the genesis of manic-depressive states', in *The Writings of Melanie Klein Volume 1*, London: Hogarth Press, pp. 262–89.

Klein, M. (1937) 'Love, Guilt and Reparation', in *The Writings of Melanie Klein Volume 1*, London: Hogarth Press, pp. 306–43.

Klein, M. (1940) 'Mourning and its relation to manic-depressive states', in

*Love, Guilt and Reparation, The Writings of Melanie Klein Volume 1*, London: Hogarth Press, 1975, pp. 344–69.

Klein, M. (1946) 'Notes on some schizoid mechanisms', in Riviere, J. (ed.) *Developments in Psychoanalysis*, London: Hogarth Press, pp. 292–317; also in *Envy and Gratitude and Other Works 1946–1963*, London: Virago, 1988.

Klein, M. (ed.) (1963) *Our Adult World and Other Essays*, London: Heinemann Medical.

Kurtz, Z. (ed.) (1992) *With Health in Mind: Mental Health Care for Children and Young People*, London: Action for Sick Children in association with SWTRMA.

Kurtz, Z., Thomas, R. and Wolkind, S. (1994) *Services for the Mental Health of Children and Young People in England – A National Review*.

Lambeth, London Borough of (1987) *Whose Child?*, report of the enquiry into the death of Tyra Henry.

Laplanche, J. and Pontalis, J.B. (1967) *The Language of Psychoanalysis*, London: Hogarth Press.

Launer, J. (1994) 'Psychotherapy in the G.P. surgery: working with and without a secure therapeutic frame', *B. J. Psychother.* 11(1): 120–6.

Lazar, and Darlington, R.B. (1982) 'Lasting effects of early education', *Monographs Soc. Res. on Cl. Dev.*, 47: 2–5, Series No. 195.

Liedloff, J. (1975) *The Continuum Concept*, London: Arkana.

Lucas, R. (1994) 'Puerperal psychosis: vulnerability and aftermath', *Psychoanal Psychother.* 8(3): 257–72.

Macy, T.J., Harmon, R.J. and Easterbrook, M.A. (1987) 'Impact of premature birth on the development of the infant in the family', *J. Consult. Clin. Psychol.* 55(6): 846–52.

Main, M. and George, C. (1985) 'Responses of abused and disadvantaged toddlers to distress in agemates: a study in the day care setting', *Dev. Psychol.* 21: 407–12.

Main, M. and Hesse, E. (1992) 'Disorganized/disoriented infant behaviour in the strange situation: lapses in the monitoring of reasoning and discourse during the parents' Adult Attachment Interview and dissociated states', in Ammaniti, M. and Stern, D. (eds) *Attachment and Psychoanalysis*, Rome: Gius, La Terza.

Main, M., Tomasini, L. and Tolan, W. (1979) 'Differences among mothers of infants judged to differ in security', *Dev. Psychol.* 15: 427–73.

Main, M. *et al.* (1985) 'Security in infancy, childhood and adulthood: a move to the level of representation', in Bretherton, I. and Waters, E. (eds) *Growing Points in Attachment, Monographs of the Society for Research in Child Development* 50(1–2).

Martin-Baros (1990) War and the psychological trauma of Salvadorean children

McCallin, M. 'The psychological well-being of refugee children', *Research, Practice and Policiy Issues*, International Catholic Child Bureau.

McCartney, K. (1984) 'Effects of quality of day care environment on children's language development', *J. Dev. Psychol.* 20: 244–60.

McCartney, K., Scarr, S., Phillips, D. and Grojek, S. (1985) 'Day care as intervention: comparison of quality programmes', *J. App. Dev. Psychol.* 6: 247–60.

McDougall, J. (1989) *Theatres of the Body: A Psychoanalytic Approach to Psychosomatic Illness*, London: Free Association Books.

McFadyen, A. (1991) 'Some thoughts on infant observation and its possible role in child psychiatry training', *ACPP Newsletter* 13: 10–14.

McGuire, J. and Earls, F. (1991) 'Prevention of psychiatric disorders in early childhood', *J. Ch. Psychol. Psychiat.* 32: 129–54.

McGurk, H., Caplan, M., Hennessy, E. and Moss, P. (1993) 'Controversy theory and social context in contemporary day care research', *J. Ch. Psychol. Psychiat.* 34(1): 3–23.

Melhuish, E.C. *et al.* (1990) 'Type of childcare at 18 months, Part 1: differences in interactional experience', *J. Ch. Psychol. Psychiat.* 31: 849–59.

Melhuish, E.C. and Moss, P. (1991) *Day Care for Young Children: International Perspectives*, London and New York: Routledge.

Meltzer, D. (1968) 'Terror, persecution and dread', *Int. J. Psycho-Anal.* 49: 396–401; reprinted in *Sexual States of Mind*, Strath Tay: Clunie Press, pp. 90–8.

Melzak, S. (1992) 'Secrecy, Privacy, Survival, Repressive Regimes and Growing Up', *Journal of the Anna Freud Centre* (September). Available from the Anna Freud Centre and Medical Foundation.

Melzak, S. (1993) 'Thinking about the internal and external experience of refugee children in Europe – Conflict and Treatment'. Published in the Proceedings of a conference on Children, War and Persecution held in Hamburg (October 1992). Available from the Child Psychiatry Department, Hamburg University and Medical Foundation.

Melzak, S. and Warner, R. (1991) *Integrating Refugee Children into schools*, London: Minority Rights Group.

Menzies, I.E.P. (1960) 'A case study in the functioning of social systems as a defence against anxiety', *Human Relations* 13: 95–121.

Menzies, I.E.P. (1970) *The Function of Social Systems as a Defence against Anxiety*, Tavistock Papers No. 3.

Menzies, I.E.P. (1975) 'Thoughts on the maternal role in contemporary society', *J. Ch. Psychother.* 4: 5–14.

Menzies Lyth, I. (1988) 'The development of the self in children in institutions', and 'Action research in a long-stay hospital', in *Containing Anxiety in Institutions: Selected Essays*, Vol. 1, London: Free Association Books.

Miller, L., Rustin, M. and Shuttleworth, J. (1989) *Closely Observed Infants*, London: Duckworth.

Mills, M. (1994) 'The Waters Under the Earth: understanding maternal depression', in Raphael-Leff, J. and Perelberg, R. (eds) *The Female Experience*.

Mills, M. and Pound, A. (1985) 'A pilot evaluation on Newpin', *Assoc. Ch. Psychol. Psychiat. Newsletter* 7.

Mills, M. and Puckering, C. (1985) 'What is it about depressed mothers that influences their child's functioning?', in Stevenson, J. (ed.) *Recent Research in Developmental Psychopathology*, London: Pergamon.

Mills, M. and Puckering, C. 'Mellow Parenting: the coding system', in preparation.

Morgan, S. (1994) 'Therapeutic communication', unpublished, Caldecott College.

Murray, L. (1991) 'The impact of postnatal depression on infant development', *J. Ch. Psychol. Psychiat.* 49.

Negri, R. (1988) 'A new approach with parents of very low birthweight new-borns', Tavistock Library, unpublished paper.

The Newpin Training Brochure (1993).

Obholtzer, A. and Roberts, V.G. (eds) (1994) *The Unconscious at Work*, London: Routledge.

Panel of Advisers for Unaccompanied Refugee children (1993) Refugee Council Leaflet.

Passey, M. (1994) *Handbook of Psychotherapy*, London: Routledge.

Patterson, G. (1990) *Depression and Aggression in Family Interaction*, London: Erlbaum.

Pearson, G., Treseder, J. and Yelloly, M. (1988) 'Personal stress', *J. Ch. Psychother.* 7(2): 152–60.

Pietroni, M. (ed.) 'Right or privilege: post-qualification training for social workers with special reference to child care (CCETSW)', in press.

Piontelli, A. (1986) *Backwards in Time*, Strath Tay: Clunie Press.

Piontelli, A. (1992) *From Foetus to Child*, London: Routledge.

Pound, A., Puckering, C., Cox, T. and Mills, M. (1989) 'The impact of maternal depression on young children', *B. J. Psychother.* 5: 241–52.

Puckering, C., Cox, A. and Mills, M. (1993) Research Report to the Department of Health.

Puckering, C., Mills, M., Rogers, J., Cox, A. and Mattsson-Graff, M. (1994) 'Mellow parenting: process and evaluation of group intervention for distressed families', *Ch. Abuse Rev.* 3: 299–310.

Punamaki, R.C. (1992) *Natural Healing Processes and Experiences of Political Violence*, Oxford: Refugee Studies Unit.

Radke-Yarrow, M. *et al.* (1985) 'Patterns of attachment in normal families and families with parental depression', *Ch. Dev.* 56: 884.

Raphael-Leff, J. (1989) 'Where the wild things are', *Int. J. Prenatal Perinatal Studies* 78–89.

Reid, S., Fry, E. and Rhode, M. (1977) in Daws, D. and Boston, M. (eds) *The Child Psychotherapist and Problems of Young People*, London: Tavistock/Routledge.

Richman, N. (1993) *J. Ch. Psych. and Psychiat.*

Riviere, J. (1952) 'The unconscious phantasy of an inner world reflected in examples from literature', *Int. J. Psycho-Anal.*; also in M. Klein, P. Heimann and·R.E. Money-Kyrle (eds) *New Directions in Psychoanalysis*, London: Karnac, 1955/1985.

Robertson, J. (1953) 'Some responses of young children to loss of maternal care', *Nurs. Times* 49: 382–6.

Robertson, J. and Robertson, J. (1953) *A Two Year Old Goes to Hospital*, Ipswich: Concord Films Council.

Robertson, J. and Robertson, J. (1969a) *Young Children in Hospital*, London: Tavistock.

Robertson, J. and Robertson, J. (1969b) *John: 17 Months: For Nine Days in a Residential Nursery*, Ipswich: Concord Films Council; New York: New York University Film Library.

Robertson, J. and Robertson, J. (1989) *Separation and the Very Young*, London: Free Association Books.

Rosenfeld, H. (1971) 'A clinical approach to the theory of the life and death instincts: an investigation into the aggressive aspects of narcissism', *Int. J. Psycho-Anal.*

Rubenstein, J. and Howes, C. (1983) 'Socio-emotional development of toddlers in day care: the role of peers and individual differences', in Kilmer, S. (ed.) *Advances in Early Education and Day Care*, San Francisco: JAI Press.

Rycroft, C. (1968) *A Critical Dictionary of Psychoanalysis*, London: Nelson; Harmondsworth: Penguin, 1988.

Saltzberger-Wittenberg, I. (1975) *Psychoanalytic Insights and Relationships: A Kleinian Approach*, London: Routledge.

Saltzberger-Wittenberg, I., Henry, G. and Osborne, E. (eds) (1983) *The Emotional Experience of Learning and Teaching*, London: Routledge.

Schamess, G. (1987) 'Parallel mother/infant/toddler group', *J. Social Work Practice* 2: 29–48.

Segal, H. (1973) *Introduction to the Work of Melanie Klein*, London: Hogarth Press and Institute of Psycho-Analysis.

Sharff, D. and Sharff, J. (1991) *Object Relations Family Therapy*, New Jersey and London: Jason Aronson.

Smith Bowen, E. (1954) *Return to Laughter,* London: Gollancz.

Soloman, Lasson and Ellis, *Handbook for the Teaching of Young Child Observation in Social Work Training*, in press CCETSW.

Spitz, R.A. (1945) 'Hospitalisation: an inquiry into the genesis of psychiatric conditions in early childhood', *Psychoanal. Study Child* 1.

Stein, A. *et al.* (1991) 'The relationship between postnatal depression and mother–child interaction', *B. J. Psychiat.* 139: 39.

Stern, D.N. (1985) *The Interpersonal World of the Infant*, New York: Basic Books.

Stern, D. (1994) unpublished lecture, Institute of Psychoanalysis, London.

Stevenson, J. (1982) *Pre-school to School: a Behavioural Study*, London: Academic Press.

Straker, G. (1992) *Faces in the Revolution*, Ohio University Press.

Summerfield, D. (1993) Addressing the Human Response to War and Atrocity.

Sutton, C. (1994) 'Parent education and training: a seriously neglected field', in *Children UK*, National Children's Bureau.

Szur, R. and Miller, S. (eds) *Extending Horizons*, London: Karnac.

Temperley, J. (1984) 'Our own worst enemies', *Free Associations* pilot issue.

Thoburn, J. (1985) *Success and Failure in Permanent Family Placement*, Avebury: Gower.

Tizard, B. and Hughes, M. (1988) *Young Children Learning*, London, Fontana.

Trowell, J.A. (1982) 'Possible effects of emergency caesarean section on the mother-child relationship', *Early Human Dev.* 2: 41–5.

Trowell, J.A. (1983) 'Emergency caesarean section: a recent study of the mother-child relationship of a group of women expecting a normal vaginal delivery', *Ch. Abuse Neglect* 7: 387–94.

Trowell, J. (1991a) 'Use of observational skill in social work training', in Pietroni, M. (ed.) *Right or Privilege: Post-Qualification Training for Social Workers with Special Reference to Child Care*, CCETSW, in press.

Trowell, J.A. (1991b) 'What is happening to mental health services for children and young families?', *ACCP Newsletter* 13(5): 12–15.

Trowell, J.A. and Huffington, C. (1992) 'Daring to take a risk: issues from the first year of the Monroe Young Family Centre', *ACCP Newsletter* 14(3): 114–18.

Trowell, J.A. and Rustin, M. (1991) 'Developing the internal observer in professional training', *Infant Mental Health Journal* 12(3): 233–45.

Troy, M. and Sroufe, L.A. (1987) 'Victimisation among pre-schoolers; role of attachment relationship history', *J. Am. Acad. Ch. Adol. Psychiat* 26: 166–72.

Uglow, J. (1993) *Mrs Gaskell*, London: Faber.

Urquhart, R. (1980) Personal communication.

Van der Kolk, B.A. (1989) 'The compulsion to repeat the traumatic re-enactment, revictimisation and masochism', *Psychiatric Clinics of North America* 12: 389–411.

Vas Dias, S. (1983) 'Some thoughts on the creation of the child psychotherapist's role in a major teaching hospital', *J. Ch. Psychother.* 9(2): 133–42.

Waddell, M. (1987) *Infantile Development, Kleinian and Post-Kleinian Theory and Infant Observation Practice*, Tavistock Clinic Paper 55, London: Tavistock.

Wilson, A. (1987) *Mixed Race Children: A Study of Identity*, Worcester and London: Billinge, pp. 21, 44.

Wilson, K. (1992) 'The place of child observation and social work training', *Journal of Social Work Practice*, 6(1).

Winnicott, D.W. (1941) 'The observation of infants in a set situation', in *Collected Papers: Through Paediatrics to Psychoanalysis*, London: Tavistock, 1958.

Winnicott, D.W. (1947) 'Hate in the countertransference', in *Collected Papers: Through Paediatrics to Psychoanalysis*, London: Tavistock, 1958.

Winnicott, D.W. (1958) 'Primary maternal preoccupation', in *Collected Papers: Through Paediatrics to Psychoanalysis*, London: Tavistock, 1958.

Winnicott, D.W. (1962) 'Ego integration in child development', in *The Maturational Processes and the Facilitating Environment*, London: Hogarth Press, 1965.

Winnicott, D.W. (1969) *Playing and Reality*, London: Tavistock.

Winnicott, D.W. (1985) *The Family and Individual Development*, London and New York: Tavistock.

Woodmansey, A.C. (1990) 'Approaches to child abuse', *J. Social Work Practice* 4: 2–29.

*Working Together under the Children's Act 1979: A Guide to Arrangements for Interagency Co-operation for the Protection of Children from Abuse* (1991) London: HMSO.

Yelloly, M. (1993) 'The dynamics of difference: poverty and wealth', *J. Social Work Practice* 7(1).

Yelloly, M.A. (1980) *Social Work Theory and Psychoanalysis*, London: Van Nostrand Reinhold.

Yelloly, M. and Henkel, M. (eds) (1995) *Learning and Teaching in Social Work*, Bristol, PA, and London: Jessica Kingsley.

Yevtushenko, Y. (1987) *Almost at the End*, London and New York: Marion Boyars.

Zulueta, F. de (1993) *From Pain to Violence: The Traumatic Roots of Destructiveness*, London: Whurr.

# Index

abuse, childhood 110, 210; community group for abused children 157–66; emotional 10, 138–9; link between physical and emotional 137–8; and violence in adulthood 268–70

adoption 95–6

after-school club 254

aggression: cross-cultural issues and racism 239–42, 246; day nursery 222, 223–5, 230–1 (individual dynamics 223–4; institutional factors 225)

Ainsworth, M.D.S. 265

ambivalence 91

'ambivalent' attachment response 265–6

anger: cross-cultural issues and racism 242, 246; mothers' group 171

anthropology 64

anti-task groups 21, 109

anxieties 2; Freud 12–13; hospital nurses 28–30; paranoid-schizoid position 173; persecutory 103; premature baby units 55–62; transition to secondary school 175–86

approved school 208; boundary controls 198, 199; delegation and staff attitudes 192–4; subcultures 205–6

army psychiatrists 22–3

assessment: observation training 47; refugee children in exile 257–8, 259–63; residential care 215–17; social work task 97–8

assigned care-takers see case assignment

asylum laws 249, 257

asylum-seekers 247, 248–9; see also refugee children

attachment: Bowlby 31–2, 264–5; day nursery 226–8; institutions 200–4, 207–8; Newpin 137, 139; pre-school intervention 148–56; refugee children 263; violence as attachment gone wrong 264–8, 271

attention, discontinuities of 201, 229

authority 194, 197–8

'avoidant' attachment response 265–8

baby clinic 63, 64–8

baby observation 33, 39–40; see also observation training

Bain, A. 201, 231; day care nursery 221–9, 231–4

Balbernie, R. 210

'Balint' groups 23

Bamford, T. 90–1

Barnett, L. 201; day nursery 221–34

behavioural problems: obstacles to improvement 101–8

belonging 196–7